SUBARU

Impreza

Foreword by Toshihiro Arai

Also from Veloce Publishing:

First published in 2003. Paperback edition printed in 2004 by Veloce Publishing Ltd., 33 Trinity Street, Dorchester DT1 1TT, England.
Fax 01305 268864/e-mail info@veloce.co.uk/web www.veloce.co.uk or www.velocebooks.com
ISBN 1-904788-35-1/UPC 36847-00335-7

SUBARU
Impreza

Foreword by Toshihiro Arai

Brian Long

VELOCE PUBLISHING

THE PUBLISHER OF FINE AUTOMOTIVE BOOKS

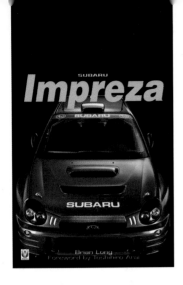

Foreword

The relationship between Subaru and I spans more than a decade, which happens to coincide almost exactly with the debut of the Impreza in Japan; we have now fought together for over ten seasons.

Subaru may not be a large manufacturer compared to some of the other Japanese companies, but I feel it has an unrivalled passion for making cars for enthusiasts. Subaru was the first to introduce four-wheel drive on a mass-production vehicle in Japan. Combined with the horizontally-opposed engine and longitudinal transmission, which give better weight distribution and a lower roll centre, the engineers have created the perfect driving machine. Not only does the Impreza handle well, it's also great fun to drive.

This 'fun to drive' element is the key behind Subaru's success in recent years. It's obvious that the Impreza, Legacy and Forester have been designed first and foremost with driving in mind - an essential factor when buying a vehicle for use in the highest levels of competition, especially rallying, but just as applicable to enthusiasts choosing a road car.

From my point of view as a rally driver, it is important not only to have a machine that is entertaining, but is also capable of winning. For Subaru, merely competing is not enough: winning is the only goal. As such, the Impreza receives engine, chassis and other major revisions on a regular basis to keep it ahead of the field. This is my reason for choosing Subaru, and I look forward to another decade of motorsport with the company.

Toshihiro Arai
SWRT Driver

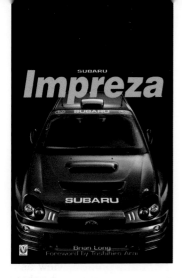

Contents

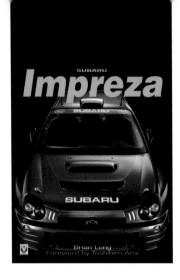

Introduction & Acknowledgements

Introduction

The Subaru Impreza went on sale in November 1992, powered by a boxer engine, and with the option of four-wheel drive on certain models; it was also available as an estate. Early 1994 saw the first STi versions join the line-up, followed by a two-door coupé shortly after. However, two years later, a 'Brand New' generation was launched.

By this time, Subaru was already making an impact on the World Rally Championship scene, with the Impreza taking over from the Legacy as the chosen weapon for the company's assault on the series. Claiming no less than three WRC titles (won in 1995, 1996 and 1997), the Impreza deservedly secured its place in history as one of the most successful rally cars of all time.

In August 2000, the all-new third generation series (or second generation, depending on your point of view) made its debut, continuing the legend and spawning another new rally car that enabled Richard Burns to take the Drivers' Championship title. As 2002 drew to a close, the Impreza received a major facelift for its tenth anniversary to take the car into a new era.

This book looks at the history of Subaru, including its fascinating early heritage, the background to the Impreza, the full story of the myriad models in Japan and major export markets, and round-by-round coverage of the Impreza's WRC challenge.

Pictures have been sourced almost exclusively from the factory and its concessionaires around the world. The remaining shots are either from contemporary catalogues or advertising, or are press cars photographed in 100 per cent standard trim at the time of launch. This book will be an invaluable tool for those searching for originality, or a useful reference when checking out a grey import - every single Japanese brochure and press release, be it issued by FHI or STi, has been referred to. In order to give an unrivalled level of detail and accuracy, any gaps in the information have been filled with the full co-operation of the works.

Acknowledgements

Although I went to the launch of the 'New Age' Impreza, in reality, this project started after a meeting in an unlikely place - the British Embassy in Tokyo. It was there that I met Takemasa Yamada (then President of Subaru Tecnica International, or STi), and Hugh Chambers of Prodrive, and, inspired by the lecture, came up with the idea for this book.

An RJC meeting later in the year brought me into contact with Kyoji Takenaka (Subaru's current President & COO), Takeshi Tanaka (Chairman & CEO) and Masaru Katsurada (the new President of STi). My proposal was met with an enthusiastic response, making me determined to follow things through. As my rough ideas gelled, Atsushi Kojima (Manager of the Corporate Communications Department and an Impreza STi owner) helped bring the project closer to reality, with Katsunori Kiyota being the poor guy who had to look after my many requests. Kiyota-san, your help and determination to overcome the various hurdles put in front of us is much appreciated.

Many thanks also to the engineers who went to a lot of trouble to answer questions; Toshihiro Arai - without doubt, Japan's finest rally driver - for writing the Foreword, and Subaru in Australia, America, Switzerland and the UK for providing pictures.

Mention should also be made of Ben Sayer and Rebecca Banks at Prodrive, Syuji Yamaga at Fellow Room, and Shinji Takahashi at Book Garage (for sourcing some of the rare early catalogues for me). I would like to take this opportunity to thank all of those people who have given me their time and support, including my wife, Miho, who once again had to translate piles of paperwork and various interviews. This book would not have been possible without you.

Brian Long
Chiba City, Japan

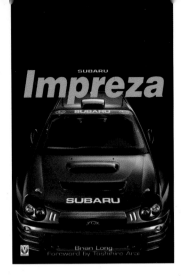

1

History of the Subaru marque

Subaru's heritage can be traced back to the time of the First World War, when, in 1917, Chikuhei Nakajima established the Aircraft Research Laboratory in Ohta, Gunma Prefecture, situated about 45 miles (70km) north of Tokyo.

Nakajima was born in Gunma Prefecture in 1884. He graduated from Naval School with honour and a reputation for being exceptionally bright, reflected in his rapid rise through the ranks of the Imperial Navy. Later, he attended the Naval University where he studied aviation (the Naval Committee for Aeronautical Research had been formed by the Japanese government in 1912).

Having acquired practical experience on the early Curtiss flying boats, Nakajima was sent to France to supervise the build and shipment of a batch of aeroplanes ordered by the Japanese authorities. However, he returned to Japan following the outbreak of the First World War, realizing how far behind his country was in the world of flight. He also

Chikuhei Nakajima (1884-1949), the man who provided the foundation stone for the Subaru marque.

realized that future warfare would almost certainly be fought in the air.

Nakajima duly left the Naval establishment to which he was attached and, with finance secured from a wealthy Kobe businessman, founded the Aircraft Research Laboratory in May 1917, initially using a disused silkworm farm as premises. Far grander buildings, which used to belong to the Tobu Railway Co., were occupied later that year.

Unfortunately, Nakajima's original backer ran into financial trouble, so a new source of funding had to be found.

The Ohta factory pictured in earlier times when aircraft production was the mainstay of the business.

Kiyobe Kawanishi, who had made his money in wool and fabrics, came to the rescue, allowing the formation of the Nakajima Aircraft Works.

With the head office registered in the centre of Tokyo, Nakajima built six aircraft for private customers in the Ohta factory in 1918. The following year 34 aeroplanes were produced, 32 of which the Imperial Army took after a successful trial. During 1920, 68 aircraft were built for the Army, 31 for the Japanese Navy, and 17 for private aviators.

The aircraft business was now a viable industry - at least on the face of it - and it was only a matter of time before the *zaibatsu* (massive, wealthy conglomerates) muscled in on the action. For instance, Mitsubishi abandoned its plans to produce motor cars in favour of entering the field of aviation, while smaller but nonetheless powerful concerns, like Kawasaki and Ishikawajima, also joined the fold.

Behind the scenes, however, Nakajima and Kawanishi had different ideas regarding policy. Small horsepower aero engines were available relatively cheaply in Japan, but Nakajima insisted on more powerful units, imported at great expense from America. A split was inevitable, with Kawanishi withdrawing from the company, and Nakajima once again needing to find a willing financier. Luckily, he did. With the help of the bank and a politician, the business was saved, with Nakajima as President.

The 1930s

Whilst it's fair to say that, although many companies suffered during the lean years of the 1920s, Mitsubishi, Mitsui, Sumitomo, and some of the other *zaibatsu*, grew even stronger, buying up smaller firms as they struggled.

Another broad observation can be made; that Japan was becoming more nationalistic. The invasion of Manchuria hit the headlines in the world's newspapers, and there was little doubt that the country was increasing its military might. All of this made the *zaibatsu* yet more powerful, as they received money for armament orders, both directly, and indirectly through their wide-ranging investments.

The Nakajima concern started producing aero engines in 1926 (Bristol

The Messerschmitt-based Kikka - Japan's first jet fighter.

Jupiters built under licence), with its own nine-cylinder rotary units coming at the end of the decade. The 'Kotobuki,' as it was called, passed its Navy trials in 1931, enabling the company to manufacture complete aircraft in-house.

Chikuhei Nakajima entered politics in 1930 (ultimately becoming Minister of Railways) and, in December 1931, his company was reorganised as the Nakajima Aircraft Co. Ltd, with his brother, Kiyokazu, named as President.

Interestingly, Japan attacked the Asian mainland from the air for the first time using Nakajima A1Ns as part of its Manchuria campaign, while Type 3 fighters were involved in the first dogfights involving the Japanese Air Force.

Forbidden to produce aeroplanes after VJ Day, the Nakajima aircraft business was renamed the Fuji Sangyo Co. Ltd. Among other things, the highly-successful Rabbit motor scooter provided the company with a lifeline, giving enough profit to keep it afloat during the immediate post-war years.

One of Japan's most famous aeroplanes from the Second World War is the Mitsubishi Zero. This legendary fighter, which made its maiden flight in April 1939, was so outstanding that production was also undertaken by the Nakajima concern. In fact, Nakajima ultimately built almost twice as many Zeros as the plane's designers.

However, the Nakajima Ki-84 Hayate was said to be an even better machine, both faster and better armed than its illustrious predecessor. Nakajima was also responsible for Japan's first jet fighter - the Kikka. It first took to the air in August 1945, but then events in Hiroshima (and Nagasaki, three days later) brought the lengthy conflict to an end.

The immediate post-war years

After the war, Japan was left in a terrible state. While not quite the witch hunt witnessed in Europe, where almost all companies and their leaders with even a suspected link to Nazi Germany were seized by local authorities, the Allied Forces broke up the *zaibatsu*, taking away their power; businesses that had thrived during the military build-up - Nakajima included - suddenly found their lifelines cut.

Having built almost 26,000 aeroplanes between 1918 and 1945 (a figure that includes an unrivalled 28 per cent of Japan's wartime production of airframes, along with 31 per cent of the nation's aero engines built during this period - a percentage surpassed only by Mitsubishi), the Nakajima Aircraft Company officially closed its doors at the end of the conflict. It was renamed the Fuji Sangyo Co. Ltd, commencing business with the

manufacture of various industrial products. The Nakajima family retained its position in the top management, however, with Kimihei Nakajima (another of Chikuhei's brothers) named as first President.

Fuji Sangyo launched the Rabbit motor scooter in June 1946. Whilst it hardly represented leading edge technology, this tiny little machine (originally powered by a 135cc engine, and with leftover tyres from fighter aircraft) sold well. Indeed, by 1968 when the Rabbit had bigger engines and had taken on a far more modern form, no less than 637,895 were built.

On the commercial vehicle front, Fuji Sangyo produced Japan's first frameless, rear-engined bus - the 'Fuji' of 1949 vintage. This was extremely advanced for the time, setting the pattern for today's buses. There were many other innovations in this field of transport, including adoption of air suspension (introduced as early as 1956), and the successful completion of Japan's first double-decker.

A year after the 'Fuji' bus was launched, due to the corporate reorganization laws in force at that time, the Fuji Sangyo concern was split into 12 independent companies, one of which took over the Prince Motor Company. However, on 15 July 1953, five of the other separate companies (Tokyo Fuji Sangyo, Fuji Jidosha Kogyo, Fuji Kogyo, Omiya Fuji Kogyo and Utsunomiya Sharyo) came together again to form Fuji Heavy Industries Limited - the foundation stone of the Subaru marque. The head office was registered in Shinjuku, Tokyo, with Kenji Kita (an ex-Nippon Kogyo Bank man) named as first President.

The origins of the Subaru automobile can be traced back to the P-1, a prototype four-cylinder car,

The first Subaru car - the P-1. Sadly, this attractive vehicle was destined to remain a prototype.

completed in 1954, and named the Subaru 1500 the following year. Only 20 of these attractive, four-door saloons (which looked similar to the contemporary Toyota Crown) were built, as, in reality, most of FHI's effort with regard to passenger vehicles was still being directed towards the Rabbit motorcycle, its line of buses, and work on diesel railcars. Interestingly, two powerplants were tried in the 1500, one of which was Subaru's own design and the other a Prince unit.

Meanwhile, Fuji Heavy Industries (FHI) was making a comeback in the aviation world, initially via the licensed production of the T-3 Mentor trainer. However, 1958 saw the maiden flight of the T1-F1 jet trainer, the first post-war jet aircraft of entirely Japanese design: before long, FHI was busy with work spanning everything from turboprop airliners to helicopters. In later years, the company fostered close links with Bell and Boeing in America, as well as important organisations closer to home, such as NASDA (the National Space Development Agency of Japan) and the National Aerospace Laboratory of Japan.

In 1960, FHI's common stock was listed on the Tokyo Stock Exchange, although, five years later, it was broken into operating divisions according to product classification. Today, the main elements of FHI are made up of the Aerospace Division, the Transportation & Ecology System Division, the Bus Manufacturing & House Prefabricating Division, the Industrial Products Division, and, of course, the Automobile Division.

The first Subaru cars

It should be noted that, even during the 1950s, Japan's motor industry was still a long way behind that of established car-building nations, and largely reliant on European technology. For this reason, it was not considered any kind of threat. In fact, when Renault complained to the French government that Hino had not been paying royalties on 4CVs built under licence, the reply came back that it was "hardly fair to pick on this poor little country which has such a task to feed hundreds of

thousands of inhabitants."

Fuji Heavy Industries decided to adopt the Subaru trade name for its automobiles, the familiar badge, first seen in the spring of 1958, being a representation of the six stars in the Taurus constellation visible to the human eye. This was actually Kenji Kita's idea - five smaller stars coming together to make one large one - and the link is quite interesting, as *subaru* is the Japanese word for Pleiades (the seven daughters of Atlas and Plieone in Greek mythology), placed in the sky by Zeus after their death. One of them, Merope, is very faint, as she fell in love with a mortal, and thus we can only see six without the aid of a telescope.

As noted earlier, the P-1 of 1954 vintage was the first Subaru, although it was destined to remain little more than a prototype. The first model to make it into series production was the Subaru 360 minicar, an altogether different beast to the P-1, announced on 3 March 1958. The original styling clay was found 40 years later, and displayed alongside a production model at a recent exhibition on the history of Japanese transport at the National Science Museum, Tokyo.

Sales of the 360 started in May. Powered by a 356cc, two-stroke, air-cooled twin, it had a 425,000 yen sticker price. The two-cylinder power unit, mounted in the back and driving the rear wheels, was originally linked to a three-speed gearbox, although a four-speed transmission was made available in the mid-1960s.

Sales of the 16bhp car were slow initially, with only 604 built in the first year. This figure quickly rose to 5111 units in 1959, and carried on rising - 22,319 were produced in 1961, by which time, the Gunma Main Plant had opened and the Sambar truck had been introduced. A shortlived convertible model was listed in the early days of the 360, later augmented by an estate version and one with a larger 423cc engine (the 23bhp Subaru 450, or K212); there had also been a rather odd-looking 'Subaru Sports' prototype exhibited at the 1961 Tokyo Show.

By now, Japan had fully recovered from the devastation of the Second World War. Cities reduced to shanty towns after heavy bombing were rebuilt, the 1964 Tokyo Olympics brought about a road-building programme (not

Rear view of the Subaru 360. This type of vehicle - and slightly larger 500cc versions of the minicar breed - was very popular in Japan at this time. Subaru ultimately listed 360 and 450 models, while Mitsubishi had the 500, 600 and Minica, Toyota produced the Publica, Hino was still building the Renault 4CV, Suzuki had its Fronte series, and Mazda the R360 and Carol.

The first production Subaru was the 360 of 1958 vintage, seen here on test.

The diminutive Subaru 360 scored a one-two victory in the T-1 Class at the 1964 Japanese Grand Prix. In total 392,016 360 series cars were built.

The 1968 Japanese Grand Prix saw the debut of a rather more traditional racing car - this Formula 3 single-seater with a tuned 1000 engine.

to mention the birth of the legendary Shinkansen, or Bullet Train), and the economy was on an all-time high. Indeed, Japan was admitted to the Organisation for Economic Co-Operation & Development (an international group for advanced industrial nations) the same year the Tokyo Olympics were held.

The management decision to build a larger saloon was therefore basically a sound one, realized in the shape of the Subaru 1000 - Japan's first mass-produced, front-wheel drive car, with development headed by Shinroku Momose. Having made its debut at the 1965 Tokyo Show, it went on sale in May 1966, powered by a water-cooled boxer four of 977cc rated at 55bhp.

An early Subaru 1000. This model, and the FF-1 series that followed in its tyre tracks, accounted for around 237,000 sales.

This four-door sedan started a Subaru tradition, continued to this day, for employing horizontally-opposed engines for its road cars. Featuring a four-wheel independent suspension, a so-called 'Sports Version' with more power and a two-door body, was launched just over a year later.

1966 also saw Subaru sign a technical co-operation agreement with Isuzu, which enabled the two companies to realign production facilities. However, the partnership was shortlived, and, while Isuzu joined forces briefly with Mitsubishi, then Nissan, and finally General Motors (GM), Subaru forged a longer lasting relationship with Nissan (not such strange bedfellows as it would at first seem, given the link between FHI and the Prince marque, which became part of Nissan in 1966). A business contract was drawn up with Nissan in October 1968, ultimately leading to a number

The R-2 made its debut in August 1969. The sportiest model was the SS, its 356cc engine developing a healthy 36bhp.

The Leone GSR of 1971 vintage.

of Nissan/Datsun cars being produced by FHI shortly after.

The Nissan agreement was signed the same year that Malcolm Bricklin started handling US imports of the Subaru 360. Bricklin had previously handled American sales of the Rabbit motor scooter (and the Lambretta, as it happens), but his promotional skills were hard-pressed to move the tiny Subaru, especially after *Consumer Report* branded it "the most unsafe car on the market." Bricklin later tried to build his own automobiles, but the project was destined to fail.

Exports to Europe, which had started in the mid-1960s, were beginning to pick up. With annual production now hovering around the 100,000 mark, the new Yajima Plant commenced operations in 1969. That year saw the debut of the R-2 (the long-awaited replacement for the 360), and also the FF-1 series, which superceded the 1000.

The 1088cc FF-1 was available in saloon, coupé or estate guise, and was sold in the USA: the founding of Subaru of America Inc. was a concerted effort to break into this lucrative market.

In July 1970, the FF-1 1300G and 1100 series made its debut. The 1267cc flat-four came in two states of tune, developing either 80 or 93bhp. The FF-1 limped into 1972, ultimately being replaced, albeit indirectly, by the Leone - a landmark vehicle in Subaru's history.

13

American advertising from 1974 outlining the key features of the Subaru range.

A Japanese advert from mid-1975 for the four-wheel dr[ive] version of the Leone Sedan.

Establishing an automotive pedigree

Under the leadership of Eiichi Ohara, Subaru was on the verge of world recognition. Its next car, the Leone (Italian for male lion), established the marque as a major player, even though sales at home were still by far the smallest of all the Japanese producers.

The Leone Coupé was the first of the line, making its debut in October 1971, and powered, sure enough, by a boxer four. The 1361cc engine developed 80bhp in standard trim (for the DL and GL grades), or 93bhp in the GS and GSR. With four-wheel independent suspension, and disc brakes on the top models, it was a modern vehicle in all respects, helping to take Subaru's car production to around 130,000 units per annum.

Soon, the two-door was joined by extra grades, a four-door sedan (with the option of a 1.4 or 1.1 litre engine), and another coupé known as the Hardtop. Perhaps the most interesting development, though, at least from a marketing point of view, was the launch of the 4WD Leone Station Wagon. Although initially aimed at business users, its potential was soon exploited, resulting in a ground-breaking design that combined the benefits of a traditional passenger car with four-wheel drive technology. Along with the boxer engine, the Subaru name became synonymous with 4WD vehicles.

Small cars weren't forgotten, however, and the Rex made its debut in the summer of 1972. Mechanically similar to the R-2 it replaced in the initial stages, the Rex featured more

modern styling (although the early R-2, which resembled the Fiat 500, was undoubtedly the prettier), and acquired bigger engines as the years passed.

Subaru built just over 100,000 cars in 1974, with around 23,000 of them reaching American shores. The following year more Leones got the option of four-wheel drive and the choice of automatic transmission; 41,587 Subarus were sold in the States, and the figure just kept rising, topping 100,000 units in 1978.

It's fair to say that the Leone was extremely popular in the States, and the GF (equivalent to the home market's Leone Hardtop) was voted 1975 'Import Car of the Year' by *Road & Track*. By this time, though, pollution and other green issues had become a major concern on both sides of the Pacific,

The Subaru 4 wheel drive wagon offers so much and asks so little:

Its full time front wheel drive becomes 4 wheel drive at the flick of a lever inside the car. Which means you can drive almost any road in almost any weather.

It combines the comfort and ride of a passenger car, the capacity of a wagon and the flexibility of a multi-purpose, 4 wheel drive vehicle.

Yet, with its SEEC-T engine, the manual transmission Subaru 4 wheel drive wagon gets 32' highway and 22' city miles to a gallon of regular based on 1976 EPA test estimates. Your mileage may vary because of the way you drive, driving conditions, the condition of your car and whatever optional equipment you might have. But this is one station wagon that's kind to you at the gas station.

What's more, it costs only $4,149.* Loaded with extras like a push-button AM radio, rear windshield wiper and washer, reclining bucket seats and power front disc brakes.

The Subaru 4 wheel drive wagon: It makes a monkey out of any other wagon on the road.

**SUBARU.
THE ECONOMY CAR FOR TODAY'S ECONOMY.**

*Total POE.—Not including dealer prep, inland transportation and taxes. Rally stripe, wheel trim rings and luggage rack are optional at extra cost.
*In California see your local Subaru dealer for price and gas mileage figures.

THE SUBARU 4 WHEEL DRIVE WAGON. CLIMBS LIKE A GOAT, WORKS LIKE A HORSE AND EATS LIKE A BIRD.

The Leone Station Wagon in US trim, 1976. In America, the 1.6 litre engine listed as an option for 1976 came as standard on 1977 model year cars.

独創の FF&4WD

世界で唯一の4輪駆動セダンによって、まったく新しい車の世界をきり拓いたスバル。この、世界でただひとつの、レオーネセダン4WDも、スバルエンジニアリングの優れた独創性をしめすひとつの例に、すぎないのです。スバルはつねに、次の時代を予見し、時代に一歩先んじた独創的な車創りに挑戦しています。

SUBARU *LEONE*

富士重工 Photo: セダン4WD シートベルトをしめて安全運転

Japanese advertising from early 1979.

The 1981 Leone Touring Wagon - quite a long way ahead in the fashion stakes, considering how popular this type of vehicle is today.

and Subaru duly launched the Leone SEEC-T series, which successfully controlled exhaust emissions without resorting to a catalytic converter.

June 1979 saw the debut of the second generation Leone. Available initially as a sedan or Hardtop Coupé, with power coming from either a 1595 or 1781cc boxer four, these earliest models were augmented by a three-door hatchback (with the option of a 1.3 litre engine, and 4WD on certain grades). Ultimately, in mid-1981, a Touring Wagon joined the line-up.

In 1980, Japan built seven million vehicles during the year to become the

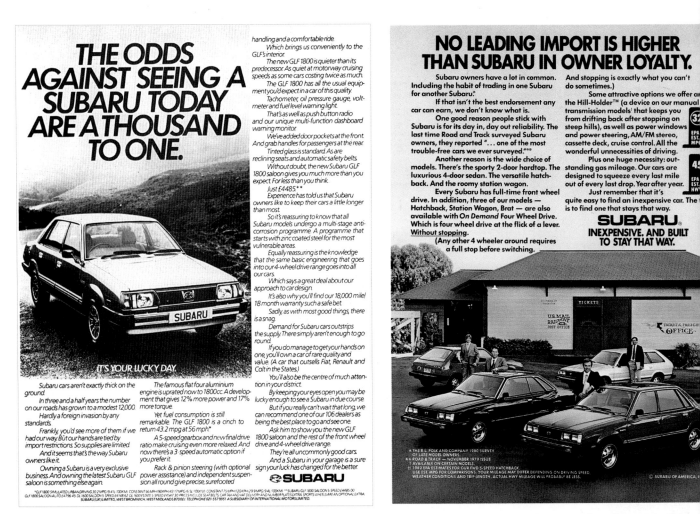

British advertising from summer 1981, using rarity as a sales point. There were only 12,000 Subarus on UK roads at that time.

US advertising showing the equivalent line-up to the Leones listed in Japan. America also had the BRAT pick-up version, the unusual name standing for Bi-drive Recreational All-terrain Transporter.

world's number one car producer. Granted, the Subaru marque only accounted for a fraction of this figure (it produced around 150,000 cars in 1979, rising to just over 200,000 units the following year), but it was a clear message that the Land of the Rising Sun could no longer be disregarded by the old school. Ironically, some of the very companies that sniggered the most in the 1950s and 1960s later became reliant on Japanese technology. And what could be more ironic than the fact that, nowadays, Britain's top car exporter is Nissan!

The second generation Rex was launched in the latter half of 1981, featuring either a three- or five-door body, and the 544cc engine carried over from its predecessor. However, as development progressed, the Rex gained the option of a turbocharger, 4WD, and a larger, 658cc engine. By the time production came to end in 1992, no less than 1,900,000 had been built; a figure that compares well with the 390,000 units from the 360 series and 290,000 R-2s.

The first 1,000,000 Leones had been built by the end of 1982, the Leone line-up now including the turbocharged RX series. The firm's increased popularity saw the Oizumi Plant commence operations in 1983 (Subaru's car production was up to around 250,000 units per annum, including the assembly of about 70,000 Nissan Cherry/Pulsar models), and there was the launch of another new model - the Domingo.

In the following year, collaboration with the Van Doorne concern of Holland resulted in the company being able to announce the successful development of the world's first electro-continuously variable transmission (E-CVT). It was duly adopted on the three-cylinder Justy, a compact, one-litre hatchback, launched that year.

The Japanese motor industry quickly moved from obscurity to worldwide dominance, at least in certain market sectors, but complete supremacy would have to wait a few more years. At Subaru, the company still had an image problem to overcome. While the marque was extremely popular in certain, highly-conservative areas in America, it had yet to gain universal acceptance; the same was

Today's roads come with standard features most cars aren't equipped to handle.

Another American advert, this time from 1984, two years later than the previous piece. By now, Subaru sales were up to around 170,000 units per annum in the States.

Today too many cars are designed without enough regard for the way most roads were designed.

Without enough regard for the hazards of everyday driving. Without enough regard for the ever present threat of inclement weather.

A car as tough as the roads it travels.

Fortunately, Subaru has designed a complete line of cars for these realities. And we started long before it was fashionable to do so.

We gave Subaru Front Wheel Drive for improved road holding. Rack and pinion steering for quicker response. Independent McPherson strut suspension for a better ride over rough roads. And a dual diagonal braking system for extra safety.

As a result, Subaru has a proven record of durability and reliability. A record achieved on real streets and highways, not just on test tracks.

You can't be sure of the road, so be sure of your car.

Since driving conditions can go from bad to worse in an instant, we've added the option of "On Demand"™ Four Wheel Drive to our Four Door Sedan and Two Door Hardtop. Making Subaru the only car company in America with a full line of front to "On Demand" Four Wheel Drive vehicles. Cars that give you more traction when the road gives you less.

This year the Two Door Hardtop incorporates our latest innovation. Turbo-Traction.™ It's our unique combination of Fuel-Injected Turbo Charging, "On Demand" Four Wheel Drive, and automatic transmission.

The result is unmatched versatility for exceptional handling under any conditions.

What's more, many dealers offer Subaru Added Security. It's the only extended service contract backed directly by Subaru.

So why settle for a car built for ideal roads, when you can have a car built for real ones.

SUBARU.
Inexpensive. And built to stay that way.

© Subaru of America, Inc. 1983

Seatbelts save lives

true in Europe. The introduction of new models and a campaign employing the World Rally Championship as a publicity vehicle would go a long way towards changing this situation ...

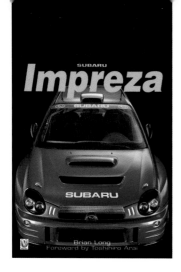

2

Creating a new image

With a background in the aircraft industry, one would expect something a bit special from a company like Subaru. After all, the field of aviation promotes high quality workmanship, leading edge metallurgy and technology, the quest for light yet strong construction of components, good packaging, and the development of reliable power without the burden of weight.

Until now, however, Subaru automobiles had been rather like the early Saabs (another aircraft maker) - a bit quirky. They had a loyal following based on practical, sensible reasoning, but few, with any honesty, would be able to look at an early Subaru and say how beautiful it was. Cute, maybe, but not beautiful.

Beyond doubt was Subaru's hard-earned reputation for building rugged and reliable machines, which also offered excellent value for money. Perhaps the American advertising slogan "Inexpensive. And built to stay that way." was closer to the truth than most lines penned by the auto industry's marketing people.

Sales in the States were very strong, although much was dependent on geographical location. At home, only Isuzu sold less cars in 1983, while very few Subarus were to be found on the roads of Europe (the Subaru range was not sold in Britain until 1977, for instance). The marque had a solid foundation on which to build, however, and all that was needed was a line-up of vehicles with more universal appeal.

Sales of the latest Leone (the third generation) started in Japan in July 1984. From a styling point of view, it was the first of a new breed of Subaru, but the longer wheelbase and wider track dimensions made possible by the new metalwork (along with a revised suspension) were practical benefits.

Refinements in the powertrain were also noteworthy, as the engines now featured sohc mechanisms instead of the previous ohv arrangements. Two basic units were available - 1.6 and 1.8 litre flat-fours, with the turbocharged version of the latter producing a healthy 135bhp.

At the end of 1985, the Leone three-door coupé made its debut. Resembling the Renault Fuego, its straight edge styling perhaps gave it the upper hand, but, if that wasn't enough, the option of four-wheel drive would definitely have swung the decision in favour of the Subaru. By the following spring, the RX/II version, with full-time four-wheel drive, had arrived on the scene.

The Leone series received what the Japanese term a 'minor change' at the time of the 1986 Tokyo Show; essentially a few cosmetic revisions, with more 4WD grades added for good measure. In October 1987 another minor change meant that an active torque split four-wheel drive system (ACT-4) was available on certain models.

Meanwhile, the two-door Subaru XT was launched in America in February 1985, going on sale in Japan four months later, badged as the Alcyone - a name derived from one of the stars in the Taurus constellation. With its rakish body (the Cd was just 0.29), this was the car that really signalled a change in Subaru's marketing stance. It was obvious after the introduction of this sporty coupé that the company was no longer satisfied with simply dominating a niche market. To increase volume - and profit - it needed products that

The new Leone was an accomplished design, with far greater universal appeal than its predecessors. It also caught the attention of enthusiasts once the RX Turbo hit the marketplace in 1985. This US advert from the time is strikingly different to earlier pieces.

The first Subaru that tests a driver's performance.

Introducing the 1985 RX 4WD Turbo. The Subaru that'll leave all your existing ideas about Subaru back in the dust.

Its body is like our Turbo Sedan. But its anatomy is like nothing else.

For one thing, the RX Turbo has sport suspension. Which gives this 5-passenger sedan all the spry handling of a sports car. Even on tight winding roads. Aided by firmer coil springs, special MacPherson struts and front and rear anti-roll bars.

It's powered by a 1.8-liter fuel injected engine with water cooled turbo and overhead cams, and also has a slick-shifting 5-speed/

Dual Range™ four wheel drive transmission.

And this muscle is backed by proper reflexes. Like manual rack-and-pinion steering, 4-wheel disc brakes (vented in front), limited slip rear differential, and, of course, the Subaru "On Demand"™ four wheel drive system.

You'll even find alloy wheels, 70-series performance radials, black trim and a rear spoiler.

Now we'd be the first to admit the RX Turbo isn't for everyone. Which is why we only made 1,500 of them.

And why you'll have to move pretty fast to catch one.

SUBARU RX TURBO
Inexpensive. And built to stay that way.

The Alcyone, as seen in Japan. In America, the Alcyone was known as the XT. Introduced with three 1.8 litre engine options (one with a twin choke carburettor, one fuel-injected, and the other turbocharged with multi-point fuel-injection), prices ranged from $7889 for the cheapest FF grade up to $13,589 for the four-wheel drive model.

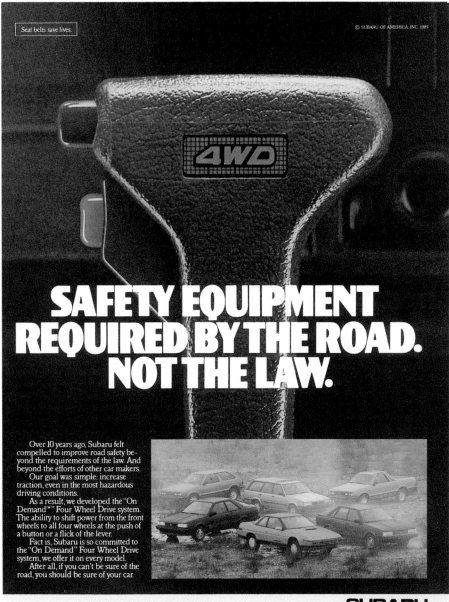

Seat belts save lives.

© SUBARU OF AMERICA, INC. 1985

SAFETY EQUIPMENT REQUIRED BY THE ROAD. NOT THE LAW.

Over 10 years ago, Subaru felt compelled to improve road safety beyond the requirements of the law. And beyond the efforts of other car makers.

Our goal was simple: increase traction, even in the most hazardous driving conditions.

As a result, we developed the "On Demand"™ Four Wheel Drive system. The ability to shift power from the front wheels to all four wheels at the push of a button or a flick of the lever.

Fact is, Subaru is so committed to the "On Demand" Four Wheel Drive system, we offer it on every model.

After all, if you can't be sure of the road, you should be sure of your car.

SUBARU.
Inexpensive. And built to stay that way.

American advertising from 1986.

The Alcyone was introduced to provide a suave and sophisticated image for the company, although Subaru's reputation for producing rugged and reliable machines was not allowed to diminish. After a respectable performance on the Singapore Airlines London-Sydney Rally, Subaru chose to enter the World Rally Championship - probably the toughest of all proving grounds - to demonstrate these established, more practical elements associated with the marque.

Subaru's WRC challenge
Subaru first appeared on the WRC scene in 1980, when two 4x4 hatchbacks were sent to tackle the Safari Rally. Finishing 18th overall, the Takeshi Hirabayashi car took Group 1 honours, but the little flat-four models were not spotted again outside of their native country.

With results improving each year on the classic Safari, the marque returned to Africa in 1983 with a team of Leone 4WD models; Yoshio Takaoka and Shigeo Sunahara finished a highly creditable fifth overall (first in Group 2), with a sister car coming home in seventh (Vic Elford's machine failed to complete the event). In New Zealand that year, Peter Bourne and Ken Fricker were 14th; enough to take Group A.

Shekhar Mehta tried his hand on the 1984 Monte Carlo Rally, coming 14th. On the 1984 Safari, Tony Fowkes took a Class win and 12th overall in the classic Kenyan event - a firm favourite with Japanese manufacturers. Later in the year, the talented Kiwi, Peter Bourne, finished eighth in New Zealand to take Group A, beating the semi-works-entered car into the bargain (Tony Teesdale came home in ninth).

With the exception of Mehta's jaunt on the Monte, at this stage, Subaru was entering only a couple of high profile events each year, particularly suited to the four-wheel drive machines. This strategy did yield a certain amount of success but, with some of the other Japanese firms supporting full World Rally Championship campaigns, it was only a matter of time before a decision would have to be taken regarding Subaru's future involvement.

1985 had seen the introduction of

---

would break into other sectors. The Alcyone/XT was a bold move and was intended mainly for the export market.

Powered by a 1.8 litre turbocharged engine (the 135bhp 1781cc unit borrowed from Leone), Subaru's new flagship model came with a five-speed gearbox, and was available with either front- or four-wheel drive; its appeal was further strengthened the following year when the Alcyone VS Turbo AT (the AT standing for automatic transmission) was launched.

A 2.7 litre model came in the summer of 1987, sporting a 150bhp flat-six, four-wheel drive with ACT-4, an electronically-controlled automatic transmission, traction control, and an electro-pneumatic (EP-S) suspension with auto levelling. At 2,929,000 yen, it was about the same price as the contemporary Mazda RX-7, so offered exceptionally good value for money, considering the array of advanced technology incorporated in the package.

Two pieces of US advertising from 1988. The four-cylinder XT was augmented by the 2.7 litre XT6 (seen here on the left) in America that year, while, at the other end of the scale, the 1.2 litre Justy became available in the States. The other advert shows the Subaru Wagon (Japan's Leone), promoting more traditional values associated with the marque.

the 1.8 litre RX Turbo, which duly made its debut on the Safari. It was a baptism of fire, but Carlo Vittuli and Robin Nixon held on to take tenth place and Group A laurels, thus giving Subaru nine WRC points. Once again, 'Possum' Bourne finished eighth in New Zealand, but this time with the new car, while other RX Turbos came home in tenth and 12th; Subaru now had 20 points. A privately entered Leone finished sixth on the Cote d'Ivorie Rally, although the event counted towards

the drivers' title only, so the Japanese maker finished the year on 20, giving it 12th place; Nissan was fourth, Toyota fifth, and Mazda tenth.

The RX Turbo had shown promise and, in 1986, a fuller programme of events was tackled, including a works effort on the prestigious Safari. Roger Ericsson took eighth on the Swedish Rally, then Mike Kirkland came sixth in Kenya, followed home by Frank Tundo in another RX Turbo; Peter Bourne retired halfway through the event, but Subaru had impressed everyone with this assault on the African classic, easily taking Class honours.

Sadly, the team was withdrawn in New Zealand after Dunlop technician, Osama Kobayashi, was involved in a fatal accident. An RX Turbo from Chile finished eighth in Argentina, although

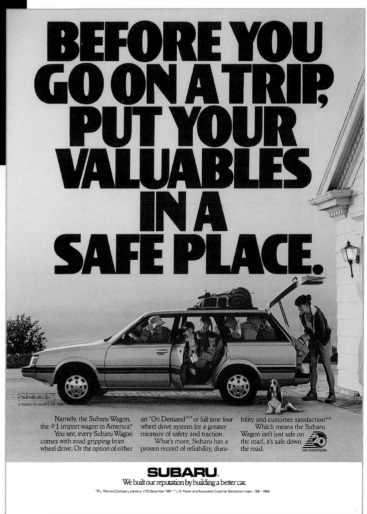

The Audi Quattro had proved beyond doubt that four-wheel drive was the way to go in the WRC arena. Subaru already knew this. This is Peter 'Possum' Bourne coming eighth on the 1984 Rally of New Zealand, and claiming Group A honours for the second year in a row.

The beautiful workings of the flat-12 'Motori Moderni' Formula 1 engine revealed by master artist Yoshihiro Inomoto. Sadly, the power unit was not given the chance to prove its undoubted potential in F1, although it was also employed in the exotic Jiotto sports car project. (Courtesy Yoshihiro Inomoto)

Subaru's WRC points remained a disappointing 13, and that was the way it stayed. Despite Bourne taking eighth in America in the last event of the year, the points only counted towards the Drivers' Championship.

In 1987, Per Eklund and Dave Whittock took 12th place on the Monte Carlo Rally, while the fastback coupé version of the model made its debut on the Safari. Four works cars were entered, with Eklund coming home in fifth, Ari Vatanen finished tenth, one place ahead of Subaru regular 'Possum' Bourne. This was enough to give Subaru the coveted Team Prize.

Ironically, it was the old RX Turbo that gave Subaru its best WRC result of the year; indeed, its best result full stop at the time - third overall in NZ, courtesy of Bourne. A privateer took ninth and Group N honours in the Ivory Coast event - the first person to finish the Bandama Rally in a production car, while Roger Ericsson was tenth in Britain's RAC Rally (Peter Bourne was forced to retire following suspension trouble).

By 1988, the RX Turbo had established itself as a strong contender in the rough road events. The Subaru team ran into trouble with the scrutineers on the Safari Rally, but overcame the problems to finish sixth (thanks to local man, Ian Duncan) and ninth. Bourne fell by the wayside in New Zealand, but Jose Celsi and Elvio Olave again did well in Argentina, the Chilean privateers finishing a very

Subaru on the 1986 Safari Rally. This is the Tundo car, which came seventh; Kirkland finished sixth (winning Group A), while Bourne crashed out of the event on the second day.

respectible fifth, taking Subaru's points total to 18. The Japanese marque ended the season with 18, incidentally, enough for ninth place.

On the 1989 Safari, 'Possum' Bourne came seventh, with teammate, Jim Heather-Hayes, in ninth. However, Bourne's hopes of doing well in his home country were dashed after he was excluded. In Argentina, he met with more bad luck, retiring in his STi-entered RX Turbo; Celsi and Olave also failed to finish, an accident putting an end to their rally.

Although Peter Bourne came home tenth in the Australian Rally, at this stage, Subaru's challenge was still rather half-hearted compared to the likes of Toyota, Nissan and Mazda - Mitsubishi was also starting to up the ante. Meanwhile, the management at Fuji Heavy Industries decided it was time to elevate the company's road car image, seeing a full-out attack on the

WRC as the ideal way to achieve this goal. A new era had begun.

Corporate news

Eiichi Ohara became Honorary Chairman in spring 1985, with Sadamichi Sasaki named as the new Chairman, and Toshihiro Tajima elected as President. A year or so later, a joint venture with Ta Ching Motors Co. Ltd was established in Taiwan (later, the Impreza was built there in CKD form), whilst in 1987, Subaru and Isuzu formed Subaru-Isuzu Automotive Inc. (SIA) in the States: production began there in 1990.

In 1988, an agreement was signed with Volvo regarding the handling of Japanese sales. It was an interesting development, as the two makers were similarly perceived - conservative but solid, although Subaru was doing all it could to shake off this staid image. Perhaps the most vivid example of this effort to make the marque more appealing to enthusiasts was the 'Motori Moderni' project. Unfortunately, the Subaru Motori Moderni F1 engine saga came to a premature end. The company supplied its jewel-like flat-12 to the Coloni team in time for a Formula One debut at the 1990 US GP. For one reason or another, Bertrand Gachot failed to pre-qualify. The same happened in Brazil, San Marino, and Canada. Not surprisingly, the project was cancelled shortly afterwards.

Meanwhile, Subaru of America (based in New Jersey) came under the control of Subaru Head Office in Japan in mid-1990, and, at the same time, Toshihiro Tajima became Subaru's Chairman, handing over the Presidency to ex-Nissan Diesel man, Isamu Kawai. By now, the company had another important new model on the market - the Legacy.

The Legacy

The Legacy, Subaru's new global car, was introduced on the home market in February 1989. Bigger than the earlier Subaru saloons and estates, it stayed true to the marque's traditional values, incorporating horizontally-opposed, four-cylinder power units combined with either front- or four-wheel drive layout.

Sales started in America in April 1989 (where it was classed as an early 1990 model), and duly began in Europe five months later. In the States, the model was sold with a 2.2 litre flat-four (rated at 130bhp), although most other markets received 1.8 litre units as well; there were 1.8 and two-litre versions for the Japanese in order for the vehicle to qualify for a worthwhile tax break.

The hottest 1994cc unit had twin-cams for each bank of cylinders, and initially produced 150bhp. However, the addition of a turbocharger added another 50bhp, while the RS Type RA (a development based on the RS Type R and launched at the end of the year) came with 220 horses under the bonnet.

In its debut year, the Legacy set a world speed record for 100,000km (the equivalent to 62,500 miles or, put another way, circling the globe almost two-and-a-half times), completing the distance at an average

Advertising for the new Legacy, as seen in Japan (above) and Great Britain. The US 1990 model year saw the American equivalent to the Leone models badged as the Loyale, and the launch of the new Legacy series (some models were built at the SIA facility in Lafayette, Indiana, to overcome import restrictions).

speed of 139.6mph (223.3kph). However, an even tougher test was in store for the Legacy ...

WRC - the Legacy era

When the Legacy made its debut in 1989, it provided the basis for Subaru's next WRC challenger. Two turbocharged 4WD prototypes were built in Ohta to allow testing in Kenya, and Prodrive was hard at work in England building cars for the 1990 season's European rounds, complete with Prodrive's own six-speed transmission.

After officially announcing the programme in September 1989, the 290bhp Legacy received homologation papers on the first day of 1990, making its long-awaited WRC debut on the Safari Rally that year. And what a debut! Markku Alen, Ian Duncan, Mike Kirkland, 'Possum' Bourne and Jim Heather-Hayes each had Group A versions, whilst local man, Patrick Njiru, was supplied with a Group N model.

Alen ran away from the field in the early stages, but sadly, after an impressive display of speed, mud in the radiator caused the engine to overheat. The Flying Finn was full of praise for the car, and, whilst the Heather-Hayes entry was the only Group A Legacy to finish (the others went out with various engine maladies), the vehicle's potential was obvious. In addition, Njiru came eighth (only two places behind Heather-Hayes) to become the first driver to complete the torturous event in a Group N machine.

In the Acropolis Rally, Alen was quick once again, but pulled out on the last day with engine trouble. Meanwhile, Ian Duncan had shipped one of the Safari cars to Greece to pull off another Group N victory (eighth overall).

'Possum' Bourne took fifth in a Japanese registered Group A model in his home rally, and Markku Alen came fourth in his home event. As the circus moved to Australia, Bourne kept up the momentum with another fourth place, although San Remo proved disappointing, with both cars retiring; the new hydraulically-controlled centre differentials were not given a chance to prove themselves.

On the RAC, the final event of

An exciting combination enters the World Rally Championship in 1990.
Subaru and Prodrive.
Subaru have a long established reputation for producing the World's leading four wheel drive road cars.
The Prodrive pedigree has been built on success; providing high quality, high performance engineering solutions that get results.
The Subaru Legacy Group A Rally Car – a joint venture of engineering excellence.

STi
SUBARU TECNICA
INTERNATIONAL

prodrive

STi and Prodrive throwing down the gauntlet in 1989.

Markku Alen on the 1990 Safari.

the season, Alen led after the first day, but turbo trouble slowed him before he finally threw in the towel; interestingly, a second car was entered for Derek Warwick (the ex-F1 star who would also campaign cars in Group C and the BTCC), although his challenge ended on the third day after he came off the road.

At year end, Subaru finished fourth, but, given the extremely tough competition (and the small number of events entered), it was a good start. 1991 held a lot of promise ...

Sure enough, Alen gave Subaru a podium finish in Sweden - his third was the best result to date for the Legacy, and equalled Subaru's top placing in a WRC event (Bourne's 1987 NZ performance). In Portugal, Alen finished fifth with teammate, Francois Chatriot, claiming sixth, while in Kenya, Ian Duncan came sixth; Subaru again took Group N honours, thanks to Michael Hughes in a locally registered Legacy.

The scenery changed as the WRC moved to the fast asphalt of Corsica: Chatriot came a gallant ninth in a Prodrive prepared car, while Alen made up for his Greek excursion with a fourth in New Zealand.

In Finland, Alen's engine blew after a good start: he was so disappointed that he signed for Toyota in the hope it would bring him the WRC crown that

he had never won, despite being one of the most successful rally drivers of all time. At least the Finn gave Subaru a fourth in Australia before he swapped his white overalls for red ones.

For the RAC, Subaru put together what looked like a dream team: Markku

Alen, Ari Vatanen and Colin McRae. A fifth for Vatanen was the best they had to show for it, however; Alen crashed out, as did the young but talented Scot, although both had led the event.

Subaru finished sixth, and there was now real hope in the Japanese

Linking road cars to success in competition is a valuable marketing tool. This Japanese advert from 1990 takes the opportunity to show the Legacy that won Group N (the production model category) in the Safari Rally that year.

Alen tackling the Swedish weather in 1991.

with a Legacy, after all).

As if to prove a point, McRae won the British Open Championship again in 1992, although it was interesting to see that his brother, Alister, came third, claiming the Group N title along the way. Another star of the future - Richard Burns - won the National Rally Championship at the wheel of a Legacy.

Meanwhile, in the WRC, with Vatanen and McRae as nominated drivers, and an improved car, Subaru hopes were high. The 1992 Legacy ran with a novel semi-automatic

Ari Vatanen on the 1991 RAC Rally.

camp, with more power in a lighter car, improved braking and development of a semi-automatic gearbox going on behind the scenes.

As well as putting in an excellent performance on the RAC, like his father before him, Jimmy, Colin McRae won the British Open Championship, earning him a well-deserved works drive with Subaru (he'd won the British title

A young Colin McRae on the 1992 Swedish Rally. His exciting driving style brought him many fans, and many trophies, too.

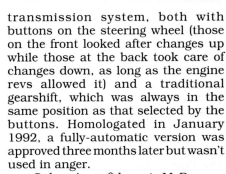

transmission system, both with buttons on the steering wheel (those on the front looked after changes up while those at the back took care of changes down, as long as the engine revs allowed it) and a traditional gearshift, which was always in the same position as that selected by the buttons. Homologated in January 1992, a fully-automatic version was approved three months later but wasn't used in anger.

Subaru's confidence in McRae was rewarded in Sweden when the 23-year old Scot took second, which was not only the best placing achieved by the Legacy, but the best WRC result for the Subaru marque.

1992 RAC Rally (Vatanen).

Per Eklund had come sixth in Sweden with a Clarion sponsored Legacy, and Noriyuki Koseki entered him and Patrick Njiru on the Safari in Group N models; the local man came eighth, while the highly experienced Swede finished ninth; Subaru took the laurels in the production category once again, giving the Japanese manufacturer a Class hat trick. In the background, testing of a prototype of the forthcoming Impreza disguised as a short-wheelbase Legacy was in progress.

1993 Tour de Corse (McRae).

RAC, with Vatanen coming second and McRae sixth, although the Scot was undoubtedly the fastest man on the event before a series of problems slowed him down. As a result, Subaru finished the 1992 season in a solid fourth place, despite a somewhat sporadic series of entries on the various rounds.

Meanwhile, the all-new Impreza had been launched in Japan, and it

Subaru's first WRC win came on the 1993 Rally of New Zealand, courtesy of Colin McRae.

Colin McRae was destined to shine again in Greece. Although he came fourth, he won as many stages as the Acropolis winner. However, New Zealand was a disaster from a Subaru point of view - Vatanen, McRae and 'Possum' Bourne all went out with engine problems.

As the teams moved to Finland and more familiar territory for Vatanen, the Flying Finn was back on form, claiming fourth, while McRae came eighth after an eventful rally. Ari was running well in Australia, too, until the transmission let go; at least Bourne came sixth to uphold Subaru honour.

The Legacy performed well on the

American advertising for the SVX, dating from spring 1992.

was this car that would ultimately carry the torch for the Subaru works rally effort. The team continued with the Legacy for the first part of 1993 but, as the WRC became increasingly competitive, the realization that a smaller, lighter base car was needed came not a moment too soon, just as it had with Mitsubishi when it changed from the Galant to the Lancer.

The Legacy went out in style, with McRae coming third in Sweden, seventh in Portugal (Markku Alen covered for an injured Vatanen to take fourth), and fifth in Corsica. Oddly, Subaru chose to run the tiny Vivio on the Safari, but without success (Njiru was the only finisher), and there was disappointment in Greece where Vatanen's Legacy led until a crash halfway through the event.

On the Rally of New Zealand, Colin McRae triumphed to give Subaru its first WRC win. Subaru's President, Isamu Kawai, had said that he didn't want STi to campaign the Impreza until the Legacy had been made into a winning car, so McRae's victory could not have come at a better time.

The New Zealand success was followed by a second for Vatanen in Australia, and an interesting result on the RAC - seventh for Richard Burns (winner of the British Championship that year), and tenth for Alister McRae

シートベルトをしめ、スピードを控えた安全運

RV
SERIES
ISUZU

V6センセーション

イルムシャーRS（オプション装

Drive with me.

いつもとはちがう道を走ってみる。
大地を駆ける風になる。

irmscher · RS

irmscher-RS
Dimensions: 4230mm × 1745mm × 1835mm
Wheelbase: 2330mm
RECARO SPORTS SEAT
MOMO 4-SPOKE STEERING WHEEL
irmscher TUNED SUSPENSION
4-LINK REAR COIL SUSPENSION
4-WHEEL VENTILATED DISK BRAKE
BRADLEY ALUMINIUM WHEEL

イルムシャーRS

V6 3.2ℓ DOHC 24VALVE 200PS(ネット)

BIGHORN

Handling by LOTUS
BASIC
irmscher
irmscher · RS

※「ネット」とは、エンジンを車両に搭載した状態とほぼ同条件で測定したもの

The Subaru line-up was quite extensive now, ranging from minicars to GTs to off-roaders - the Isuzu Bighorn (seen here) was also sold as a Subaru, including the 'Handling by Lotus' version introduced in early 1992.

(Colin, his brother, was driving the Impreza, which had made its debut on the 1000 Lakes). Ultimately, Subaru finished third in the 1993 World Championship, beating the mighty Lancia team, and McRae came fifth in

the Drivers' title chase.

Road car developments
The SVX was introduced at the 1991 North American Motor Show. The space-age bodywork, with styling based

on a Giugiaro concept, hid a water-cooled, 3.3 litre flat-six linked to a four-speed, electronically-controlled automatic transmission with four-wheel drive. Sales of this new 240bhp model began in Japan (where it was badged as the Alcyone SVX) in September that year, signalling the end of the original Alcyone; 98,918 examples had been built in all.

The SVX certainly moved the Alcyone up a notch, from sports coupé to Grand Tourer, with the established European marques firmly in its sights. The British *Fast Lane* magazine carried out an interesting comparison test with the rather more expensive four-litre Jaguar XJS, observing: "Just one drive in that scenic British backdrop was enough to tell us that the £27,999 SVX was seriously well-developed. A week wafting along motorways, ambling through traffic and whistling through more picturesque scenery taught us the SVX offered fitting opposition to Jaguar, pedigree or no pedigree ... For us, there can be no doubt that the Subaru SVX is one of the most significant Japanese cars we've ever tested."

While hardly in the same league as the SVX flagship, the Legacy quickly gained a strong following, its image enhanced by a successful WRC programme. By the summer of 1991, Legacy sales topped the 10,000 units a month mark in Japan, and the figure

The STi story

Subaru's STi division (STi standing for Subaru Tecnica International) was founded on 2 April 1988, as a wholly-owned subsidiary of FHI. With a capital of 250 million yen, the business, based in Mitaka, Tokyo, was formed with three main objectives: to plan and manage Subaru's motorsports activities; to develop and manufacture specialist components for aftermarket use (this also led to the sale and repair of complete vehicles); training of technicians.

It should be noted that the record-breaking Legacy was the responsibility of STi, while 1989 also saw the company named as the entrant on a number of World Rally Championship events, although the following year brought with it an official works programme employing the Legacy.

An STi version of the Legacy was introduced in 1992, paving the way for future production models and limited editions. The STi President at the time of the Impreza project was Ryuichiro Kuze, incidentally, who remains an honorary board member to this day, as does Isamu Kawai.

was set to rise again once the Legacy Touring Wagon (bringing with it the availability of the 2.2 litre powerplant for the home market) augmented the existing range.

Meanwhile, the Vivio replaced the Rex in March 1992, reflecting Subaru's progress. Its lineage could be traced back to the first Subaru - the 360. Following its predecessors through the decades, one can see with each new generation a giant step towards

modernity. The Vivio, with accomplished styling and state-of-the-art, 658cc engine (which developed almost 100bhp/litre in supercharged guise), almost completed a full reshuffle of the line-up which had seen every model move upmarket.

Subaru had now built ten million cars, but there was one more introduction before the year came to an end. The final piece of the jigsaw: enter the Subaru Impreza ...

Prodrive

The other part of the Legacy equation was Prodrive, founded in 1984 by David Richards and Ian Parry out of a motorsport marketing and consultancy business. Ex-Talbot man, Dave Lapworth, soon joined the organization, bringing with him the engineering expertise necessary to make the business a success.

Dave Richards, born in Orpington in 1952, had been Ari Vatanen's co-driver, allowing the Finn to win the Acropolis Rally in 1980 and 1981. In addition, the team won the Brazilian and Finnish rounds in 1981, not to mention the World Championship crown.

The Ford Escort campaigned by Vatanen and Richards had been sponsored by Rothmans, and Prodrive duly formed the Rothmans Porsche Rally Team. It won the 1984 Middle East Rally Championship, and came second in the European Championship.

The Prodrive operation moved from Silverstone to its present headquarters in Banbury in 1986, the year in which the team bagged a hat trick of Middle East titles.

By 1987, Prodrive had formed a close bond with BMW, preparing cars for both WRC and BTCC competition. The Banbury concern won its first WRC event that year, when Bernard Beguin took a BMW M3 to victory in the Tour de Corse. The M3 also took the British Touring Car Championship in 1988, 1989 and 1990.

With the BMW era coming to an end, at least from a rallying point of view (the Prodrive M3s were still successful in the BTCC), a relationship was forged with Subaru. By 1991, Prodrive had its own engineering division, allowing other motorsport teams and mainstream manufacturers access to its project design consultancy facilities.

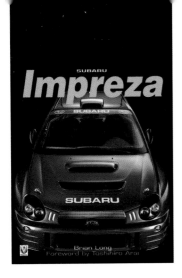

3

The first generation models

The Impreza was basically an indirect replacement for the Leone, as the two models had similar overall dimensions (the Legacy was a much bigger automobile), and whilst it continued for the time being, the highly-successful Leone was discontinued in the near future. By the time sales ceased in early 1994, a total of 3,790,380 Leones had been built.

Announced on 22 October 1992, instead of continuing with the Leone moniker, a new name - Impreza - was apparently chosen in order to give this latest car a fresh, youthful image. Indeed, even the sales brochure

Above: A swan in flight was used as the Imprezza's styling theme, although a vivid imagination was necessary to see it in the finished product. It was an accomplished design, however, and all-round visibility was very good, thanks to a low bonnet line, large glass areas and thin pillars.

Right: Early design proposals included some interesting variations for the tail treatment. Some reflected the final Sports Wagon design but with the rear section executed completely in glass; others hinted at conventional five-door hatchbacks with Ford Scorpio or Peugeot 309-style back-ends, while some were a touch more original, resembling a scaled-up Honda CRX. One-fifth scale clays were used for final design analysis and aerodynamic testing. Once the styling was settled upon, a full-sized clay was produced for evaluation. After signing-off, another model was made in glassfibre, complete with windows and a full interior, in order to finalize the detailing.

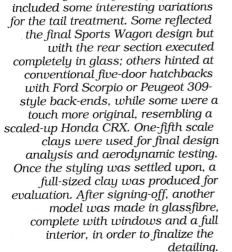

An interview with the project leader

Miho Long: The Mitsubishi Lancer is an obvious arch rival for the Impreza, but which other vehicles did you consider to be the main competitors for your new car?

Hideshige Gomi: We had an image of an affordable, high class vehicle in mind - one that the majority of people could use on a daily basis. This was true across the entire Impreza range, so for me, the Honda Civic presented the greatest threat, followed by cars like the Toyota Corolla series, the Nissan Sunny and Mitsubishi Lancer. During development, the high powered version of the Lancer did not exist, so the biggest direct rival for the WRX was the [Nissan] Pulsar GTi, with the Skyline GT-R being the benchmark in the sector.

Miho Long: How closely did you work with the STi engineers in the design of the Impreza in view of its WRC mission? Or did FHI complete the vehicle first and then leave it to STi/Prodrive to make it into a competitive car?

Hideshige Gomi: The WRX was developed fully at FHI. It was after we had finished that it went to Prodrive for conversion into a competition car.

Miho Long: Did the majority of development time go into the WRX, or were the lesser models given equal attention? And in retrospect, are you surprised by the worldwide popularity of the original WRX?

Hideshige Gomi: The bread-and-butter sedan and station wagon models were the main focus of attention in the early stages. It was as the range developed that the WRX came into being. Although something like it had been on my mind from the very start, I wanted to get the basic cars right first - the WRX was such an attractive project, people would have devoted all their time and energy to the turbocharged machine, thus neglecting the others, and that couldn't be allowed to happen.

To answer the second part of your question, from my point of view, I was fairly sure the WRX was going to be a hit with enthusiasts. But I have to say the level of support the model received certainly took me by surprise.

Miho Long: Were there any areas of the vehicle that you would have liked to change before the launch, or were you completely satisfied with the Impreza package?

Hideshige Gomi: As far as I was concerned, there was nothing left to do with the Impreza. I was very happy with it as it was.

Miho Long: How did you feel after the Impreza's first WRC victory?

Hideshige Gomi: It took a while for the Impreza to score its first win, so I felt relief as much as anything. At the same time, though, I was quietly confident that the Impreza would one day be a World Champion car. We had designed it to be a winner, so it was only a matter of time before it fulfilled its destiny.

Hideshige Gomi, the man who headed the original Impreza project, pictured recently. The Chief Designer was Masashi Takahashi, while Takeshi Ito was in charge of the engineering; Masaru Katsurada was involved with development of the chassis.

catchline 'New Driver's Basic' although not of great meaning to native English speakers, was used in an effort to appeal to enthusiasts.

The new Impreza line-up included a four-door saloon in FF guise (powered by 1.5 litre sohc unit), and in 4WD form, the latter using 1.6 and 1.8 litre sohc engines for motive power; there was also a two-litre WRX saloon with a turbocharged twin-cam boxer and 4WD. In addition, the Sports Wagon, expected to account for around one in four sales, came in front-drive form (with the 1.6 litre engine) or with a 4WD layout employing a 1.8 litre power unit.

The saloon - or Hardtop Sedan in Subaru lingo - was refreshingly different to the Leone, with softer, rounded lines designed not to date quickly. The same styling policy was applied to the interior, which had a very upmarket appearance compared to other vehicles in its class.

The body was light and strong, and designed to conform with all known safety standards at that time (side door beams were standard, incidentally). It employed galvanized steel for the floorpan and wheelwells, while all the other panels were treated via coatings, underseal, or wax in cavities, to enhance the vehicle's longevity; the metal used was chosen because it gave a good paint finish. The frameless side windows were more than just a styling gimmick; a lot of thought had gone into reducing the number of

Japanese advertising for the new Impreza. Kyle MacLachlan featured in domestic publicity material (including the first catalogues), no doubt because of the Twin Peaks boom in Japan at that time. Note the 'SW' badge on the Sports Wagon C-post, which appeared on very early cars only.

components involved, thus increasing build quality whilst speeding up production. It also reduced the time necessary to replace them in the field.

The sporty WRX, which formed the basis for the new Subaru WRC challenger, was distinguished by an aluminium bonnet with vents and a

massive air scoop in the centre, a different grille with a deep spoiler and integrated foglights beneath it, side skirts, a lowered rear valance, and a rear spoiler (for some reason, the rocker panel extensions and rear pieces were left off the Type RA). At this time, the aerodynamic appendages were quite conservative, although, as the years passed, they became more efficient and increasingly prominent.

With a wheelbase of 2520mm (99.2in.), the overall length was listed at 4350mm (171.3in.), width was 1690mm (66.5in.), and height was 1415mm (55.7in.). On most models, the track measured 1470mm (57.9in.) at the front and 1465mm (57.7in.) at the back; ground clearance was 165mm (6.5in.) on 4WD models, or 155mm (6.1in.) on FF grades, which - naturally - reduced the overall height by 10mm (0.4in.).

The WRX was pretty much the same with regard to dimensions, although it was 10mm (0.4in.) shorter and used the track measurements listed for the other standard grades, which were 10mm (0.4in.) narrower at each end. It also had the lower ground clearance, so overall height was listed at 1405mm (55.3in.), and had a larger 60 litre (13.2 Imperial gallon) fuel tank in place of the usual 50 litre (11 gallon) version. As for weight, the WRX was 1200kg dry (2640lb), whilst the basic WRX Type RA weighed 30kg (66lb) less - about the same as a top HX model, but substantially more than the 990kg (2178lb) quoted for the base car.

In the author's humble opinion, the estate, or Sports Wagon, was not quite as attractive, although the paintwork colour made a big difference, either hiding or accentuating the rather chunky rear pillars: one journalist likened the styling to "the whacky AMC Pacer." The glass in the tailgate was interesting, though, running high up into the roofline. The Sports Wagon shared its leading dimensions with the run-of-the-mill saloons, although the vehicle weight increased slightly and the load carrying capacity was naturally far greater.

Masaru Katsurada, the man behind the Legacy, was in favour of using conventional in-line, four-cylinder engines for the smaller capacity units, as they are obviously much cheaper to produce. However, it was decided to follow Subaru tradition. As such, the four engines listed for the Impreza were all compact, all-aluminium alloy, flat-four boxer units - the two smaller fuel-injected sohc

powerplants were new, while the other two were borrowed from the Legacy series. Smooth running and reliability were the key areas of development, although power was not neglected for the sake of enthusiasts.

Starting with the 1.5 litre engine (code EJ15), this had a bore and stroke of 85.0 x 65.8mm, giving a cubic capacity of 1493cc. The single overhead camshaft on each bank of two cylinders, driven by a cogged belt at the front of the engine, acted on roller rocker arms to operate the four valves per pot with hydraulic adjustment incorporated into the design; the single sparkplug was placed in the centre of the head. With a compression ratio of 9.4:1, it developed 97bhp at 6000rpm, along with a maximum 95lbft of torque 1500rpm lower down the rev range.

The fuel-injected EJ16 was a sister unit, with the same stroke but a slightly bigger 87.9mm bore to give 1597cc. Listed with an identical 9.4:1 compression ratio, there was a 3bhp gain in power and a 7lbft gain in torque, both maxima being produced at the same revs as those quoted for the smaller powerplant.

The 1.8 litre EJ18 had previously been employed in the Legacy series. With multi-point fuel-injection and a high efficiency intake manifold, this had the same bore measurement as the EJ16 but a longer 75.0mm stroke, resulting in a capacity of 1820cc. This, combined with a slightly higher 9.5:1 compression, took maximum output up to 115bhp at 6000rpm, and 113lbft at 4500rpm.

For the WRX, there was the Boxer Turbo from the Legacy RS and GT grades, albeit slightly modified. Designated the EJ20, this was an all-alloy flat-four with a 1994cc capacity (92.0 x 75.0mm). It featured twin camshafts on each bank, thus enabling direct activation (via a cam follower with hydraulic adjustment) of the four valves per cylinder - one of the main differences between the Impreza and Legacy unit. With fuel-injection, a Mitsubishi TD04H turbocharger, intercooler and an 8.5:1 compression ratio, it developed a healthy 240bhp at 6000rpm, along with 224lbft of torque. The two-litre cars came with twin exhausts, incidentally, whereas all other models had a single pipe exiting on the nearside.

The five-speed manual gearbox

was designed with smooth shifts in mind. With fifth outside a conventional 'H' pattern to the top right (and reverse directly below it), the internal ratios were 3.636, 2.105, 1.428, 1.093 and 0.825 on FF models, or 3.545, 2.111, 1.448, 1.088 and 0.825 on 4WD cars; final drive was 3.90:1 on both.

A special, close ratio gearbox came with the WRX, with 3.454 on first, 2.062 on second, 1.448 on third, 1.088 on fourth and 0.825 on top. The Type RA version was different again, with internal ratios of 3.454, 2.333, 1.750, 1.354 and 0.972; both WRX models had a 4.111:1 final drive.

An electronically-controlled, four-speed automatic was fitted on all cars that came with the two pedal option. With a seven position selector for more precise control, it was linked to the engine computer in a bid to provide smoother shifts. A 'Manual' button gave greater control in bad traction situations, allowing the car to start off in second, while in standard operating mode, the transmission adapted to driver input, noting throttle action so that someone with a heavy right foot got a more sporting shift pattern than one who drove on a light throttle.

The four-speed ECT (not available on the WRX) came with a 2.785 ratio on first, 1.545 on second, a direct third and an overdriven 0.694 top gear on all grades; the final drive was listed as 4.44:1 for the majority of cars, although the 1.8 litre 4WD models came with a 4.11:1 ratio instead.

Although front-wheel drive was the starting point for the Impreza's layout, Subaru's 4WD expertise was a big selling point. Four-wheel drive cars fitted with the electronically-controlled automatic gearbox were treated to Subaru's active torque split system, which featured a multi-plate transfer clutch (MP-T) which not only compensated for road conditions on a full-time basis, but also sent more power to the back under acceleration and to the front under braking to account for weight transfer. In normal operating conditions, the split with this 'box was 60:40.

For manual cars with 4WD, there was a bevel gear centre differential with viscous coupling. This full-time 4WD system normally split torque 50:50, but the viscous coupling compensated as road conditions changed, sending power to the wheels

Part of the first Japanese catalogue; these pages feature the sporty, 1.8 litre HX Edition S saloon.

with the most traction. The rear differential (a newly designed, compact unit for normally-aspirated vehicles, weighing in at less than half of an older, more conventional item) featured a limited-slip device.

There was one other transmission, but only for the manual Sports Wagon with the 'AirSus' package. This was a dual range 4WD system with 'Hi' and 'Lo' settings; the low range provided 1.6 times more traction than the high range, and automatically raised the car's ride height by 40mm (1.6in.) once activated.

On the subject of suspensions, the Impreza came with a fully independent set-up, designed to give a long wheel stroke, good stability, and a reduction in friction and unsprung weight. Based on the Legacy layout, MacPherson struts were employed up front, combined with lightweight, L-shaped lower arms. At the back also were large diameter struts with integral coil springs, but this time put together with parallel transverse links; a trailing arm arrangement was used for location. An anti-roll bar came as standard up front, with a rear one also specified on the higher powered machines.

Sure enough, the WRX came with a much harder suspension, with special springs and bushes and beefier anti-roll bars - 19mm (0.75in.) diameter up front, and 18mm (0.71in.) at the rear. In addition, the shock absorbers

incorporated a linear control valve, the front lower arms were of cast aluminium alloy to save weight, and ball-joint links were used for the front anti-roll bar. The Type RA featured further uprated, stronger components - the equivalent level to those used on the rally circuit.

Finally, Subaru's own electro-pneumatic air suspension (EP-S) was available on the Sports Wagon HX grade. This gave four-wheel auto levelling, and a greater ride height, either automatically (when the low range was engaged on the transmission) or via a switch.

Power-assisted rack-and-pinion steering was standard for all cars, mounted on a steering support beam for extra rigidity, and therefore better response. A 16:1 ratio was specified for the majority of the range, but two-litre vehicles had a quicker 15:1 rack. Although the HX Edition S and WRX models came with a leather-trimmed Nardi three-spoke steering wheel (the Gara III type), most cars had a Subaru three-spoke item, or a four-spoke one (like that found in America) if the optional airbag was fitted.

All normally-aspirated (NA) cars had 260mm (10.2in.) diameter vented disc brakes up front; these were combined with drums at the rear to give a good handbrake. Brake lines were split diagonally, with a rear pressure control valve coming as

standard for added safety. A 230mm (9.0in.) diameter brake servo was standard on the NA cars, although those with ABS had a different set-up. The optional ABS system was a four-channel, four-sensor type (with G-sensor), incidentally, and brought with it rear discs and a minimum of 14-inch wheels to give the necessary clearance.

The WRX had two-pot calipers working on ventilated discs that were 277mm (10.9in.) in diameter and 24mm (0.9in.) wide at the front, with equally large (266mm, or 10.5in.) but narrower vented discs at the back. Like the cars with ABS, the WRX came with tandem boosters - a combination of 180mm (7.0in.) and 200mm (8.0in.) diameter components. ABS was an option on the strict WRX (it was not available on the WRX Type RA), and added 10kg (22lb) to the vehicle's kerb weight.

Wheel and tyre combinations were just as complicated, with cheaper grades having 165 SR13 rubber on steel rims, and the CX and HS 175/70 tyres on 14-inch steel rims trimmed with wheel covers (naturally different to those found on the CS, while the CF grade had to do without); the HX saloon had its own unique wheel trims and fatter 185/70 R14 Yokohamas.

Meanwhile, the HX Edition S sported 15-inch wheels and tyres; actually, the same five-spoke alloys fitted to the WRX models. These were shod with 195/60 rubber on the top

Impreza
WRX

4WD Pure Sports Sedan

This page and next three: The WRX catalogue. The layout was nice from an engineering point of view, with the engine placed near the bulkhead and the transmission within the wheelbase, all low down and symmetrical. Early testing was carried out in Germany and France. The first WRX had a 7000rpm redline, incidentally. Markings were white on black, although the various calibrations glowed light green once the lights were switched on.

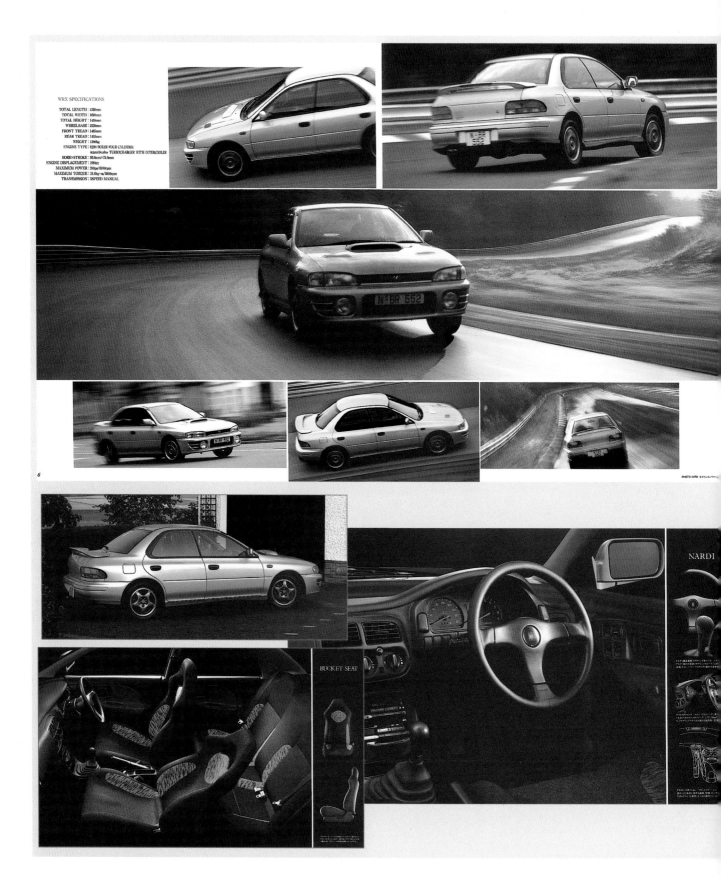

WRX SPECIFICATIONS

TOTAL LENGTH : 4340mm
TOTAL WIDTH : 1690mm
TOTAL HEIGHT : 1405mm
WHEELBASE : 2520mm
FRONT TREAD : 1465mm
REAR TREAD : 1465mm
WEIGHT : 1200kg
ENGINE TYPE : EJ20 BOXER FOUR CYLINDER
4cam16valve TURBOCHARGER WITH INTERCOOLER
BORE×STROKE : 92.0mm×75.0mm
ENGINE DISPLACEMENT : 1994cc
MAXIMUM POWER : 240ps/6000rpm
MAXIMUM TORQUE : 31.0kg-m/3600rpm
TRANSMISSION : 5SPEED MANUAL

6

PHOTO : WRX ライトシルバーメタリック

NARDI

BUCKET SEAT

シマムパワー240ps. BOXER TURBOのフルパワーを生かし切る、タイム4WDのトラクション。

240ps 2.0ℓBOXER 4cam 16valve

アクセルワークにダイレクトに反応するアクセルレスポンス。そして、高回転まで持続する伝説的なパワーフィール。インプレッサWRXのパワーユニットは、オールアルミ合金製BOXERによる16バルブ、EJ20-TURBO。スバルが熟成を続けてきた水平対向4気筒エンジンである。水平対向（ボクサー）のエンジンは低振動で、シリンダーブロックの剛性の高さとあわせ、低速から高回転までのメカニカルノイズを抑える...

FULL TIME 4WD SYSTEM

BOXERエンジンの高性能なパワーをフルに生かし切るのが、機敏に反応した高速域のスピリティ。そして、4WDの装備をつくりだすナチュラルなハンドリング...

INTERCOOLER TURBO

BOXER、そしてエキパルブの本来の力をでもある最初のターボの伸びの力を余分なく発揮するために、大容量高性能型の水冷ターボチャージャーを採用し、高出力タイプのターボンブレードと...

TRANSMISSION

4本のバックギアの高回転域の時に生み出されるのギア比選定がなされたトランスミッション。レフト式横列・ダブルダブレ式...

...ージしたラインを正確にトレースするために。...ーティサスペンション&高剛性ボディ。

CHASSIS TECHNOLOGY

いかに高度なパワーユニットやサスペンションを装備していても、ボディの剛性が低ければ...

SAFETY & RECYCLE

セイフティなインプレッサWRXの...

KE SYSTEM

...はもちろん、信頼のおける十分なコントロール性を備えたブレーキシステム...

①フォグランプ(WRX)
バンパー埋め込み式の大径フォグランプ。夜間の悪天候時の視界確保に威力を発揮する。

②リヤスポイラー(WRX)
ハイマウントストップランプを内蔵したリヤスポイラー。高速走行時の安定性を向上するとともに、後続車へブレーキングを確実に知らせる。

③電動チルト&スライドサンルーフ
(WRXにメーカー装着オプション)
ワンタッチでチルトアップ&ダウン＆ワンタッチ操作可能。

④アルミホイール&ハイグリップタイヤ
軽量化により15サイズのアルミホイール、ワイドなリムサイズによりタイヤの接地性を上げ、郊外での限界域のグリップを確保し、タイヤには205/55 R15サイズのブリヂストン・ポテンザ RE71を採用。すぐれたグリップ能力と操縦特性を発揮する。WRX typeRAには、コンペティションレベルのグリップとラクションを発揮する専用開発のブリヂストン・エクスペディア205/50 R15ラジアルタイヤを採用。

⑤パワーウインドゥ(WRX)

⑥サイドウインドゥ&ベンチレーター(WRX)
前後同時にすばやく車室内を換気可能にする。

⑦オーディオシステム(WRX)
AM/FM電子チューナーラジオ一体型のフルロジックフロントロード・カセットデッキ＆4スピーカーを組み合わせた、ADDZESTブランドの高機能オーディオシステム。CDプレーヤーやCDオートチェンジャーにも対応したシステムアップも容易である。

⑧カップホルダー

⑨オートエアコン(WRXにメーカー装着オプション)

⑩センターコンソール

⑪スポットマップランプ(WRX)

⑫大容量トランクルーム
・バンパーレベルから広く開口するトランクは、ゴルフバッグ4セットが入る大容量を確保している。

オーディオシステム(KENWOOD)

オーディオシステム(ADDZEST)

3連メーター(油温計、電圧計、内外気温度計)

15インチアルミホイール(ディッシュタイプ)

エアロスプラッシュ

カーペットマット(スポーティ・ブラック)

コンペティション・ユース・オンリー

Impreza
WRX typeRA

ターゲットは、コンペティション・フィールド。
コン教練で一段と過酷になっていく、
行くパワー・オンを発揮するため、
インタークーラー・ウォーター・スプレーやクロスミッションを装備、
最終仕上げのポテンシャルに向けたのが、WRX typeRA。

主要装備
・フォグランプ ・アルミフード ・アルミ製大径リヤスポイラー ・カーボン製大径リヤスポイラー ・バケットシート
・パワーウインドゥ ・ジュニア ・15インチアルミホイール ・ブリヂストン・エクスペディア 205/50 R15 ラジアルタイヤ
・リヤスポイラー ・4輪ベンチレーテッドディスクブレーキ ・インタークーラー・ウォーター・スプレー ・クロスミッション

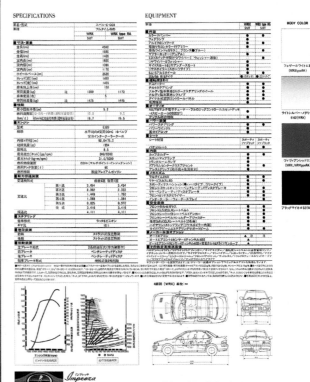

SPECIFICATIONS　　　　　　　EQUIPMENT

Impreza

normally-aspirated car, while the WRXs came with 205/55 Bridgestones (Potenza RE71 type on the WRX and Expedia on the Type RA).

The official accessories list included five alloy wheel options - a multi-spoke BBS design (15-inch), the 6J x 15 WRX-style rims, a six-spoke Subaru wheel (also 15-inch), and a couple of 14-inch choices, including a criss-cross one and the seven-spoke design sold as an optional extra in the American market. The WRX had a six-spoke 16-inch wheel and tyre combination listed in its accessory section, the alloy's design resembling two sets of three-spokes welded together.

Equipment levels varied quite a lot depending on the grade. In addition to certain items already mentioned, all cars came with halogen headlights, tinted glass (including a laminated windscreen), a tachometer, digital clock, radio, door pockets, driver's footrest, shoulder height adjustment on seatbelts, and remote releases for the boot and fuel filler door. The cheapest models sported grey cloth seat facings, whilst moving up to the CS brought better quality cloth (in two-tone grey and pink, extended to the door trim), power windows, locks and mirrors, plus a radio/cassette unit. The CX, meanwhile, built on this specification with more supportive seats (with height adjustment) trimmed in a mixed grey cloth, air conditioning (an option on lesser grades), rear armrests, rear heating, a four-speaker stereo, maplight, high-mount rear stoplight, and colour-keyed door handles.

The HX was the luxury model, and the interior reflected this. While the specification was similar to the CX, a grey, velour-type fabric was used to trim the seats. In addition, the strict HX (i.e. not the Edition S) had a chrome side window moulding. Although this latter item was not carried over to the equivalent Sports Wagon, most of the estates had roof rails.

The HX Edition S used the same trim materials as the CX, but had a more sporty appearance, highlighted by the alloy wheels, rear spoiler (incorporating an auxilliary brake light), foglamps, a Nardi steering wheel, leather-trimmed Nardi gearknob (manual cars only, although the automatic shift lever was covered in

The Hardtop Sedan Range

Grade	Engine	Trans.	Price (yen)
2WD CF	1.5 litre	5-sp.Man.	1,129,000
		4-sp.Auto.	1,222,000
2WD CS	1.5 litre	5-sp.Man.	1,229,000
		4-sp.Auto.	1,322,000
2WD CX	1.5 litre	5-sp.Man.	1,470,000
		4-sp.Auto.	1,563,000
4WD CF	1.6 litre	5-sp.Man.	1,329,000
		4-sp.Auto.	1,422,000
4WD CS	1.6 litre	5-sp.Man.	1,429,000
		4-sp.Auto.	1,522,000
4WD HX	1.8 litre	5-sp.Man.	1,819,000
		4-sp.Auto.	1,912,000
4WD HX Edition S	1.8 litre	5-sp.Man.	1,929,000
		4-sp.Auto.	2,022,000
4WD WRX	2.0 Turbo	5-sp.Man.	2,298,000
4WD WRX Type RA	2.0 Turbo	5-sp.Man.	2,108,000

The Sports Wagon Range

Grade	Engine	Trans.	Price (yen)
2WD CS	1.6 litre	5-sp.Man.	1,370,000
		4-sp.Auto.	1,463,000
2WD CX	1.6 litre	5-sp.Man.	1,656,000
		4-sp.Auto.	1,749,000
4WD HS	1.8 litre	5-sp.Man.	1,549,000
		4-sp.Auto.	1,642,000
4WD HX	1.8 litre	5-sp.Man.	1,859,000
		4-sp.Auto.	1,952,000
4WD HX Edition S	1.8 litre	5-sp.Man.	1,977,000
		4-sp.Auto.	2,070,000
4WD HX 'AirSus'	1.8 litre	5-sp.Man.	1,980,000
		4-sp.Auto.	2,073,000

leather on this model), and the option of an electric tilt-and-slide sunroof.

The WRX had bucket seats with integrated headrests, trimmed in black fabric with a red, patterned insert. The same seats were carried over to the Type RA version, as was the Nardi steering wheel and matching gearknob. The WRX was much the same as the HX Edition S in other respects, although air conditioning was now relegated to the options list (automatic air con was a maker option, and a manually-adjusted cooler was available as a dealer extra). The Type RA, meanwhile, had a very spartan specification, with less sound deadening, no foglights, no audio equipment, no air conditioning (although manual air con was available as a dealer option), and certainly no electrical goodies - even the maplight and digital clock were missing - and the door mirrors became basic black items, all in a bid to save weight. Interestingly, though, only the RA came

with a dash-mounted switch for the intercooler water spray.

On the practical side, the saloon featured a large boot, and the estate offered a flexible cargo area due to the fold-down rear seats. The Sport Wagon boosted 25.5 cubic feet of luggage space with the seats in place, increasing to 62.1 with them folded.

A so-called 'Winter Pack' was offered, with such things as a wiper de-icer. Whilst Japan is hot most of the time, the islands stretch a long way, from Hokkaido in the north to the Okinawa chain in the south. Believe me, Hokkaido can become a frozen waste in the depths of winter. Heated front seats and heated door mirrors were listed as options, too.

With sales starting from 1 November, Subaru was aiming to move 5000 units a month on the domestic market. The Impreza had a fairly limited range of colours according to grade, with Feather White, Lavender Mist Metallic, Dark Grey Metallic, Carmine

Red, Belgian Green Metallic, Majorca Blue Metallic, Light Silver Metallic and Black Mica listed for the standard saloons, whilst Vivienne Red replaced the white shade on the estate range. The WRX came in Light Silver Metallic, Vivienne Red and Black Mica, although the Type RA was available only in Feather White or the same bright red hue as its more civilized stablemate.

As for chassis codes, the 1.5 litre Sedan range carried the E-GC1 designation, while the 1.6s were classed as E-GC4s, and the 1.8s as E-GC6s; the two-litre WRXs were given the E-GC8 code. On the Sports Wagon side, the 1.6 litre models were designated E-GF3, and the 1.8 range was known as E-GF6 ; the only exception was the HX 'AirSus' grade, which carried the letters E-GFA.

So, what did the press think? The respected Japanese journalist, Aritsune Tokudaiji, described the WRX as a "poor man's [Skyline] GT-R" and felt it was a much better car to drive than the equivalent Mitsubishi. However, he was less than impressed - excuse the pun - with the styling, which he considered a bit conservative.

Jack Yamaguchi tried the WRX Type RA. "I'll get right to the point," he said. "Subaru's new Impreza WRX is sizzling hot. I had the Type RA car for sampling, which is the basis for a competition machine. It has no radio, no air conditioning, no power windows. The WRX can be distinguished from the rice-and-miso-soup Impreza sedan by its nose job, a full length grille, a huge hood opening and a couple of gaping holes that can accommodate rally driving lights.

"On public roads around our hallowed Mount Fuji, I had a taste of the Impreza WRX's tremendous performance and roadholding. The car is ideally sized, beautifully balanced, and immensely tossable and catchable. And the howl of the turbocharged flat-four soaring to 7000rpm was a sheer delight."

The Impreza in America

The Impreza replaced the Loyale (the American name for the Leone) in the Stateside line-up. Introduced to the US market in spring 1993, there were basically four grades on the four-door sedan (two of which came with the option of four-wheel drive), and two for the five-door Sport Wagon, listed with

The Subaru Impreza

BEAUTY IS ONLY SKIN DEEP.

—

UNLESS YOU FIND GALVANIZED STEEL

AND A HORIZONTALLY-OPPOSED ENGINE

ATTRACTIVE.

Introducing the exciting new Subaru® Impreza.™ A class act that's going to redefine the subcompact class for 1993. The only car in the class offering features like All-Wheel Drive, 4-channel ABS, driver's-side air bag and the reliable engineering you expect from Subaru. Come see why the new Impreza is going to quickly graduate to the head of its class.

See your local Subaru dealer for details.

Subaru. What to drive.™

©1992, Subaru of America, Inc.

American advertising announcing the Impreza's arrival.

both front-wheel drive and 4WD.

All of the early US spec cars employed the same EJ18 engine as that found in the 1820cc Japanese models. The fuel-injected unit therefore featured a sohc arrangement operating four valves per cylinder on each bank but, despite a higher 9.6:1 compression ratio, maximum power was slightly down on that quoted for the home market. For America, the 1.8 litre flat-four produced 110bhp at 5600rpm,

and 110lbft of torque at 4400rpm.

As in Japan, the Impreza was offered with either a five-speed manual gearbox (the internal ratios were altered in order to give longer gearing, although the 3.90:1 final drive was carried over from the home market), or a four-speed, electronically-controlled automatic transmission. With the latter option, the internals were the same as those listed in Japan, but a different final drive was specified.

40

The fully independent suspension was carried over, with most cars having only a front anti-roll bar. The brakes were also the same disc/drum set-up as those found on home market models on the cheaper grades (vented discs up front, with drums at the rear), although the LS came with ABS and discs all-round. The LS also featured wider, 175/70 HR14, all-season rubber (mounted on 5.5J steel rims) in place of the standard 165/80 SR13 tyres on 5J steel wheels.

Exchange rates were far from favourable at this time, at roughly 100 yen to $1, having been nearer 160 yen at the start of the decade. However, in line with a stated policy to "keep the quality high, the maintenance easy, and the price reasonable," Subaru managed to put together a competitive package.

Going up against the likes of the Honda Civic, Toyota Corolla and Nissan Sentra, the $10,999 Base saloon came with power steering (set at 3.2 turns lock-to-lock), a tilt column, driver's airbag, reclining front seats with cloth trim, tinted glass, black side protection mouldings, a front chin spoiler, tachometer, remote trunk and fuel filler door releases, and intermittent wipers.

Adding another $500 to the invoice brought the L-Base grade. This came with higher quality cloth trim (which extended to the door panels), wheel covers, and dual mirrors (the Base grade only had one, on the driver's side) finished in black. Like the Base, this was available in manual, front-wheel drive guise only.

The L grade was the next step up the ladder, with prices starting at $12,999 for the five-speed fwd model (specifying an automatic gearbox added $800 to this), while the four-wheel drive versions came in at $14,499 and $15,299 for the manual and automatic respectively. In addition to the features found on the L-Base, the L came with air conditioning, power windows, mirrors and door locks, a four-speaker radio, digital clock, and a bigger wheel and tyre combination on 4WD cars.

Top of the range was the automatic-only LS ($15,699, or $17,199 with 4WD). The extra money got you ABS brakes with discs all-round, front and rear anti-roll bars, cruise control, colour-keyed door mirrors, handles and side mouldings, velour upholstery and cloth headliner,

and an upgraded stereo.

As for the Sport Wagon, the front-wheel drive L was the cheapest in the line-up with a $13,399 sticker price. In addition to the features found on the equivalent saloon, the estate had a split fold-down rear seat and rear wash/wipe facility. The automatic was again $800 more, and four-wheel drive added $1500.

Like the LS saloon, the Sport Wagon version was only available with automatic transmission, with prices starting at $16,099 for the FF car; 4WD models were listed at $17,599 before options. Metallic paint was a no-cost option, but seven-spoke alloy wheels added $500 to the price, with a CD player not much cheaper at $495.

Motor Trend observed: "At the press introduction, our drive through the twisties in the mountains above Santa Barbara, California, showed us a front-drive, five-speed manual Impreza that was stable, quiet, quick, and well balanced. Steering felt precise and responsive, and plenty of low and mid-range torque from the flat-four got us to the top with little shifting and grunting. While the automatic all-wheel-driver was exceptionally sure-footed, uphill treks took a bit longer due to the added weight. Stopping was uneventful and fade free.

"Inside is pleasingly middle-of-the-road, with one exception: there's an amazing absence of noise in the passenger compartment. Subaru went the extra mile to ensure solidity of this product. Double-walled sheetmetal on the firewall, cushioned with foamed asphalt, liquid-filled rear suspension bushings, and extra stiffening in the wheelwells all contribute to the lack of squeaks, rattles, and tiresome noise."

The magazine recorded a 0-60 time of 12.1 seconds for the four-wheel drive LS (the heaviest sedan in the line-up), so it was hardly a ball of fire, but easily in touch with its direct competitors, and quite a way ahead of them in the braking distance department. There was no doubt, though, as Mac DeMere stated, that: "The Impreza needs more strength to turn its all-wheel drive into a decisive competitive advantage."

Car & Driver also felt the new Subaru could do with a few extra horses under the bonnet: "To make up for the lack of ultimate thrust, Subaru endows the Impreza with user-friendly handling and a host of upmarket features. Front-

drive Imprezas handle with predictable understeer; all-wheel drive models feel even more secure in dry situations and impressively stable in wintry conditions. It won't dislodge a 600SL from the prestigious parking spaces at the Ritz-Carlton Huntington, but the Impreza garners its own prestige in other ways, such as passing four-wheel drive Isuzu Troopers atop black ice Wyoming highways at 60mph without a twitch.

"All Imprezas have linear, progressive engine-speed-sensitive power steering. Base models get by with rear drum brakes, while the LS gets fadeless four-wheel disc brakes with anti-lock control that bring it down from 70mph in just 170 feet. When the anti-lock system is engaged, automatic-equipped cars shift to third gear to help prevent lock-up.

"The interior is worldly in its own way, assembled from rich-looking, fully grained plastics and high quality switchgear. At close hand are intuitive climate controls and a world-class 80 watt AM/FM cassette player (with an optional Clarion CD player). Large white-on-black instruments dominate the driver's view, behind a grabby tilt steering wheel packed with a standard airbag (a passenger bag will be along in 16 months). The door mounted power window and lock buttons look exactly like those on a Civic, while the cruise control is conveniently located between the steering wheel spokes, as on a Lexus. The cupholder blocks the radio faceplate when in use, but otherwise the ergonomics are flawless ... The seats lack sufficient fore-aft support to make the Impreza an ideal cross-country hauler, but in everyday use they are as supportive as Phil Donahue."

Road & Track tried the cheapest Sport Wagon version for its test of April 1993. Douglas Kott noted: "A blindfolded passenger with an ear for engines could pick out the characteristic slight growl of the flat-four, and the driver can feel a bit of low-frequency rumble through the shift lever and the throttle pedal. But it's a fairly smooth engine overall, and it needn't be wound to its 6000rpm redline to extract enough oomph to keep pace with or be slightly ahead of the normal traffic flow. And the Impreza is an enjoyable car in traffic, with light efforts for clutch and brake, and a shift linkage that feels precise and robust, with a touch of rubberiness. Just be sure to pick your drag-race opponents very carefully.

"Though reasonably nimble and well balanced through our slalom test, the Impreza just doesn't have the crisp handling edge of a Nissan Altima or Mazda Protege in everyday driving; what makes the Subaru so unflappable when the conditions are sloppy causes its chassis to feel numb when the asphalt dries and grip is there for the taking. The flip side to all this is ride quality that's excellent for the class. Subaru's chassis engineers have done a fine job juggling springs, shocks and anti-roll bars to produce a platform that has pleasant, non-floaty ride motions and a lack of jiggle over poor pavement."

In a four-way test pitching the five-speed, mid-range Impreza against the Toyota Corolla, Geo Prizm and Eagle Summit (a Mitsubishi in disguise), *Consumer Report* noted a number of problems with the interior, and was especially critical regarding entry to and egress from the back seats, particularly for taller adults. The Toyota and Geo were voted better cars on this occasion, but it's interesting to note that Subaru quickly devoted a lot of attention to improving the interior. As the seasons passed, in addition to gaining some serious enhancements in the performance department, the model made a distinct move upmarket.

The new car in Europe

The Impreza made its European debut at the 1993 Geneva Show. A couple of months later, on 17 May, the model was given its official UK launch. Imports were limited by the voluntary quota system at this time, introduced nearly two decades earlier when Japanese cars threatened to flood the market. However, these archaic restrictions were soon relaxed, with another 34,000 vehicles allowed into Britain (an increase of 20 per cent, split between the various manufacturers) at the time of the Impreza's announcement.

The Impreza certainly arrived with a splash. A great deal of money was spent on publicity, including an eight-page advertising supplement in the issue of *Autocar & Motor* closest to the launch date. Available with either the four-door saloon or five-door estate body, all UK spec cars had four-wheel drive. There was a choice of 1597 or

Subaru at the 1993 Geneva Show.(Courtesy Pool Photo, Geneve/Subaru Schweiz AG)

Left & below: The front and rear covers from a Haymarket Advertising Supplement dating from May 1993. It appeared as an eight-page section in Autocar & Motor, *and featured some stunning photography by Andrew Yeadon.*

1820cc litre power units (with a 9.5:1 compression ratio, they were rated at 88bhp/95lbft and 101bhp/109lbft, respectively), and the option of electronically-controlled automatic transmission with the bigger engine. The manual 1.8 litre machines had an official 0-60 time of 9.7 seconds, with top speed quoted as 118mph (189kph).

James Thomas at *Autocar & Motor* noted: "It's the five-door Impreza which is the more interesting of the two. It will either go down as a lesson in skillful packaging, or as one of 1993's more conspicuous marketing cock-ups.

"This is the model that will be crucial to the success of the Impreza in the UK, where estate cars have been Subaru's best sellers. In line with this, the projected sales split is likely to favour the five-door over the four-door by roughly four to one."

Rather interestingly, Thomas pointed out: "Both versions grip tenaciously, turn into corners with aplomb and understeer in a predictable fashion. The chassis could handle the sort of increase in power that would make the Impreza truly sporting."

There was talk about bringing the WRX to Britain, but it never really came to anything. However, Subaru UK did import six early WRX models in 1993 - three of which went to Prodrive, while the others were ultimately sold as second-hand cars.

Thomas concluded: "There's little doubt Subaru will sell all the Imprezas it is allowed to import. The real question is, how many would it sell if unrestricted? Quite a few, we'd wager."

Major options included ABS brakes (a conventional disc/drum set-up was standard), air conditioning, an electric sunroof, alloy wheels to replace the 14-inch steel rims, and roof rails for the estate. In the guide to the 1993 Earls Court Show, it was noted: "Subaru arrives at the London Motor Show with a comprehensive line-up of four-wheel drive models to suit everyone's taste.

"Following a spring launch, which significantly increased the company's market coverage, is the latest Impreza - one of the most important models ever to be introduced by Subaru.

"Offering a totally new concept, both in terms of styling and practicality, the Impreza's vibrant good looks target a broad range of customers and age groups with wide-ranging interests and active lifestyles.

"Sophisticated four-wheel drive, the hallmark of Subaru motoring, has been matched to newly-developed 1.6 and 1.8 litre fuel-injected engines with either manual or automatic transmission. All five models in the Impreza range are generously equipped to GL specification and feature as standard central locking, power steering, electric windows, headlamp washers, height-adjustable driver's

The UK range			
Grade	Engine	Trans.	Price
1.6 GL 4WD (five-door)	1.6 litre	5-sp.Man.	£12,499
1.8 GL 4WD (four-door)	1.8 litre	5-sp.Man.	£12,499
		4-sp.Auto.	£13,498
1.8 GL 4WD (five-door)	1.8 litre	5-sp.Man.	£12,999
		4-sp.Auto.	£13,998

The four-door Impreza in 1993 UK trim.

seat and tilt-adjustable steering wheel.

"Both the Impreza four-door saloon and five-door models maintain Subaru's reputation for superlative handling and ride characteristics, with the reassurance of four-wheel drive.

"Following on from the success of its Legacy Turbo stablemate, the Impreza is contesting the World Rally Championship series in the hands of top driver, Ari Vatanen. He competes alongside British Open Rally Champion, Colin McRae, who also has his sights set on victory at the forthcoming RAC Rally, this time with the Prodrive-prepared Impreza which will be a central feature of the Subaru stand."

The Impreza was sold alongside the Justy, Vivio, Legacy and £30,499 SVX in the UK, and at the start of 1994, three new entry level, front-wheel drive grades were added: the Impreza 1.6 LX and 1.6 GL saloons, and the 1.6 GL station wagon. With prices on these models ranging from £9999 to £11,249, it was now a very comprehensive line-up.

Home market developments

On 1 June 1993 a special edition, four-wheel drive, 1.6 litre, CF Limited was

announced. This saloon came with air conditioning (usually a maker option) and central locking (something not listed at all for the CF grade) as standard, along with unique fabric upholstery, colour-keyed door handles and power door mirrors, and wheel trims. Just 500 were produced, finished in shades of either white, red or dark grey, and priced at 1,429,000 yen in manual guise.

A couple of weeks later, the CS Limited made its debut, based on the two-wheel drive version of the Sports Wagon. With manual air conditioning, roof rails, colour-keyed door handles and remote control mirrors, and special fabric trim coming as part of the 1,439,000 yen package, it offered very good value for money. As with the CF Limited, only 500 were available, with automatic transmission adding 93,000 yen.

The second generation Legacy was introduced at the 1993 Tokyo Show. Displaying slightly softer lines than the original, it was nonetheless similar from a styling viewpoint. It was mechanically similar, too, except for the availability of a new 250bhp twin-turbo powerplant; a year later, a 2.5 litre 250T model joined the line-up.

43

ラヴと
ドリームがあるかぎり、
スポーツワゴン。

ウィークデイは、アスレチック・ジムかインドア・テニス。
音楽のレッスンやカルチャークラブもいいかもしれない。週末は、もちろん太陽がいっぱいの海。
白銀のリゾートでのんびりもご機嫌にちがいない。走って楽しくて、しかも大好きな人と
アクティブな時間がいっぱい持てるクルマが欲しい…。なんて考えていたらこんなワゴンができました。
スポーツワゴンは、ほかにはちょっとないクルマです。
僕たちのエネルギーは、やっぱり恋と夢なんだって
スポーツワゴンに乗っていると、思うこのごろです。

IMPREZA SPORTS WAGON
for Couple of New Age.

Japanese advertising for the 1994 model year Sports Wagon WRX.

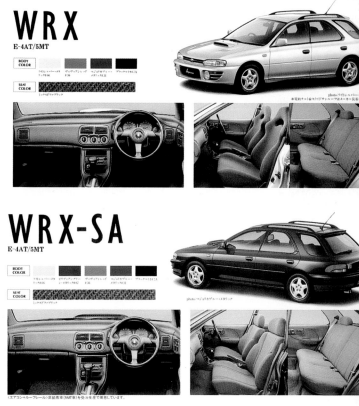

Sections of the brochure produced for the new Sports Wagon WRX and WRX-SA grades.

Two new four-wheel drive Impreza models were introduced at the same time - the turbocharged Sports Wagon WRX and the Sports Wagon WRX-SA, although an automatic version of the WRX saloon was also announced in time for the Makuhari Messe event.

Although the compression ratio was the same, the two-litre, twin-cam engine employed in the new E-GF8 Sports Wagon models produced 220bhp at 6000rpm, along with 206lbft at 3500rpm - both figures slightly less than those quoted for the equivalent saloons, though maximum torque was produced a lot lower down the rev range, thanks to a remapped ECU. The manual transmission was the same as that employed on the saloon. However, the automatic version came with variable torque distribution - the VTD system borrowed from the Alcyone SVX. With this set-up, the 0-60 dash could be covered in under seven seconds!

Like its WRX sedan brethren, the estate version had an aluminium bonnet, the distinctive front bumper/

airdam arrangement, side skirts and a lowered rear valance. Naturally, the 15-inch alloy wheel and tyre combination was also carried over, as was the braking system concealed within the rims. One unique feature was a roof spoiler, and the WRX (but not the WRX-SA) was also fitted with a modified boot spoiler.

Inside, the WRX had bucket seats, and both grades got a slightly different Nardi wheel. A stereo radio/cassette came as standard, as did fully automatic air conditioning (now standard on all WRXs except the Type RA), remote control central locking and colour-keyed power door mirrors with fold-in facility.

The Sports Wagon WRX was introduced at 2,495,000 yen (or 2,618,000 yen in automatic guise), while the WRX-SA was 100,000 yen cheaper. There was also a special order version of the SA grade, minus the air conditioning and roof rails, which sold for just 2,193,000 yen.

As already noted, the automatic

WRX saloon came with the innovative VTD-4WD system, which usually split torque 35:65, resulting in more natural handling. Of course, as conditions changed, power - 220bhp for the two-pedal machine - was distributed to whichever wheels had the most grip which, for sporting drivers, was probably ideal. The automatic car also had a new steering wheel (the same Nardi item as that fitted to the WRX estate models) and revised suspension rates, but was otherwise pretty much the same as its manual stablemate. It was priced at 2,598,000 yen.

The Impreza in competition

The Prodrive concern had been approached for its thoughts on developing the Impreza even before final production car plans had been approved, way back in winter 1990. Apart from the obvious differences in overall dimensions, the Legacy and Impreza were quite mechanically similar; this was the initial stage of producing a machine that would be

44

Publicity shots showing the front, rear and cockpit of the Impreza rally car.

competitive from day one.

There were subtle differences in the engine, such as the adoption of an air-to-air intercooler instead of a water-to-air one (although a water spray nozzle was fitted on the bonnet, directly over the intercooler), a new IHI (Ishikawajima-Harima Heavy Industries) turbo, which now featured overhead camshafts that operated directly onto cam followers to reduce weight, friction and the number of moving parts.

The fuel-injected and turbocharged Impreza produced over 300bhp in Group A trim, along with 339lbft of torque - slightly more than the old Legacy, albeit higher up the rev range at 5000rpm. The boxer four was kept cool via radiators for the engine water and intercooler, and there was a heat exchanger for the engine oil.

The Prodrive six-speed transmission, based on the earlier STi manual gearbox (with constant mesh and a large number of Hewland internals), was quite a remarkable piece of engineering, using electronics to control shifts and the dog clutch. The driver could choose between semi-automatic modes (using either steering wheel-mounted flippers or the gearlever, which automatically moved, with the help of high pressure compressed air, into the right position to match the gear selection) or, after switching off the other system, full manual operation.

The Impreza employed mechanical front and rear differentials, combined with an electronically-controlled hydraulic centre differential. Like the road cars, the suspension was via simple MacPherson struts at both ends, although large diameter vented brake discs were specified all-round, fitted with a water-cooling facility for faster tarmac events.

Compared with the Legacy, it had the same track measurements, but was shorter (both overall and in the wheelbase), narrower and not so quite so high. Minimum weights dictated no difference in that department, although the lighter vehicle enabled the engineers to place ballast to give the Impreza better weight distribution, quoted as 55 per cent front, 45 per cent rear.

Homologated in April 1993 (number A5480), rally driver, Colin McRae, observed: "Compared with the Legacy, the Impreza feels quite different. It feels quite nervous to start with - it's twitchy and changes direction a lot quicker, and has gained more power. The Impreza is certainly harder to drive but quicker, and I'm really trying to change my driving style to suit it. Nowadays you have to be so tight. Driving on a special stage is like driving on a race track - as soon as you start to slide around, you're losing time. The Impreza may feel like it wants to be driven sideways, but if you drive it straight it's going to be quicker."

The 1993 rally season

The Legacy was used by Subaru for most of the 1993 season, although, in the background, development of the Impreza was moving at a rapid pace. The main drivers in the 555 Subaru team at this time were Ari Vatanen, Markku Alen and Colin McRae.

Vatanen, one of the author's heroes, was born in Finland in 1952, and began rallying at the age of 18. He won his first WRC event in 1980, and was declared World Champion the following year driving a Ford Escort. It was a link with the past when he joined the Subaru camp at the end of 1991, as Dave Richards (MD at Prodrive) used to be his co-driver.

Alen - another Flying Finn - had won an enormous number of rallies, and was robbed of the Championship title in 1986. After a lengthy career with Fiat and Lancia, he moved to Subaru in 1990, before signing for Toyota in 1992. For 1993, he was back in blue overalls, albeit briefly.

McRae, born in Scotland in 1968, came from good stock - the son of Jimmy McRae, ex-British Open Champion. After an appearance on the 1991 RAC, he was given a seat in the Subaru works team the following season, and quickly showed his potential. A British champion like his father, he won his first WRC event in 1993 (in New Zealand). Was this the first victory of many?

1993 rally record

The Impreza made its WRC debut on the 1993 1000 Lakes Rally. Ari Vatanen and Bruno Berglund were in one car, although Colin McRae was doing well in the increasingly important Asia-

Ari Vatanen.

1993 1000 Lakes Rally (Vatanen).

Ari Vatanen congratulating fellow Finn, Juha Kankkunen (Toyota), on winning the 1993 1000 Lakes.

Markku Alen.

Pacific Championship, so missed the round in Finland in order to compete in Malaysia. Markku Alen was given his seat but, having entered a corner too fast, crashed out on the very first stage. Needless to say, John Spiller (Subaru's Team Manager) was not amused, and Alen, who had been so successful with Fiat and Lancia, did not drive for the Japanese team again.

However, the Impreza so nearly won on its debut. Vatanen moved into the lead on stage 26, only to be struck down by an unusual piece of misfortune, as described in the October

1993 issue of *MotorSport*: "The next stage was due to start at 8.24pm and crews were having their front light clusters fitted at service. Ironically, this proved to have a diminishing rather than beneficial effect on Vatanen's forward visibility. The Impreza has been put through all manner of tests, including spells in the wind tunnel, both with and without the front light cluster fitted. But it had never undergone wind testing in the rain with the cluster fitted.

"Without the cluster, rain is channelled to assist the turbocharger cooling, but when the cluster was fitted the airflow was disturbed so much that, on the stage, rain water found its way into the heater system, with the

1993 rally record

No.	Driver/Co-driver	Position	Reg. No. (Group)
1000 Lakes (27-29 August)			
2	Ari Vatanen/Bruno Berglund	2nd	L555 BAT (Gp.A)
5	Markku Alen/Ilkka Kivimaki	dnf	L555 STE (Gp.A)
RAC (21-24 November)			
5	Ari Vatanen/Bruno Berglund	5th	L555 STE (Gp.A)
2	Colin McRae/Derek Ringer	dnf	L555 BAT (Gp.A)

1993 RAC Rally (Vatanen).

result that the windscreen interior immediately misted up, and continued to do so all the way to the end. Peering through the less than transparent screen, and having to wipe it every few seconds with a glove, distracted Vatanen so much that he lost time and dropped back to second place, two seconds behind his rival."

Ultimately, the Flying Finn finished second, sandwiched between two Toyota Celicas. It was an impressive debut, although neither Alen or Vatanen used the steering wheel-mounted controls for the semi-automatic gearbox on competitive stages, Ari instead using them on road sections between legs in order to become familiar with the system.

As the WRC circus moved to Australia, the location dictated the rally would be contested with the Legacy, as spares and everything else necessary to back up a works entry were already in place in the Antipodes following the earlier NZ round. The 555 Subaru Rally Team didn't enter the San Remo or Catalunya Rallies, so the RAC was next on the calendar.

Out came the Imprezas again for the final round in the 1993 Championship, augmenting the Legacy Turbos of Richard Burns and Alister McRae. Vatanen claimed three fastest stage times, although a brief excursion ruined his chances; he ultimately came in fifth. Colin McRae, however, took nine stages and went into the lead on the third day, only to have his radiator hole which led to his engine overheating. He retired as a result, but both car and driver had been spectacular whilst running.

As noted in chapter two, Subaru finished the 1993 season in third place, although only a small part of the WRC challenge had been campaigned with the Impreza. For 1994, the Impreza was the vehicle chosen to represent the marque in this most demanding of motorsport arenas.

Incidentally, in the Asia-Pacific Championship, Subaru won the first three rounds, and then the fifth and final round of the series (thanks to Colin McRae and 'Possum' Bourne, respectively), handing the title to the Japanese manufacturers. In addition, the Kiwi driver was declared APC Champion.

America's 1994 model year

A total of 104,179 Subarus were sold in the States during 1993 (almost exactly the same number as recorded for 1992), 23,577 of which were Impreza models; around 30 per cent of these were four-wheel drive cars.

For the 1994 model year, dual airbags became standard on the higher grades, while ABS braking was now available, albeit at extra cost, on the L. This was also the last season in which the Loyale was sold (as an estate only for 1994), so the Impreza was now an important player in the Subaru line-up, taking its place between the Justy and the Legacy, while the SVX (priced at $34,295 in its most expensive form) continued as the flagship model.

In standard $11,200 guise, the Impreza Base grade was much the same as that of the previous season, although the L-Base was discontinued. Instead, it was now simply known as the L, and came with the 14-inch wheel and tyre combination. Prices on this model started at $12,000, with four-wheel drive adding $1500 and automatic transmission a further $800. In addition, there was the Preferred Equipment Package ($1950), which gave the owner dual airbags, air conditioning, power windows, mirrors and door locks, a four-speaker stereo radio, and a digital clock. Major options included the aforementioned ABS braking system, an electrically-operated sunroof, cruise control and a cassette player.

The LS was available with four-wheel drive only for 1994, with the sedan priced at $18,550 and the Sport Wagon at $18,950. Moquette velour trim was used (extending to the door panels), with a power sunroof, uprated stereo and cruise control adding to the luxury.

The Impreza in Australia

Like most other export markets, the Impreza was included in Australian price lists from spring 1993. The 4WD Wagon was still available as the entry level Subaru at this time, with the Impreza slotting in beneath the Liberty (the Australian name for the Legacy) and the $72,950 SVX.

The front-wheel drive, 1597cc LX Sedan was the cheapest car in the Impreza line-up, at $3000 less than the 1820cc GX Sedan which commanded $24,995 (or $26,995 with 4WD), while the five-door version - the Sports Wagon, in other words - came in at $25,895 in FF guise, or $27,895 with four-wheel drive. A four-speed, electronically-controlled automatic transmission option augmented the standard five-speed stickshift.

By the end of the year, prices had increased by around $1500, although the Impreza range remained the same. In fact, the only difference in the Subaru line-up was the lack of a Leone-based car; the SVX was up to $78,000 at this stage.

However, a new model was on the horizon, and *Wheels* was quick to make the most of a pre-launch test drive. Michael Stahl wrote: "Forget tail-wagging wheelspin, axle tramp, induction roar, flailing fists, masses of metal being torn from rest. High-performance used to mean offence to the eye, ear and nostril. Today it's a different world. Silent, compact, searingly efficient. Like a Beretta hidden in a purse. Or the Subaru Impreza WRX.

"This apparently innocent sedan, built to carry Subaru's future hopes in world championship rallying, might just be the car to define high-performance 1990s-style. It is of smallish to medium size (laughably tiny two decades ago), with quite a large engine of 2.0 litres (again, maybe one-third what was needed in '73). But with a techno-fest of multi-valves, turbocharging and constant four-wheel drive, it'll melt most of your 'modern' V8s quicker than a laser beam and even take the shine off a legend or two.

"Very few cars can scythe from a standstill to 100kph [62mph] in under seven seconds, or cover the standing 400 metres in less than 15. Australia's fastest ever muscle car, the Ford Falcon GTHO Phase III, was one of them. This little red Impreza WRX - with just 1200km under its still-tight belt - has already equalled that, with every sign that the best is yet to come."

The Impreza WRX finally made it to the Antipodes in March 1994, with a $39,990 sticker price. Although it looked the same from the outside, it had a number of subtle differences compared to the home market WRX.

For starters, the fuel-injected engine developed less power due to a different turbo set-up, lower compression ratio and a remapped ECU. With a 8.0:1 compression ratio and Mitsubishi TD04L turbocharger, the Australian spec flat-four developed 211PS (208bhp) at 6000rpm and 201lbft of torque at 4800rpm.

Slightly softer springs were employed to augment the standard WRX shock absorbers, ABS came as part of the package (acting on discs all-round, but ventilated at the front only), and the interior featured grey cloth trim and a Momo four-spoke steering

The WRX made it to Australian shores in spring 1994.

The very first WRX-STi saloon, seen here fitted with the optional five-spoke, 16-inch alloy wheels. Note the pink grille emblem used exclusively on the STi cars.

wheel (the Nardi gearknob was retained, however); air conditioning, a sunroof, power windows and central locking came as standard.

"Summing up the Impreza WRX's abilities is pretty easy," stated *Car*. "It makes plenty of so-called sports cars look silly, not only because it is faster, but it handles, grips and rides with absolute aplomb. Plus it carries four people and luggage. Looks pretty good, too. And it's cheap enough, considering all that performance. What else could you want?"

Wheels magazine did a comparison test with the $33,825 Mitsubishi Lancer GSR, and concluded: "The Lancer GSR is the better buy, but the Impreza WRX is the better car. It's worth stretching the budget just that few thousand further."

Meanwhile, the price of estate models was reduced slightly during the summer of 1994 and the GX 4WD saloon was deleted soon after. Otherwise things stayed pretty much

the same going into the 1995 model year.

The STi road cars

In its May 1994 issue, *Car Graphic* carried out an interesting three-way comparison test between the new Celica GT-Four WRC, the Subaru Impreza WRX, and the Lancer GSR Evolution II. The Subaru had the least power (240bhp) but it was also the lightest - and cheapest - of the three, which made up for the shortfall of 15 horses on the Toyota (by far the heaviest of the bunch), and the extra 20bhp lurking under the Mitsubishi's bonnet.

Whilst the new Toyota covered the standing quarter in 13.5 seconds (almost exactly the same time as that posted by the Subaru), the 'LanEvo' was 0.7 seconds quicker. The 0-60 time was a similar story, with the Celica recording a far from shabby 5.5 seconds (again, about the same as the Impreza, on 5.6), but the Lancer managed to do the same exercise in just 4.7 seconds.

Engine of the first STi model. This is a contemporary shot provided by the factory (as used in the brochure), so the tower brace bar is the correct one for the type. Note also the myth regarding red intake manifolds: very early cars had a normal finish. A red crackle finish was introduced on Version II cars, but even then those based on the Type RA did not have this distinctive feature. The intercooler was mounted at the rear of the engine at an angle, high up, just beneath the bonnet scoop.

All were fast - very fast, in fact - but the Mitsubishi was absolutely devastating.

Summing up, it was observed that the "GT-Four is the refined, but costly all-rounder. The Lancer is the hard-driving road racer. The Impreza falls somewhere in between ... The winner? We'd go for the Lancer on account of its sensational performance, its brilliant handling, and sheer fun factor."

However, Subaru already had an answer to this stronger competition. On 20 January 1994, STi President, Ryuichiro Kuze (a leading light in the Legacy project, who had joined FHI in 1953), announced the STi versions of the Impreza WRX saloon and estate. Incidentally, internally, all Imprezas were given the Type B designation at this time, as earlier cars had the Type A moniker.

Anyway, the WRX-STi range was based on the five-speed manual WRX Sedan and the manual WRX Sports Wagon. As one would expect, the STi models received a number of high performance modifications, carried out at the STi works at that time (contemporary promotional material proudly stated: "Handcrafted and tuned by STi" - nowadays all cars are finished on the same line at the Yajima Plant).

Not least amongst these upgrades was a highly tuned, blueprinted engine. For the STi version, the estate gained the same Mitsubishi TD05H turbo, cylinder block and camshaft profile as the hot saloon, so both had identical performance figures (the catalogue Sports Wagon WRX had 20bhp less than its four-door counterpart).

The engine featured forged pistons and pins, STi's lightweight hydraulic 'valve lash' adjuster (HLA) system, polished intake ports, a remapped ECU (which also increased turbo boost pressure a touch), an STi nozzle on the intercooler water spray, uprated intercooler ducting and a silver finish on the intercooler itself, and a large diameter Fujitsubo exhaust system (Fujitsubo is a legendary name in Japanese enthusiast circles). Ultimately, the modified power unit (readily identified by a discreet little 'Handcrafted & Tuned by STi' badge on the fan belt cover) gave 250bhp at 6500rpm, and 227lbft of torque at 3500rpm.

STi badging also extended to the front airdam, underneath the 'WRX' sticker on the bootlid, on the nose (in the shape of the signature cherry pink grille ornament - lesser cars had a black one), and embedded in the unique rear spoiler employed on the saloons. These early cars also had an STi chassis plate on the offside suspension tower, detailing build numbers and build date. The massive rear spoiler was actually quite heavy, but with the various badges and a colour-keyed front bumper grille, it was a useful identifying feature.

Under the skin, an aluminium front strut tower bar (oval section, with STi pink fixing bases) stiffened the suspension, and uprated front brake pads enhanced stopping performance. As with the Type RA, Bridgestone Expedia 205/55s were mounted on dark silver 6J x 15 rims as standard, but 16-inch STi Electra R two-piece aluminium alloys were offered as an option; an STi rear mechanical limited-slip differential was also listed as an optional extra.

Sharing exactly the same gearbox (internal ratios were identical) and final drive as the catalogue WRX, independent tests gave the estate a 0-60 time of 6.1 seconds, with the standing quarter clocked at 13.9.

Inside, the Nardi steering wheel featured a carbonfibre-style insert and red stitching, the latter carried over to the special STi gearknob. Escaine (manmade suede) was used to trim the front seats and door panels, with the STi logo set into seatbacks. Interior colours were officially listed as off-black for the Sedan and grey for the Sports Wagon; exterior paintwork came in Vivian Red, Light Silver Metallic or Black Mica - the same shades as those offered on the standard WRX.

The Sedan was priced at 2,778,000 yen, with the Sports Wagon commanding 2,858,000 yen. Due to the nature of the car's 'production,' the company was intending to sell only 100 units a month, although it was stated that sales of this special version would finish at the end of September. Due to the modifications, each car came with a thick document outlining the changes from standard in order to satisfy Japanese law; oddly, the model was never homologated, so could not enter sanctioned motorsport events.

Not long after the STi made its debut, a Tommykaira version was launched. Tommykaira is a highly respected independent Japanese company that has been tuning and building specialist cars for a number of years. Its first Impreza-based model, built around the basic WRX Type RA Sedan (2,850,000 yen), the standard Type RA (3,780,000 yen) or the cooking WRX saloon (3,980,000 yen), was known as the M20b.

From the outside, the M20b was distinguished by an enormous rear spoiler (with twin blades), although the front airdam was also quite different - smoother than the catalogue version, and featuring a large aperture where the grille usually sits (the lower air intake was a similar shape).

Engine modifications included a new, high efficiency intercooler, a lightweight flywheel and revised electronics to take power up to 260bhp at 6500rpm, with maximum torque quoted as 242lbft, coming in at 5300rpm.

The base car brought with it a couple of gearing options, of course. As one would expect, the hike in power - combined with a close ratio transmission - made for some pretty interesting performance figures: the standing quarter could be dismissed in 13.9 seconds, while 0-60 took 5.9 seconds.

The standard shock absorbers were carried over, but mated with harder springs, while the brakes were treated to special aftermarket pads; larger, 17-inch wheels and tyres completed the mechanical specification. As for the interior, there was an abundance of carbonfibre embellishment, Recaro seats, a different steering wheel, an aluminium gearknob, and unique red-on-black gauges (featuring a 260kph speedo - domestic models usually came with one marked up to 180kph).

On the standard road car side, four days after the announcement of the STi models, the CS Limited II was launched. Like its predecessor the CS Limited, it was based on the 1.6 litre fwd Sports Wagon and shared the same upmarket specification. On sale until September (no restriction on numbers this time, simply a cut-off date), it was priced at 1,399,000 yen in manual guise.

Comparing earlier prices reveals

The five-door WRX-STi, also equipped with the Electra R wheels; the same alloys as those employed on the stock WRX models were standard fare.

Subaru at the 1994 Geneva Show, when the turbocharged Impreza made its European debut. (Courtesy Pool Photo, Geneve/Subaru Schweiz AG)

that the CS Limited II was actually cheaper than the original model, and several lower grades were reduced in price at this time. The basic CF saloon was now just 1,117,000 yen, although the HX range stayed the same, and the WRXs were slightly more expensive. The standard WRX saloon was now listed at 2,475,000 yen - an increase of 177,000 yen since introduction.

Basically, specifications remained the same, although there were a few detail changes. All Sports Wagon models gained a WRX-type front grille, and the HX Edition S model now had a standard silver finish on its five-spoke alloys, as did the WRX estates. In addition, the HS version was dropped from the line-up and replaced by the 4WD CS (introduced in September 1993). The home market Hardtop Sedan range continued unchanged.

Europe's hot models

The turbocharged Imprezas eventually found their way into European showrooms (initially just UK and Switzerland) following a successful debut at the 1994 Geneva Show. These cars had significantly less power than their Japanese counterparts, developing only 208bhp at 6000rpm on a 8.0:1 c/r, in order to make the engine run on poorer quality, 95 RON unleaded fuel and meet stricter noise standards, in addition to the usual concerns about emissions.

Autocar & Motor announced the arrival of the latest machine whilst covering the Geneva exhibits: "A bargain basement 208bhp Subaru Impreza Turbo goes on sale this week for just £17,500.

"Performance is in the Escort Cosworth league - rest to 60mph takes

Opposite and next page, top: An English language brochure for the Turbo dating from November 1991. As an advance information tool for the export version of the WRX, not all of the specs add up. Right-hand drive with a kph speedo would usually indicate Australia, but the Nardi steering wheel is not correct for that market (a Momo four-spoke wheel was used). Whatever, it is an interesting guide to the contemporary Turbo.

SUBARU IMPREZA TURBO 4WD

IMPREZA
2.0-litre DOHC 16-valve Turbo 4WD

BORN TO RUN

PURE DRIVING EXCITEMENT

Viscous LSD Centre Differential 4WD

5-speed manual transmission

DRIVE TRAIN

A full-time 4WD system employed in the IMPREZA TURBO 4WD is the culmination of over 20 years of SUBARU experience in 4WD technology. To match the high power of the turbocharged engine, a viscous limited slip differential (LSD) is used. This improves performance in low-traction conditions and enhances cornering potential when traction is good. Clutch size and gear ratios of the 5-speed manual transmission have been carefully aligned with the power and torque curves of the turbocharged 2.0-liter engine for smooth, precise shifting. The torque distribution of the compact, centre differential is basically 50:50, but varies progressively when front and rear wheels rotate at different speeds.

The 4-wheel strut suspension, provides precise control while maintaining its capability to put the power on the road. The suspension layout has been tuned to yield a long wheelstroke, low friction, and high lateral rigidity in order to enhance driving stability as well as the driver's "feel" for the road.

Viscous LSD

One of the greatest pleasures for genuine car lovers is the feeling of control. Since the debut of the popular "LEGACY," SUBARU has earned the reputation for being "driver-oriented". The new "IMPREZA TURBO 4WD" is no exception. Agile and sophisticated, it brings a new dimension to the words "Joy of Driving."

The sleek and tightly muscled look of the IMPREZA TURBO 4WD is like that of a well trained athlete. Smoothly integrated aero parts including air dam skirt, side and rear spoilers, and a functional air scoop gives this impression.

SRS air bag system (front passenger air bag is available in certain areas only)

ENGINE

The same 2-litre turbo engine that lead the LEGACY to victorious triumph in WRC competition can also be found under the bonnet of the IMPREZA TURBO 4WD. New developments have kept this 16-valve DOHC powerplant's output at the top of its class. Technical charms include direct valve actuation, a high-output turbo unit, and an air-cooled intercooler. It combines the sharp response and acceleration of a turbo with the smooth low-rpm torque that only a horizontally opposed DOHC engine can provide.

ENGINE
EJ20-TURBO
WITH INTERCOOLER

SAFETY

The "high dimension driving experience" of the IMPREZA TURBO 4WD could not be achieved without reliable safety features. 15" ventilated disc brakes are fitted on the front wheels while 7+8 inch tandem boosters provide power assist. The 4-wheel Antilock Braking System is a full 4-sensor, 4-channel system that's lightweight, compact, and extremely reliable-for top-of-the-class braking performance. Passive safety measures include side door beams in both front and rear, fully-adjustable seatbelt system, and SRS air bag system.*

(* Available in certain markets only.)
(SRS: Supplemental Restraint System)

ABS unit

Front ventilated disc brake

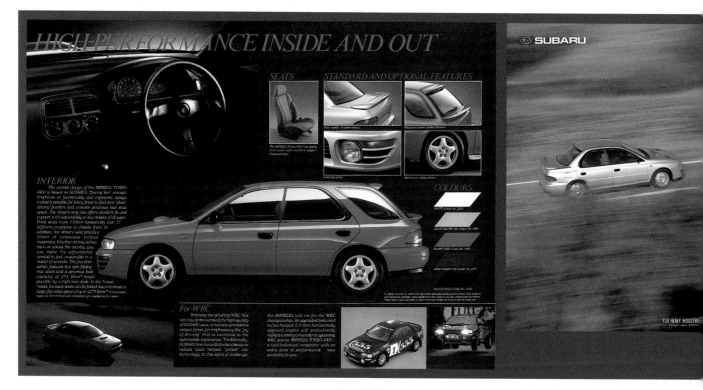

SUBARU

The WRX estate as it first appeared in Britain.

a claimed 6.3 seconds and top speed is 142mph - but price is in top-spec Mondeo territory.

"Under the power-bulged, aluminium bonnet sits an uprated version of the Legacy RS quad-cam intercooled two-litre turbo four. Maximum output is up to 208bhp from the Legacy's 197bhp, thanks to turbo and fuel-injection system improvements.

"But power hike is at the expense of a peakier torque curve. Maximum torque is up from 193lbft at 3600rpm to 201lbft at 4800rpm.

"Power is directed through Subaru's full-time four-wheel drive system with viscous centre coupling and limited-slip rear differential. The suspension features struts all-round with trailing arms at the rear to improve wheel control."

Launched in the UK at just £17,499 for the saloon and £17,999 for the estate, it was badged the 'Turbo 2000' in Britain and the 'GT' in other European markets. Sporting all of the WRX body appendages and well-equipped - ABS brakes operating on discs all-round, power-assisted steering (with adjustable column and driver's airbag), Nardi leather gearknob, central locking, five-spoke 6J x 15

Dashboard arrangement of the same car. Note the so-called 'Bright' switch; only fitted to export models, it was installed to override the clock dimmer when the lights were turned on.

52

alloy wheels shod with Michelin rubber, power windows and mirrors, a four-speaker stereo radio/cassette unit, headlight wash and leveling facility (something not found on home market cars), front foglights, 'Rallyweave' cloth trim, a digital clock and an immobilizer - the Impreza really was something of a snip.

There was an immediate waiting list, not least because the Impreza offered exceptional value for money, especially in England where car prices were - and often still are - ridiculously inflated. For the same kind of money, enthusiasts had very little choice in the new car market, especially if they demanded a modicum of practicality.

The Daily Express World Car Guide for 1995 observed: "Weird it may look but Subaru's Impreza is full of surprises. When it was launched a year ago as a 'hatch and a half,' no-one quite knew what to make of it.

"Then only four-wheel drive models were available, but this year the range was expanded to include cars with front-wheel drive, too.

"Star of the range is the new, ultra-powerful Turbo which offers Escort Cosworth-rivalling performance at something of a bargain price. A swoopy-looking Impreza two-door coupé is available in other countries, as well."

Gearing was quite different on the European turbo, with ratios of 3.454 on first, 1.947 on second, 1.366 on third, 0.972 on fourth and 0.738 on top (the same as those listed for Australia). With a 4.11:1 final drive (Australia got a 3.90 item), official factory figures for the 208bhp Turbo quoted a 0-60 time of 6.6 seconds, a 142mph (227kph) top speed, and an average fuel consumption figure of 29.9mpg, although the latter was liable to be a lot less if the driver had a heavy right foot.

It was available in White, Flame Red, Deep Green Metallic, Light Silver Metallic or Black Mica (although, unlike the home market, metallic and mica finishes were classed as a cost option). One of the few things that consistently drew complaints was the rather dull grey interior and a less than perfect gearchange, but otherwise it was a hit with the motoring press, even after 12,000 miles (about 20,000km) with the car in the case of the *Autocar*. It was also a hit with the buying public, and soon accounted for almost half of

One mean, magnificent son of a Subaru.

A Subaru Impreza 2000 4WD Turbo road car specially prepared by 'Prodrive' - suppliers of the 555 Subaru World Rally Team, with various performance and luxury options including sportssuspension, choice of wheels and tyres, and a revised interior to include sports seats or full leather trim.

IMPREZA TURBO 2000 4WD
Saloon or 5 door 2.0 litre
16V 4 Cam, ABS
Turbo Intercooler 4WD
208 BHP @ 6000 rpm
Max Speed 137 mph *
0-60 in 5.8 secs *

prodrive

Now exclusively available for inspection or demonstration at the dealers listed below.

SCOTLAND	THE NORTH	LONDON AND THE MIDLANDS	CENTRAL AND SOUTH WEST	SOUTH EAST
Fraser Anderson Ltd	KTGreen	Deep Leap SUBARU ISUZU	DAVID HENDRY CARS	Barretts
111 Drip Road, Stirling Stirlingshire 0786 472088	Leeds / Otley Road (A660) Pool in Wharfedale, W. Yorks 0532 843535	Ringshall Berkhamsted 0442 842273 / 842384	Kingfisher Mill, Park Road Malmesbury, Wiltshire 0666 824369	The Westgate Canterbury, Kent 0227 766932

Advertising for the Prodrive version of the Impreza Turbo 2000. Prodrive offered performance items for the Impreza from the time of the model's launch, although some parts tended to be the same regardless of the powerplant.

the UK Impreza sales.

Prodrive was quick to work its magic on the model, although the first limited edition of 25 cars left the engine untouched. Modifications were restricted to the suspension (lowered and further stiffened compared to the catalogue version), new wheels and tyres (five-spoke, 7J x 16 alloys shod with 205/50 ZR-rated Pirellis), and a few cosmetic changes to the interior: Recaro seats and a carbonfibre-look gearknob and trim pieces were added, and there was the option of a sports steering wheel if the owner could do without an airbag.

The UK line-up still included the four other Subarus, although the latest generation Legacy was listed. As noted earlier, the two-litre car was not available in all European markets straight away; the French, for instance, had a 1.6 GL and 1.8 GL four-door, and a 1.6 LX augmenting the same grades in the five-door range. These five models were all that was available for the start of the 1995 season, with prices ranging from 97,800FF to 117,000FF.

The export version of the WRX would eventually find its way into most of Europe, South Africa and South America but, for the time being at least, the North American market had

to do without the 'Super Scooby.' Of course, the Australians were already enjoying the turbocharged model.

Developments at home

In late September 1994, several changes were made to the Subaru Impreza line-up, introduced in plenty of time for the forthcoming Tokyo Show. Distinguished by the Type C designation, these latest models - including some new grades - featured a number of refinements. Fortunately for enthusiasts, the WRX series received the most attention.

The saloon version of the WRX and its sporty Type RA variant gained a few more horses under the bonnet, courtesy of a hike in turbo boost pressure from 600 to 650mmHg. Power was enhanced from 240bhp to 260bhp at 6500rpm (which more than made up for the 30kg, or 66lb, weight increase), whilst torque output increased a fraction, up to 227lbft at 5000rpm.

Incidentally, the RA came with a stiffer, closed deck cylinder block, and the HLA clearance adjustment system was dropped in favour of solid spacers acting on the sodium-filled valves. As a result, the Type RA rev limit increased from the standard 7000rpm to

7500rpm, and both WRX grades reverted to manual transmission only.

Regarding the five-speed gearbox, internal ratios were the same as those specified in the first catalogue. However, while the strict WRX retained its 4.111:1 final drive, the Type RA was given the 3.90 gearing employed on the lesser four-wheel drive models.

A bigger wheel and tyre combination was adopted on both models, with attractive 6.5J x 16, five-spoke rims coming shod with 205/50 rubber. Otherwise, things were pretty much the same on the outside, with the exception of colour-keyed door handles for the WRX (the Type RA continued with black door handles and mirrors), stronger headlight bulbs for the RA, and improved windscreen wipers and an automatic aerial for the WRX models, which was now located on the nearside rear wing instead of the driver's-side A-post.

Inside, the front bucket seats were carried over but with better trim, including Escaine accents in place of the rather dated tiger-print cloth. There was also a new - albeit similar - leather-wrapped Nardi three-spoke steering wheel with matching gearknob.

Equipment levels were basically the same, although the stereo radio/cassette unit (by Addzest) was updated to the latest version. Fewer WRX accessories were listed than before, but included the same auxiliary gauge pack (located in the centre console, the three meters monitored turbo boost,

Japanese advertising for the 1995 model year WRX.

battery condition, and outside temperature), various items of stereo equipment, a navigation system, and a rather solid-looking sump guard.

Now available in Feather White, Light Silver Metallic, Active Red, Cosmic Blue Mica or Black Mica, the WRX was priced at 2,498,000 yen. The Type RA version (which came in white or red only) was extremely reasonable, listed at just 2,198,000 yen.

The WRX-SA Sports Wagon was dropped, leaving just the one estate with the famous WRX insignia. This continued with the 220bhp engine, but at least received the latest 16-inch wheels and tyres. Available in silver, red, blue or black, it was priced at 2,399,000 yen with a manual transmission, or 2,522,000 yen if the automatic gearbox was specified.

The HX Edition S grade - both in saloon and estate guise - was made a touch sportier by way of a colour-keyed, WRX-style front grille and airdam (the latter with integrated foglights), and full bucket seats up front. The Sports Wagon version got roof- and tailgate-mounted rear spoilers (the Edition S Hardtop Sedan had always had a wing on the bootlid).

The majority of Sports Wagon models got more flexible rear seating, and a useful side storage tray that could be removed in a one-touch action. Four new estate grades were introduced: the CS Extra, CS-X, HX Edition L, and the 1.5 litre CS. The latter was a new, entry level model (with a corresponding specification to the 1493cc CS saloon), while the CS Extra (in 1.6 litre 4WD form only) introduced a value package for younger families; the CS-X was basically a catalogue version of the CS Limited II, and the HX Edition L estate (with a 1.8 litre engine and four-wheel drive) was a slightly less sporty option than the Edition S, with more emphasis on luxury equipment. It took the place of the old HX model in the line-up, whilst the HX 'AirSus' and CX variations were dropped.

There were fewer changes to the Hardtop Sedans, with only one new grade (available in 1.5 FF or 1.6 4WD guise; the CS Extra replaced the old CS) and dropping of the strict HX, but

all received a revised front grille - different to that fitted to the estates, and a vast improvement on the original, it must be said. Air conditioning was now standard on all Imprezas except the basic 1,017,000 yen CF saloon, and new trim and paint options were introduced to freshen-up the range.

The 1994 rally season

The FIA introduced a rotation system for the 1994 WRC. Taking in ten rounds, makers had to enter nine of these to qualify for the manufacturers' crown, calling for complete dedication in a works-backed programme.

On the Subaru front, the main change to the Impreza for 1994 was adoption of a hydraulic front differential, which could be adjusted from within the car, and Pirelli rubber instead of Michelin. As for the drivers, Carlos Sainz replaced Ari Vatanen, and Colin McRae continued as the other regular member of the team.

Carlos Sainz.

Colin McRae.

Sainz was born in Madrid in 1962. Starting with Ford, his career really took off when he signed for Toyota in 1989; the following year, he was declared World Champion. In 1991, he came second, but reclaimed his WRC crown in 1992 before a disappointing year with Lancia. Hopes were high for both Subaru and the Spaniard ...

1994 rally record

The Monte was blighted by poor crowd control, causing McRae to go off the road (snow had been shovelled into the road on a blind corner) and ruining his chances of a decent finish in the

1994 Monte Carlo Rally (Sainz).

1994 Rally of Portugal (McRae).

1994 Tour de Corse (Sainz).

Italian advertising showing Carlos Sainz on his way to a fine victory in Greece.

NUOVA SUBARU IMPREZA 4WD 2.0 TURBO 211CV

1ª

RALLY DI
**NUOVA
ZELANDA**

RALLY DELL'
ACROPOLI

RALLY DI
**COSTA
SMERALDA**

Un'impresa dopo l'altra! Le potenti Subaru Impreza Turbo 4WD guidate da Mc Rae, Sainz e Liatti trionfano nelle prove del Campionato Italiano e Mondiale Rally. Dai percorsi di gara, la versione stradale della nuova Impreza - Berlina e Compact Wagon - oggi arriva nella tua città e ti aspetta in tutte le Concessionarie Subaru. Trazione integrale permanente, differenziale autobloccante posteriore, motori 1.8 e 2.0 Turbo con iniezione elettronica multi-point, con Impreza viaggia tutta la tecnologia Subaru, la grande casa giapponese che ti offre una gamma completa di auto a trazione integrale con garanzia di tre anni a chilometraggio illimitato. Nuova Subaru Impreza. Una scelta vincente.

Corri a vederla dalla più vicina Concessionaria

BERLINA	2.0 Turbo	4WD	211 CV
COMPACT WAGON	2.0 Turbo	4WD	211 CV
BERLINA	1.8	4WD	103 CV
COMPACT WAGON	1.8	4WD	103 CV

Pensa Integrale. Scegli Subaru. SUBARU

1994 Rally of Argentina (Sainz).

1994 1000 Lakes Rally (Sainz).

1994 San Remo Rally (Sainz).

process. Despite problems with the centre differential towards the end of the event, Sainz claimed a good, solid third place (he'd won the event in 1991), and McRae recovered to take tenth.

In Portugal, McRae's charge was halted by an underbonnet fire, but Sainz took fourth after a consistent performance, winning five stages along the way. Subaru chose to run the 265bhp Group N Impreza WRX-RA in the Safari, with Patrick Njiru coming an amazing fourth; Richard Burns finished next in line.

The more familiar Imprezas returned in Corsica, equipped with new 'active' central differentials which improved driveability no end; they were also running with 18-inch wheels and tyres. Sainz was fighting for the lead when his anti-roll bar broke, causing a costly puncture.

Carlos Sainz and Luis Moya on the finishing ramp in Finland.

Nonetheless, he still came second, although McRae went out early following an accident.

At this stage, Subaru was lying second in the Championship (on 58 points against Toyota's 77), while Carlos Sainz was in a clear third place, ten points behind Didier Auriol. Carlos then won in Greece to give the Impreza its maiden victory and him joint lead, whereas Colin was unlucky not to win. Scrutineers failed to close the bonnet properly after an inspection, resulting in a broken windscreen. Thus, it was agreed that he could continue at the head of the field with a fresh screen. However, at midnight, he found himself excluded in this most extraordinary of circumstances.

McRae's luck didn't improve in Argentina, where he went out with accident damage, although Sainz was once again in a hard-fought battle with Auriol which, ultimately, the Toyota driver won by a margin of just six seconds! At least there was some consolation for the Spaniard, as he took the lead in the Drivers' Championship.

Now with active front and centre differentials, the Subarus were very competitive in New Zealand. Four cars were entered, as NZ counted towards the Asia-Pacific Championship, as well as the WRC. Unfortunately, Sainz, Burns and Bourne all went out, but McRae saved the day with a stunning victory - his second on the island and his first with the Impreza, a car that had not been kind to him up until this point.

Only one car was sent to contest the 1000 Lakes, but Sainz came away with a trophy for third place, keeping him in touch with Auriol, although Toyota was now unbeatable in the maker's section. In San Remo, the Spanish driver came second, with McRae fifth: Auriol won, which virtually sealed the Championship.

Sainz was still in with a chance as Auriol struggled on the RAC (the last round of the season), but went off the road, handing the title to the Frenchman. On a brighter note, Colin McRae won in front of his home crowd, leading the event from the third stage until the finishing ramp.

Subaru finished second in the 1994 World Rally Championship, beaten only by Toyota. In the Drivers' title chase, Carlos Sainz was second,

1994 rally record

No.	Driver/Co-driver	Position	Reg. No. (Group)
Monte Carlo (22-27 January)			
2	Carlos Sainz/Luis Moya	3rd	L555 REP (Gp.A)
7	Colin McRae/Derek Ringer	10th	L555 SRT (Gp.A)
Portugal (1-4 March)			
3	Carlos Sainz/Luis Moya	4th	L555 STE (Gp.A)
5	Colin McRae/Derek Ringer	dnf	L555 BAT (Gp.A)
Safari (31 March-3 April)			
5	Patrick Njiru/Abdul Sidi	4th	GM52-MU7032 (Gp.N)
7	Richard Burns/Robert Reid	5th	GM52-MU7033 (Gp.N)
Tour de Corse (5-7 May)			
3	Carlos Sainz/Luis Moya	2nd	L555 REP (Gp.A)
7	Colin McRae/Derek Ringer	dnf	L555 BAT (Gp.A)
Acropolis (29-31 May)			
3	Carlos Sainz/Luis Moya	1st	L555 REP (Gp.A)
7	Colin McRae/Derek Ringer	exc	L555 BAT (Gp.A)
Argentina (30 June-2 July)			
2	Carlos Sainz/Luis Moya	2nd	L555 REP (Gp.A)
6	Colin McRae/Derek Ringer	dnf	L555 BAT (Gp.A)
New Zealand (29-31 July)			
2	Colin McRae/Derek Ringer	1st	L555 BAT (Gp.A)
6	Carlos Sainz/Luis Moya	dnf	L555 REP (Gp.A)
10	'Possum' Bourne/Tony Sircombe	dnf	L555 STE (Gp.A)
11	Richard Burns/Robert Reid	dnf	L555 SRT (Gp.A)
1000 Lakes (26-28 August)			
2	Carlos Sainz/Luis Moya	3rd	L555 REP (Gp.A)
San Remo (9-12 October)			
10	Carlos Sainz/Luis Moya	2nd	L555 REP (Gp.A)
4	Colin McRae/Derek Ringer	5th	L555 BAT (Gp.A)
RAC (20-23 November)			
4	Colin McRae/Derek Ringer	1st	L555 BAT (Gp.A)
2	Carlos Sainz/Luis Moya	dnf	L555 REP (Gp.A)
9	Richard Burns/Robert Reid	dnf	M555 STE (Gp.A)

Richard Burns after finishing second in the 1994 Rally of Thailand, which gave him third place overall in the 1994 APC.

whilst Colin McRae, after a chequered season full of ups and downs, was fourth.

The increasingly-important Asia-Pacific Championship took another step closer to the limelight in 1994, taking in six rounds including the prestigious Hong Kong-Beijing Rally (won by Subaru's 'Possum' Bourne, incidentally). In fact, after a convincing season, challenged only by the Mitsubishi of Kenneth Eriksson, the 1994 Asia-Pacific titles went to Subaru and Bourne, respectively.

A new STi model

The WRX Type RA STi model debuted on 17 November 1994. Similar to the earlier Impreza modified by STi, it was based exclusively on the Type RA and given a higher state of tune - and a number of other enhancements - to bring it in-line with the Lancer Evolution.

The engine featured forged pistons, reinforced heads with polished ports, and a special STi ECU which increased turbo boost pressure. A unique water spray nozzle (complete with a large capacity STi reservoir) was again adopted for the air-to-air intercooler, the latter featuring uprated ducting and a silver finish. Even though the compression ratio remained at 8.5:1 (the same as the standard WRX and the last STi version), the end result of these tweaks was a significant increase in power and torque output, now quoted as 275bhp at 6500rpm and 235lbft at 4000rpm, respectively. Stronger engine mountings were adopted as a consequence, along with a double cooling fan for the radiator, although the standard Type RA exhaust system (with twin pipes exiting from the back) was used this time.

Power's one thing, but unless it can be effectively transmitted to the road, it means very little; for this reason the driver was given more control over the 4WD system. STi developed a

Tail of the WRX Type RA STi, introduced in November 1994.

The WRX Type RA STi was a formidable opponent for the Mitsubishi Lancer Evolution.

Interior and engine bay of the WRX Type RA STi. Both pictures appeared in the brochure, so provide an excellent guide for those looking for originality. Being Type RA-based, the intake manifolds had a natural finish, and note the latest tower brace bar.

system whereby a switch mounted by the handbrake allowed five-step adjustment of the car's power distribution, from a rearward bias of 35:65 to 50:50; an instrument panel indicator informed the driver of the centre-diff ratio selected.

In addition, a two-way, four-pinion, mechanical limited-slip differential was adopted, and the rear axle shafts were uprated to deal with the extra torque developed by the engine. Topped by a leather gearknob with red stitching, the gearbox was given an STi 'quickshift' linkage with stronger bushes, although all the ratios (including that of the final drive) were carried over from the latest WRX Type

RA catalogue model. Steering wheel-mounted, F1-style shifts were being investigated, but were dismissed at this time.

Outside, the lower front grille (under the bumper) was colour-coded like the earlier STi model, but the WRC-style foglight covers and roof vent were new additions. A larger rear spoiler was part of the package and, although not as dramatic as its predecessor, was both lighter and more efficient; naturally, it incorporated a high level rear brake light. Although hard to tell, the bonnet vents were also modified to enhance engine bay cooling - they were opened fully as on the works rally cars.

Gold-coloured, 6.5J, five-spoke,

aluminium alloy wheels were adopted at this stage, shod with 205/50 VR16 Bridgestone Potenzas, and with the same five-bolt fixing as that found on the entire Impreza range. Earls stainless steel mesh brake hoses could be glimpsed through the spokes, and there was a modified handbrake to make handbrake turns easier to execute - a sign of the car's rally breeding.

Special badging included the signature STi pink grille ornament (although the one with six stars that Subaru used in the WRC could be specified), a small oval badge on the trailing edge of the front fenders, and a similar sticker to that found on the previous STi special for the bootlid; the 'Type RA' insignia was underneath the offside rear combination lamp. Of course, the engine proudly carried its oblong STi label, and the carbonfibre and die-cast aluminium front strut tower bar also made reference to the FHI Aerospace Division that developed the bracing piece.

As for the interior, like the original special model, STi's own bucket seats were fitted up front. Black with grey Escaine inserts, they featured integral headrests, red stitching and the STi logo. The steering wheel also looked familiar, being a Nardi three-spoke item with a carbonfibre-style insert ring and red stitching on the leather wrapping. Incidentally, for this car there was the option of a 13:1 steering rack instead of the standard WRX ratio of 15:1, and the power steering system came with an oil cooler and large capacity pump.

Available in Feather White only (being based on the RA, the door mirrors and handles were finished in black, by the way), Subaru was hoping to shift 50 units a month, priced at a very reasonable 2,728,000 yen apiece. Ultimately, the WRX Type RA STi proved extremely popular and stayed in limited production at the STi works until the latter part of 1996, although it continued with a new name for a year before that.

Meanwhile, *Car Graphic* tried the latest STi model, pitting it against the Mitsubishi Lancer Evolution III. Ultimately, the 1200kg (2640lb) Impreza got the nod on tarmac, while the 'LanEvo' was the most impressive on loose surfaces. Straight line performance was a close match, too, with the Subaru covering the standing quarter in 13.3 seconds and the 0-60 dash in 5.3 - both times were 0.5 seconds slower than those quoted for the hard-charging Mitsubishi.

Other Japanese road models
Announced just before Christmas 1994, the two-door Impreza Retna series went on sale from 7 January 1995. Interestingly, this was still a Type C model, and even carried the same chassis designation as the

Japanese advertising for the two-door Retna series, designed by Masashi Takahashi. The same picture was used in the contemporary catalogue.

equivalent saloon, even though the coupé body was very different. It was what was under the skin that mattered more to Subaru, and it did, indeed,

America's 1995 Sport Coupé was a variation of the home market Retna model.

look very familiar.

Four models were available: a front-wheel drive version, equipped with either a manual or automatic gearbox and powered by the 1.5 litre EJ15 unit, or a 4WD variant with the same transmission options but the slightly more powerful EJ16 lump up front. The suspension and other chassis details were carried over from the saloon, with disc/drum braking, power-assisted steering, and 13-inch wheels and tyres.

Power windows, central locking, colour-keyed mirrors (with remote adjustment) and door handles, and wheel trims were included in the package, with prices ranging from just 998,000 yen to a still very reasonable 1,515,000 yen. Automatic models came with air conditioning (optional on others), and a stereo radio/cassette was listed on all but the cheapest grade. A Clear View Pack for those living in the north of Japan was the only major option.

The coupé's styling was attractive enough, set off by well-chosen colours which included Active Red, Light Silver Metallic, Cosmic Blue Mica and Splash Green Mica. Dimensions were exactly the same as those listed for the saloon, while the lightest car in the range weighed in at around a tonne.

With the introduction of the coupé model and the continued success of the existing range (the WRX-based cars were immensely popular), in March 1995 Subaru posted record monthly sales of the Legacy and Impreza lines in Japan.

Big changes in America
Front-wheel Impreza sales held steady during 1994 (17,240 units were sold - a slight increase on the previous year), but 4WD models were suddenly much more popular, accounting for 13,675 of the 100,000 Subaru vehicles sold in the States that year. The 1995 model year brought about the end of the Loyale and the Justy, but some significant changes in the Impreza range made up for the loss of these two lines.

For starters, the Sport Coupé model was added. Based on the home market Retna model, the American version was far more in keeping with its looks, powered by either the familiar 1.8 litre flat-four or the 16v 2.2 litre unit from the Legacy, the latter (with

automatic transmission only) pumping out a healthy 135bhp.

The Base model specification was pretty much the same, although the Sport Coupé gained full wheel covers (165/80 tyres on 13-inch rims was standard fare for FF models, with 14-inch wheels shod with 175/70 HR-rated rubber for the four-wheel drive cars).

Moving up to the L grade brought air conditioning, power mirrors, a four-speaker radio/cassette unit, a tachometer, better trim, and wheel covers for the four-door saloons and the estate; the two-door model also gained foglights and a rear spoiler. If the 2.2 litre engine was specified, bigger 195/60 HR15 tyres and a rear anti-roll bar came as part of the package.

Alloy wheels and anti-lock brakes were an option on the cheaper grades, but standard on the top models. The 2.2 litre LX, quickly identified by its colour-keyed door mirrors, came fully loaded. Priced at $17,495 in two-door guise, the saloon was $300 cheaper, while the station wagon version was $100 more.

Finally, the Sport Wagon at last lived up to its name with the introduction of the Outback series (the upgrade was available on the Legacy estate as well, incidentally). The five-speed, 1.8 litre Outback was the most expensive car in the 1800 range, priced at $15,950, while the 2.2 litre version (automatic only) cost $1000 more.

The extra money brought together a nice package for younger, more active buyers, or for those who simply wanted to add some 'street cred' to their practical purchase. Two-tone paintwork was a distinguishing feature, combined with a roof-mounted luggage rack, mudguards and wheel trims to cover the 14-inch steel rims. Air conditioning and a four-speaker radio came as standard, with the 2.2 litre model also sporting power door mirrors, a radio/cassette and rear anti-roll bar.

Subaru shipped a WRX Sports Wagon to America for journalists to try, even though there was still little hope of the model being sold in that market. Andrew Bornhop was impressed, nonetheless, especially with the handling. In the May 1995 issue of *Road & Track*, he observed: "On my own private little rallycross course, the beauty of the WRX's rear-biased AWD system came to light. Unlike most 4WD

cars that behave like a typical front-driver and understeer when driven hard into a corner, the WRX turns in nicely, aided by a quick lift of the throttle. Then, after getting the WRX settled, a progressive reapplication of the throttle brings on - surprise, surprise - power-on oversteer in a situation that would have most all-wheel drivers pushing like a pig. For lap after lap I charged into the corners deeper and came out harder, with each power-on exit feeling more and more like one that McRae might pull off."

Car & Driver rated the automatic transmission very highly: "Under full throttle, the transmission cracks off gear changes at an ambitious 6700rpm. These are rifle-shot, blink-of-the-eye shifts that are, at the same time, surprisingly smooth. Downshifts are equally impressive. Punch the throttle at a 60mph [100kph] cruise and you instantaneously summon - *sans* lurch - not only a lower gear but also 5400rpm on the tach, thigh-deep in the flat-four's sweet spot. Very satisfying.

"If the question is 'What's the quickest way to deliver your Victoria's Secret catalogue mid-blizzard?' the answer may well be this ingratiating little mongrel. We'll gladly assist with the adoption papers."

The WRX STi Version II
It's fair to say that demand for the Type RA STi took everyone by surprise, although it shouldn't have. The WRX accounted for a large percentage of Impreza sales, and Mitsubishi had already proved there was a lucrative niche market for homologation specials - the first 2500 Lancer Evolutions sold so quickly (in just three days, in fact) that another batch of 2500 was produced. With the Evolution II, which went on sale in early 1994, the 5000 run was sold in around three months, so there was definitely an eager bunch of enthusiasts ready to snap up homologation specials like this as soon as they were built.

However, the STi facility at Mitaka was simply not geared for volume production. It was therefore decided to introduce the Version II range, which was built on the Subaru production line at the Yajima Plant in limited - but nonetheless far greater - numbers. Orders for the Type RA STi continued to be taken, although the Version II moniker was now applied to this model,

EQUIPMENT

SPECIFICATIONS

スピードはひかえめに、安全はスバルの願い。シートベルトをしめて安全運転を。

'95 World Rally Championship

WRCイメージを手に入れる。

世界の頂点で闘うワークスカーのイメージを添った
STiバージョンII 555。
オプションの555 SUBARU ステッカーセット、
スピードライン製アルミホイールを装着すれば、
WRCの様をバージョンIIのポテンシャルとともに再現できる。
さらに、スポーツワゴンSTi バージョンII 555も登場。
バージョンII 555を手に入れるのは、誰だ。

WRX STi Ver.II 555はセダン500台／ワゴン100台の限定生産車です。

PURE SPORTS SEDAN / SPORTS WAGON WRX

STi Ver.II 555

BODY COLOR VARIATION

SPORTS WAGON WRX STi Ver.II 555

富士重工業株式会社

外装色：ラリッシュバージレッド

ファクトリーチューンに乗る。

WRC「世界ラリー選手権」をはじめ、
スバルのモータースポーツ活動を統括するスバル・ファクトリー、
STi（スバル テクニカ インターナショナル）のノウハウを注ぎ込んだ
スペシャル・チューニングマシン、それが、STi バージョンIIである。
最高出力ダン275ps、ワゴン260psのSTi チューニングエンジン。
そして、迫力のエクステリアとインテリア。
鍛え抜かれたそのポテンシャルは、走りを愛するものすべてを魅了する。

チャンピオンマシンと走る。

'95全日本ラリー選手権、Cクラスを圧倒したパフォーマンス。
コンペティションフィールドはもちろん、ストリートでも味わうために。
待望のWRXtypeRA STi バージョンII登場。
ハードラストレに加え、最高出力27.5psのハンドクラフテッド・チューニングエンジン、
"ドライバーズ・コントロール・センターデフ"採用の4WDシステムを搭載。
チャンピオンマシンをベースポテンシャルの更なる強化。
いま、もっとも進化したWRXの走りがここにある。

'95 All Japan Rally Championship

C-class CHAMPION

PURE SPORTS SEDAN / SPORTS WAGON WRX

STi Ver.II

BODY COLOR VARIATION

SPORTS WAGON WRX STi Ver.II

PURE SPORTS SEDAN WRX type RA

STi Ver.II

BODY COLOR

ドライバーズ・コントロール・センターデフ

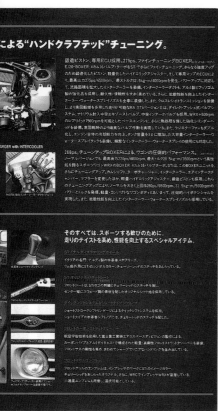

Brochure for the STi Version II models.

too, with only the engine receiving STi's handbuilt treatment.

The Version II cars made their official debut on 22 August 1995 in five variations: the WRX STi Ver.II Pure Sports Sedan and Sports Wagon, the WRX STi Ver.II 555 Pure Sports Sedan and Sports Wagon, and the WRX Type RA STi Ver.II. The latter, essentially produced for competition purposes, was built to order, whilst the 555 saloon was limited to 500 units and the equivalent estate restricted to just 100 cars.

Taking the strict WRX STi Version II cars first, the saloon engine developed 275bhp at 6500rpm, along with 235lbft of torque at 4000rpm. The STi models gained red induction manifolds at this stage but, rather oddly, this distinctive feature was not seen on the Type RA-based cars, only the more civilized versions. All cars still carried a label on the fanbelt cover, although it now read 'Tuning by STi' - the reference to handcrafting was deleted.

While the powerplant for the saloon had basically the same specification as the STi Type RA (although hydraulic valve adjustment meant a 7000rpm rev limit), the Sports Wagon had to make do with 260bhp and 227lbft. In other words, the estate came with the standard WRX saloon engine (the contemporary WRX Sports Wagon had 40bhp less, of course). All non-RA Version II cars came with a five-speed manual transmission, the gearing being the same as the standard WRX (including the 4.11:1 final drive).

Compared with the 1994 Type RA STi, the lack of a roof vent was a useful distinguishing feature on the new car, as were the WRX side skirts, rear valance and body-coloured door handles and mirrors, rear wiper, and bronze glass in place of green. Otherwise it was very similar, even down to details like the grille colouring and side emblem; the attractive 16-inch wheel and tyre combination was also carried over from the original Type RA STi (although the Type RA had Potenza rather than Expedia rubber).

Equipment levels were much nearer those of the standard WRX, with the saloon priced at 2,748,000 yen and the estate just 11,000 yen more. Coachwork colours included Feather White, Active Red and Light

Silver Metallic.

The limited edition '555' cars were, in reality, the same as the run-of-the-mill Version II models, with the exception of paint colours and a number of minor details. However, with blue coachwork and availability of a sticker set and gold Speedline Electra S alloys, they could be made to look just like a WRC Impreza. While the estate was less convincing, of course, it was certainly striking.

Apart from the Sports Blue paint, the 555 models were given rally-style mudflaps and a roof vent, although the latter was simplified for series production and had a better finish than the earlier STi cars. In view of the lack of air conditioning on the Type RA, the vent was a necessity for hot, Japanese summers, but purely a cosmetic addition on the 2,878,000 yen '555' saloon (it was not part of the 555 Sports Wagon package, priced slightly lower at 2,849,000 yen).

As for the WRX Type RA STi Version II, it was almost impossible to tell it apart from its immediate predecessor part from the addition of polished exhaust trim. The engine, chassis, body and interior modifications were all carried over. Unlike the other Ver.II models, the WRX Type RA STi Ver.II had the same internal ratios and 3.90:1 final drive as the model it replaced; it also had a 'Type RA' badge by the rear light. Available in white only, it was priced at 2,728,000 yen.

A UK Special

The price of turbocharged Impreza motoring went up by £500 at the start of 1995 (the price of normally-aspirated models remained the same), and then, the so-called 'Series McRae' Impreza was launched in mid-1995 to commemorate Colin's victory in the previous year's RAC Rally.

A year or so later, Allan Muir at *Autocar* observed: "The car that makes you feel like a rally star is Prodrive's Subaru Impreza Turbo Series McRae. Prodrive, the Oxfordshire company that runs the Subaru rally team, takes an £18,499 Impreza Turbo 2000 and adds nearly 10 grand's worth of go-faster bits and a striking wheels/tyres/paint package that turns the oddball four-wheel drive saloon into a serious performance car.

"An uprated engine management system, Prodrive exhaust silencer and

Ramair filter give the standard 208bhp two-litre flat-four a claimed 15% power and torque boost. That takes it to around 240bhp, with a corresponding improvement in mid-range response. Prodrive makes no performance claims, but the Series McRae feels capable of shaving half a second off the standard car's 5.8 second 0-60 time and topping 140mph [224kph].

"Subaru's boxer engine has never felt stronger or sounded more charismatic, with a deep burble at low and medium revs that gives way to a surprisingly sweet note at the top end.

"Prodrive also uprates the springs, dampers and anti-roll bars, then fits a striking set of Speedline wheels and Pirelli P-Zero tyres. The modifications tighten the car up noticeably and turn an already capable chassis into a real peach - grippy yet adjustable, neutral with just a hint of power oversteer on the exit of corners.

"The cabin comes in for attention too: Recaro front seats, retrimmed rear seats and door inserts, plus fake carbonfibre (or wood) on the fascia and gearknob. The fake trim we can take or leave, but the seats are well worth the money.

"With the bespoke dark blue mica paint, the Series McRae costs £28,300; add all the bits to an Impreza of another colour and it costs £27,500. That's serious money for an Impreza, but you have to remember that it's rare (just 200 have been built so far) and that it's now capable of out-performing some far more expensive machinery. Colin McRae ought to like it."

Timing ultimately proved very good, as a few months after the launch of the Series McRae, Colin was crowned World Champion. With deep blue paintwork, gold-coloured alloys, power sunroof, special badging on the tail and front wings, monogrammed seats, plus an individually numbered plaque (mounted on the lower part of the centre console, it stated 'Series McRae by Prodrive' and carried the car number), the model was a nice package for enthusiastic drivers.

Incidentally, Subaru displayed the 'Streega' concept car at the 1995 Earls Court Show - an estate based on Impreza mechanicals, and featuring four-wheel drive, traction control and a flat-four power unit tuned to give 246bhp. Needless to say, it did not find its way into the showrooms.

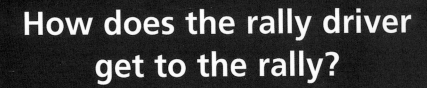

The Prodrive performance conversion continued to be popular in the UK, as this piece of 1995 advertising clearly proves. Prodrive's limited edition, 'Series McRae,' made its debut that year.

The 1995 Tokyo Show

A few days before the doors opened to the public at Makuhari Messe, Subaru announced the Impreza Gravel EX series - the EX an abbreviation of express. This was the Japanese market equivalent to the Outback in the States, although power was provided by the 220bhp WRX Sports Wagon unit in this case.

With a turbocharged two-litre engine and 4WD, performance lived up to the new car's looks of WRX-style bodywork finished in striking two-tone paintwork, roof-rails, a bull-bar up front and spare wheel housing on the tailgate. To complete the package the Touring Pack - which came with front foglights, five-spoke, 15-inch alloy wheels shod with wide 205/60 rubber (multi-spoke BBS alloys were listed as an individual option) and an expensive

**Prétentieuse, non.
Simplement parfaite.
Quand on est aussi bon
on n'a pas besoin
de le clamer.**

TURBO 4WD
Des différences de caractéristiques techniques peuvent apparaître selon les marchés.

**Si l'arrièe de l'IMPREZA est
aussi beau c'est pour que
les autres conducteurs
ne vous en veuillent
pas de les dépasser.**

**"La voiture est un palais."
Les sièges de l'IMPREZA
le trône d'un roi : vous.**

*Part of the French catalogue for the 1995 model year
Impreza range.*

Il y a une IMPREZA idéale pour tous les goûts.

65

Subaru displayed this car - the Operetta - as one of its concept vehicles for the 1995 Tokyo Show. Reaction was mixed, but it would have almost certainly sold in limited numbers had it been given the chance.

Kenwood stereo - was an option.

With the choice of four two-tone paint schemes and weighing in at 1310kg (2882lb) in its lightest form, the manual version was priced at 2,349,000 yen; an automatic transmission added 30kg (66lb) to the kerb weight and 123,000 yen to the invoice.

The 1995 Tokyo Show also saw the debut of the Subaru Operetta. Based on the two-door Retna, it was a full four-seater cabriolet, with an electrically-operated hood and a roll-over loop replacing the B-post. Finished in red with cream leather upholstery setting off the interior, sadly, it was destined not to enter production.

At the end of October, the C'z

Wagon made its debut. Based on the front-wheel drive 1.5 litre CS and the 4WD 1.6 CS Extra, this was a value-for-money package that included special trim, a driver's airbag, power windows, remote control door mirrors (with parking facility), central locking, air conditioning, a four-speaker radio/cassette with electric aerial, and full wheel trims. With prices starting at 1,389,000 yen, it was available in Light Silver Metallic, Active Red, Belgian Green Metallic and a new colour - Passion Blue Mica.

The Australian market

Australian prices were reduced slightly in spring 1995, with the entry level LX starting at a very reasonable $19,990.

The turbocharged WRX was listed at $41,990 at this time, but exchange rates pushed the cost of Subaru motoring back up again a few months later, the WRX, or Rex, as it became known to enthusiasts in the Antipodes, shooting up to $44,490.

Prices started at just under $22,000 for the 1996 model year, with the WRX now commanding $44,990; the Lancer GSR was just $35,240 at this time. However, in the spring, pricing was revised once again (with the emphasis on value-for-money), and a number of new grades were added, including a WRX estate. The full line-up appears in the accompanying table.

Australia also received a limited edition model at this time, the $46,990 Impreza WRX Rallye. As Bob Hall wrote in the March 1996 issue of *Wheels*: "The deep blue WRX Rallye is a special version of the familiar WRX, limited to 120 cars here in Australia but sold in Japan complete with '555' ciggie livery.

"Fortunately, our cars come neat, the only exterior announcement of its arrival beyond the attractive solid blue paintwork being the gold-painted [five-spoke] alloy wheels.

"Changes inside are limited to a different seat fabric and all-new front seats. These are heavily sculpted, laterally retentive sports seats with (surprise) a heavy World Rally Championship flavour."

Actually, the car Hall was referring to with the 555 stickers was an STi model, and therefore quite different to the Australian special. Nonetheless, he concluded: "With the changes to the WRX Rallye being of a purely cosmetic nature, it follows that dynamically this WRX behaves just like every other WRX. It is an exceptionally entertaining drive, comfortable for four adults, fast, occasionally furious, and, well, different ... It's one of the great buys of the Western World."

The 1995 rally season

For 1995, manufacturers were forced to enter in each of the eight WRC events. There was also a new scoring system, in which the points from two cars were put forward for each round. Consistency and teamwork were therefore more important than ever.

The Sedan range		
Grade	*Transmission*	*Price*
1.6 LX	5-sp.Man.	$19,990
1.6 LX	4-sp.Auto.	$21,790
1.8 GX	5-sp.Man.	$26,990
1.8 GX	4-sp.Auto.	$28,790
1.8 GX (4WD)	5-sp.Man.	$29,490
1.8 GX (4WD)	4-sp.Auto.	$31,290
2.0 WRX	5-sp.Man.	$44,990

The Five-Door range		
Grade	*Transmission*	*Price*
1.6 LX	5-sp.Man.	$21,990
1.8 GX	5-sp.Man.	$27,490
1.8 GX	4-sp.Auto.	$29,290
1.8 GX (4WD)	5-sp.Man.	$29,990
1.8 GX (4WD)	4-sp.Auto.	$31,790
1.8 Sportswagon	5-sp.Man.	$26,290
1.8 Sportswagon	4-sp.Auto.	$28,090
2.0 WRX	5-sp.Man.	$45,490

Australia's WRX Rallye, limited to just 120 units.

1995 Monte Carlo Rally (McRae).

1995 Monte Carlo Rally (Liatti).

1995 Swedish Rally (Sainz)

1995 Rally of Portugal (McRae).

1995 Tour de Corse (Sainz).

1995 Rally of Portugal (Burns).

1995 Tour de Corse (Liatti).

1995 Rally of New Zealand (Burns).

1995 Rally of Australia (McRae).

Peter Bourne getting a soaking in NZ.

On the technical front, new, smaller bore restrictors limited airflow going into the turbocharger, thus levelling the playing field - all the major teams were getting around 300bhp from their two-litre engines. Interestingly, Subaru ran a 1995 spec car in the 1994 Catalunya Rally (classed as an F2 event that year) and found that engine revs were up to 1000rpm lower at the top end - the SWRT quoted maximum outputs of 300bhp at 5500rpm, and 325lbft of torque (at 4000rpm) for the 1995 season.

New gear ratios, revised camshaft profiles, and a change in the compression ratio and ECU were adopted to overcome the power loss caused by the restrictors, while a 'bang-bang' system (something employed by all of the leading teams in one form or another) was incorporated to reduce turbo lag. However, new tyre regulations also caused problems for the engineers, as the latest style rubber appeared to lose optimum efficiency quicker than earlier tyres,

The rally car featured an 'active' four-wheel drive system, incorporating an electronically-controlled front differential. To transmit the power to the road, Subaru continued to employ Pirelli tyres, mounted on 15-inch, eight-spoke alloys for gravel events, or 18-inch, six-spoke items for tarmac; in both cases, the wheels were made by the Speedline concern. As for the brakes, four-pot AP calipers were fitted at both ends.

Both Carlos Sainz and Colin McRae renewed their contracts, and the third car was driven by either Richard Burns or Pierro Liatti, the Italian. Born in 1962, Liatti was a tarmac specialist with a European championship under his belt, but he was only given three drives, the same number as Burns.

1995 rally record

Despite recent regulation changes, all the major teams remained on a par. Indeed, Toyota, Ford, Subaru and Mitsubishi shared the top four places in Monte Carlo. Subaru led all of the first day, initially through McRae until he left the road briefly, handing the lead to Sainz. The Spanish driver then stayed in front for the remainder of the event - even a momentary electrical failure on the final night couldn't stop him. Both Liatti and McRae slid off the same bend in the notorious Sisteron

No.	Driver/Co-driver	Position	Reg. No. (Group)
1995 rally record			
Monte Carlo (21-26 January)			
5	Carlos Sainz/Luis Moya	1st	L555 REP (Gp.A)
6	Pierro Liatti/Alex Alessandrini	8th	M555 STE (Gp.A)
4	Colin McRae/Derek Ringer	dnf	L555 BAT (Gp.A)
Sweden (10-12 February)			
4	Colin McRae/Derek Ringer	dnf	L555 BAT (Gp.A)
5	Carlos Sainz/Luis Moya	dnf	L555 REP (Gp.A)
6	Mats Jonsson/Johnny Johansson	dnf	M555 STE (Gp.A)
Portugal (8-10 March)			
5	Carlos Sainz/Luis Moya	1st	L555 REP (Gp.A)
4	Colin McRae/Derek Ringer	3rd	L555 BAT (Gp.A)
6	Richard Burns/Robert Reid	7th	M555 STE (Gp.A)
Tour de Corse (3-5 May)			
5	Carlos Sainz/Luis Moya	4th	L555 REP (Gp.A)
4	Colin McRae/Derek Ringer	5th	L555 BAT (Gp.A)
6	Pierro Liatti/Alex Alessandrini	6th	M555 STE (Gp.A)
New Zealand (27-30 July)			
4	Colin McRae/Derek Ringer	1st	L555 BAT (Gp.A)
6	'Possum' Bourne/Tony Sircombe	7th	M555 STE (Gp.A)
14	Richard Burns/Robert Reid	dnf	L555 REP (Gp.A)
Australia (15-18 September)			
4	Colin McRae/Derek Ringer	2nd	L555 BAT (Gp.A)
5	Carlos Sainz/Luis Moya	dnf	L555 REP (Gp.A)
6	'Possum' Bourne/Tony Sircombe	dnf	M555 STE (Gp.A)
Spain (23-25 October)			
5	Carlos Sainz/Luis Moya	1st	L555 REP (Gp.A)
4	Colin McRae/Derek Ringer	2nd	L555 BAT (Gp.A)
6	Pierro Liatti/Alex Alessandrini	3rd	M555 STE (Gp.A)
RAC (19-22 November)			
4	Colin McRae/Derek Ringer	1st	L555 BAT (Gp.A)
5	Carlos Sainz/Luis Moya	2nd	L555 REP (Gp.A)
6	Richard Burns/Robert Reid	3rd	M555 STE (Gp.A)

stage, but, whereas the Italian was able to continue to take a top ten finish, the unlucky Scot's rally came to an end.

Sweden was an event best forgotten for Subaru, as all three cars retired with engine maladies caused by jammed oil pressure relief valves. Interestingly, the Lancer Evolution scored its first WRC victory. The battlefield was set; apart from Ford's challenge, the rally scene was dominated by Japanese marques, all of which were armed with competitive machinery. A new era had begun ...

The Imprezas were back on form in Portugal, with Carlos Sainz recording his second win of the season (in a lightweight car with more power), Colin McRae getting on the podium, and Burns finishing in the top ten with the third car. This enabled Subaru to close the gap on Mitsubishi (which had been 54 points after the Swedish debacle) to 26, with Toyota sandwiched in-between.

Round four saw the teams move to Corsica (the Safari was an F2 event that year), where the Imprezas were strangely off the pace, scoring only two fastest stage times between them. However, the team scored valuable points, and Sainz stretched his lead in the Drivers' Championship.

Carlos Sainz was absent in the next round following a mountain bike accident in which he injured his right shoulder, but Colin McRae claimed his hat trick of wins in New Zealand to equal Sainz's achievement. Moving across the water to Australia brought a great deal of drama: Sainz holed his radiator, causing retirement on the first day, and Bourne had an accident, leaving only McRae to uphold Subaru's honour. He did well, coming second, but Toyota and Mitsubishi were now neck-and-neck, with the Subaru team 38 points adrift of the leaders. In addition, in the Drivers' title chase, Juha Kankkunen took the lead, pulling clear of the field. With only two rounds to go, things weren't looking good for the 555 SWRT.

There was more drama in Spain, with Toyota disqualified (which ultimately led to TTE's absence from the WRC scene until the 1997 1000 Lakes Rally), and team orders in the Subaru camp robbing Colin McRae of a well-deserved victory. The idea was to keep Sainz in the team, so it was doubly ironic - given the TTE ban - that the Spaniard signed for Toyota a day after he'd been handed the win. Politics aside, though, the Impreza performed superbly, taking the top three places, with privateer Ivan Postel also finishing in the top ten.

Going into the RAC, Mitsubishi was just two points ahead of Subaru, while Sainz and McRae shared the lead in the Drivers' Championship. It looked set to be a nail-biting finish - and it was. The Mitsubishi challenge ended early after a strong start, leaving the Imprezas a clear run. But they still had to finish, and there was the Sainz-McRae battle to consider as well.

Sainz took the lead on day two, although McRae's outright speed (he had fastest time on nearly two-thirds of the stages) won through. He beat the Spanish driver by 36 seconds to become Britain's first - and youngest-ever - World Champion. With McRae and Sainz finishing in the first two places, and Burns coming third in another works car, Subaru secured the Manufacturers' crown as well.

After the RAC, Subaru finished on 350 points, 43 ahead of Mitsubishi, and 127 ahead of Ford (Toyota's points had been taken away by the FIA after the infamous Catalunya turbo incident) to claim its first WRC title.

Ryuichiro Kuze was naturally delighted, not only with winning the

1995 Catalunya Rally (Liatti).

Carlos Sainz celebrating a home victory, although controversy surrounded the event.

1995 RAC Rally (Sainz).

Championship trophy, but also with the steady progress of the Impreza since its introduction. Asked what was next, he said: "Winning once is not enough. We have to win again in order to join the ranks of the legendary makers. We want our customers to drive their Subarus with pride."

In the Drivers' Championship, Colin McRae overcame a bad start to the season and team orders in Spain to take the crown. Sainz, who missed the NZ round, was second, a long way ahead of Mitsubishi's Kenneth Eriksson in third, who, to be fair, was concentrating effort on the Asia-Pacific Championship, which he easily won.

1995 RAC Rally (Burns).

Road car update
The start of 1996 saw the introduction of another new Impreza model, the HX-20S, powered by a normally-aspirated

Photo:スポーツワゴン HX-20S

インプレッサ、20S誕生。

2.0ℓ BOXER+シンメトリー4WDシステム。走りの違いは、全身に現れる。

これは、スポーツワゴンの最も新しいカタチかもしれない。水平対向2.0ℓ BOXER
16VALVEの、自然吸気のリニアな吹き上がり。ゆとりの排気量がもたらすトルク
フルな走り。そして、WRC世界ラリー選手権での数々の勝利が実証した、信頼
のスバル4WDシステム。ドライバーの思いのままの走りに、さらに磨きをかけた。
インプレッサ20S、走りを予感させる精悍なフォルムに、すべては現れている。

主な装備 ●フロントスカート一体カラードバン
パー ●大径フォグランプ ●リヤスポイラー
（ルーフ＆ウエスト） ●サイド＆リヤアンダー
スカート ●オートエアコン ●4スピーカー高機
能オーディオ（KENWOOD） ●赤外線リモコ
ンドアロック ●15インチアルミホイール ほか

ナルディ製本革ステアリング
（VINCENTE）

フロントバケットシート
（オリジナルファブリックシート地）

インプレッサ スポーツワゴン HX 20S誕生

スバル、'95WRC世界ラリー選手権 世界チャンピオン獲得。

インプレッサは'95 WRCシリーズ全8戦中、V5を達成。メーカー＆ドライバーチャンピオンのダブルタイトルを獲得。
世界のあらゆる路面コンディションでスバル4WDシステムの基本性能の高さを実証した。

インプレッサの快挙です

スバルのことなら フリーダイヤル 0120-052215

*インプレッサのカタログをご希望の方は、はがきに住所、氏名、年齢、職業、電話番号、現在お持ちのお車の車名、
形式を明記の上、〒100-91 東京中央郵便局私書箱1639号スバル事務局月刊プレイボーイ係までご請求ください。

SUBARU 富士重工

Japanese advertising for the HX-20S, announced in January 1996.

---

part of the 1,899,000 yen package; automatic transmission added 93,000 yen, while ABS, an SRS airbag system and sunroof could be specified as maker options. Colours included red, silver, black and blue.

A few days after the announcement of the HX-20S, the special edition WRX V-Limited was launched to commemorate the success of Subaru and Colin McRae in the WRC series. Going on sale from 1 February, the V-Limited came in two different guises: standard 2,555,000 yen trim (with the normal WRX providing the starting point) or, for 268,000 yen more, a model based on the Type RA STi for serious enthusiasts.

The 260bhp WRX V-Limited was restricted to 1000 units, with a serial number allocated to each car, printed on an aluminium plaque. Special features included gold-painted STi five-spoke alloys, ABS brakes, green-tinted glass, and an FIA approved emblem on the tail (stating that Subaru was 1995 World Rally Champion) with the same roundel carried over onto the back of the STi seats (the door trim was revised to suit the black/grey upholstery). This model was available in Sports Blue, Feather White or Black Mica.

Rather fittingly, the WRX Type RA STi Ver.II V-Limited - to give it its proper title - was restricted to 555 units, all finished in the same Sports Blue shade. Unlike the car it was based on, the V-Limited version came with air conditioning; in reality, a necessity in a hot country like Japan if the vehicle was to be used on the road. The white victory emblem was again a feature, as was the numbered plaque, but this time the seats featured an STi logo and the signatures of Colin McRae and Derek Ringer, and the grille ornament had the six stars mark as used in the WRC.

Incidentally, a number of Legacy models were also announced to celebrate getting the double title, with prices ranging from 2,177,000 to 2,766,000 yen. The timing on the Impreza special was perfect, however, as the '555' limited edition models launched a few months earlier had already sold out.

While the range and prices of Impreza models remained unchanged for the UK's 1996 model year, at the start of 1996 proper, normally-aspirated, two-litre cars were added to

---

(NA), two-litre engine. Sharing the same bore and stroke measurements as the WRX's EJ20 unit, with fuel-injection and a 9.5:1 compression ratio, it developed 125bhp at 5500rpm, along with 126lbft of torque at 4500rpm. This latest engine (also designated EJ20) eventually found its way into other markets, notably the UK and Australia.

From the outside, the HX-20S looked like a WRX, with all the same aerodynamic appendages and large front foglights, although the five-spoke alloys were 15-inch instead of 16-inch. Air conditioning, front bucket seats, cloth trim, power-assisted steering, and green-tinted electric windows came as

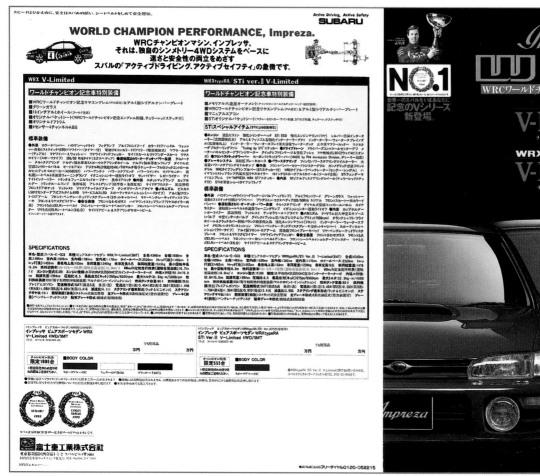

the line-up. The 115bhp, 2.0 GL saloon was priced at £12,749, with the estate version commanding £13,249; automatic transmission added £1000 on both. Shortly after, the 2.0 Sport sedan and station wagon were introduced, featuring WRX-style bodywork but without the expensive bonnet. With a manual gearbox only, they cost £1000 more than the equivalent GL grade.

Other European markets duly got the 1994cc NA car during 1996. Prices in France at this time ranged from 99,900 FF for the 1.6 GL to 169,900 FF for the 2.0 GT Turbo; the normally-aspirated, two-litre machine had a 126,900 FF sticker price. A number of sporty limited editions were also launched, not surprisingly strengthening the marque's links with its successful rally campaign.

For the US 1996 model year, all Impreza models came with four-wheel drive. In addition, apart from one coupé

grade - the entry level 1800 Brighton - the 135bhp, 2.2 litre engine was made the standard powerplant for the range. In effect, the five-speed Brighton replaced the earlier Base grade, although a more upmarket specification was adopted, with air conditioning and a radio/cassette coming as part of the $13,495 package.

The coupé was also available in L and LX guise, with both of the latter options having the choice of manual or automatic transmission. The L spec sheet was similar to that of last year's namesake, but there was no direct equivalent to the LX. With prices starting at $17,295, the LX came with such goodies as velour trim, ABS brakes and alloy wheels, and the four-door model gained a rear spoiler (already standard on the two-door L grade).

The sedan was listed in L (manual or automatic) and LX forms (automatic only), with prices ranging from $15,595 to $17,795. The estate, meanwhile,

came in five-speed L, four-speed LX and Outback guise (the latter with either gearbox). Only one Outback grade was available for 1996, boasting ABS brakes, power windows, two-tone paintwork with colour-keyed bumpers (incorporating a rear step) and custom stripes, luggage rails, special upholstery and wheel trims, and raised white lettering on the 185/70 HR14 all-season tyres. The five-speed Outback was priced at $17,595, and automatic transmission added $800.

American Impreza sales for 1996 were basically similar to those of the previous year, although the ratio of FF to 4WD models shifted quite dramatically. In 1995, 24,415 units were sold, 76 per cent of which were four-wheel drive variants. During 1996, sales levels held steady at 24,687 units, but, with the changes announced at the start of the season, four-wheel drive models now accounted for 97 per cent of the total.

A couple of special estate models were launched for the Japanese market in May 1996: the 1.8 litre C'z-L and the 1.5 litre C'z-II. The 1.8 litre car was based on the 4WD automatic HX Edition L, and built on the already high standard specification with a driver's airbag, a CD player (in addition to the four-speaker radio/cassette), Escaine trim and a roof spoiler. Available in silver, black or red, it was priced at 1,799,000 yen.

The C'z-II was essentially the same as the earlier C'z launched seven months earlier, except it was limited to south-west Japan, and was cheaper, despite having a CD player as standard. The manual car

was just 1,399,000 yen, while automatic transmission added 93,000 yen.

Mention should be made at this point of the Australian market RX model, introduced at the end of the 1996 season. Priced at just $29,990, it gained the WRX bodykit and alloys, but not the latter's engine or aluminium bonnet (with its air scoop). Instead, power was provided by a torquey, normally-aspirated, two-litre unit like that found in Japan's HX-20S grade; inside, the emphasis was on luxury (air conditioning, cruise control, electric windows, and so on, were all part of the standard package). A total of 400 were shipped south before the 1997 cars began landing on Australian shores.

The 1996 rally season

Colin McRae, the reigning World Champion, continued with Subaru, as did Pierro Liatti, who was given a full programme of events this season.

Sainz's wish to go to Toyota was scuppered by the TTE ban, but the 555 SWRT had already decided that his place would be taken by Kenneth Eriksson after Catalunya; he eventually went to Ford. Incidentally, Eriksson, born in Sweden in 1956, was the Group A World Champion in 1986, and had a long career with Mitsubishi before signing for the Subaru team.

1996 rally record

Due to the rotation system, the classic Monte was not part of the WRC calendar for 1996, so the season started with the Swedish Rally. Subaru struggled with stud problems on the first day, but McRae fought back to claim third and Eriksson came fifth on his debut for the team; Didier Auriol, without a drive after the TTE affair, drove as a guest but failed to adjust to the car. Ultimately, he claimed tenth place.

The second round moved to another extreme - in Kenya. McRae led

The 1996 Outback Sport for North America.

An attractive publicity shot showing the Australian WRX Sports Wagon.

in the early stages, but a rear suspension collapse on the second day after he hit a rock ended his chances of a win. In fact, trouble with the Bilstein shock absorbers plagued the 555 SWRT for most of the event, but the Impreza somehow remained competitive. The works entered the Impreza Sport Wagon in Group N, and came away with a

Pierro Liatti, pictured with co-driver Fabrizia Pons.

Kenneth Eriksson.

Colin McRae about to start the 1996 Acropolis Rally.

1996 Acropolis Rally (McRae).

The SWRT pictured in Greece.

convincing Class win.

Indonesia was the third round of the WRC and the second in the Asia-Pacific series, so was of particular importance to the Japanese manufacturers. However, all of the expected top runners went out for one reason or another (accidents in the case of McRae and Eriksson), leaving Pierro Liatti (now with the highly experienced Fabrizia Pons by his side) to pick up the points for Subaru - he came second, just behind Sainz. Subaru won Group N, incidentally, with Michael Lieu taking a highly creditable sixth place with his WRX-RA model.

McRae led the Acropolis from start to finish, challenged only by Tommi Makinen, and, with Liatti and Eriksson both claiming top five places, Subaru opened up its lead in the Championship to 40 points. This win at least made up for the Scot's disappointment in Greece in 1994; in a proud display of his heritage, he was led up the winner's ramp by a bagpipe player.

Argentina was not kind to Subaru generally, and McRae in particular. He first hit a spectator who wanted to get a little too close to the action, then a hefty rock which damaged the rear subframe (resulting in delays to change it) before he rolled into retirement. Eriksson was running well in second until a puncture on the final day cost him precious time, dropping him to third, while Liatti finished seventh.

Colin's luck didn't improve in

1996 San Remo Rally (McRae).

Finland, where he retired with seriously modified bodywork. Eriksson took fifth to prevent a total disaster for the 555 SWRT, but it wasn't enough to stop Mitsubishi Ralliart taking the lead in the Championship.

On the other side of the world, the Australian round (part of the APC as well as the WRC) will be remembered for the stage at Bunnings which was completely waterlogged. It was later cancelled, but not before a lot of works machines had stalled in a bid to get across deep water. Eriksson came second (sealing the Asia-Pacific title for the Swede), McRae came fourth and Liatti seventh.

San Remo saw a return to form for the talented Scot, who led from the end of day one and never looked back. Liatti was running well on the faster tarmac, but retired with electrical problems (the car simply wouldn't start

Service halt during the 1996 San Remo classic.

Pirelli advertising proclaiming its role in Subaru's 1996 WRC title.

on day three). Eriksson drove sensibly to take fifth.

The final round was held in Spain in 1996. Spectators witnessed an impressive performance from Pierro Liatti, who led for most of the rally before he was caught by Colin McRae. This 555 SWRT dominance, combined with a poor showing from Mitsubishi, secured Subaru a second consecutive World Championship.

Before closing this section, mention should also be made of the RAC Rally, which was listed as a W2L event. Finishing only eight minutes down on Armin Schwarz in a TTE-prepared Toyota Celica, Masao Kamioka brought an ex-works Impreza (still carrying the M555 STE number plates) to a remarkable second place; the same driver had claimed fourth in Portugal, another round of the W2L Championship.

Subaru ended the 1996 season on 401 points - 79 more than Mitsubishi, and 102 more than Ford in third. However, while Subaru retained its WRC title, Colin McRae couldn't; he came second, whilst Kenneth Eriksson occupied fourth place, one slot ahead of Pierro Liatti.

The works teams were much in evidence in the Asia-Pacific Championship, with Subaru claiming a one-two-three in Thailand (the opening round), so Indonesia was disappointing, with only Liatti scoring any points. Eriksson won in Malaysia, and, whilst Richard Burns pipped him to the post in NZ, the Swede's second place in Australia secured the APC title for him. However, Subaru's poor performance in the Hong Kong-Beijing Rally handed the Manufacturers' crown to Mitsubishi.

1996 rally record

No.	Driver/Co-driver	Position	Reg. No. (Group)
Sweden (9-11 February)			
1	Colin McRae/Derek Ringer	3rd	N1 WRC (Gp.A)
2	Kenneth Eriksson/Staffan Parmander	5th	N555 WRC (Gp.A)
3	Didier Auriol/Bernard Occelli	10th	N555 BAT (Gp.A)
10	Pierro Liatti/Mario Ferfoglia	12th	N555 SRT (Gp.A)
Safari (5-7 April)			
2	Kenneth Eriksson/Staffan Parmander	2nd	N555 WRC (Gp.A)
1	Colin McRae/Derek Ringer	4th	N1 WRC (Gp.A)
3	Pierro Liatti/Mario Ferfoglia	5th	M555 STE (Gp.A)
16	Hideaki Miyoshi/Tinu Khan	8th	GM52-MU7031 (Gp.N)
14	Patrick Njiru/Rick Matthews	9th	GM52-MU7032 (Gp.N)
Indonesia (10-12 May)			
3	Pierro Liatti/Fabrizia Pons	2nd	L555 SRT (Gp.A)
1	Colin McRae/Derek Ringer	dnf	N1 WRC (Gp.A)
2	Kenneth Eriksson/Staffan Parmander	dnf	N555 WRC (Gp.A)
Acropolis (2-4 June)			
1	Colin McRae/Derek Ringer	1st	N1 WRC (Gp.A)
3	Pierro Liatti/Fabrizia Pons	4th	N555 SRT (Gp.A)
2	Kenneth Eriksson/Staffan Parmander	5th	N555 WRC (Gp.A)
Argentina (4-6 July)			
2	Kenneth Eriksson/Staffan Parmander	3rd	N555 WRC (Gp.A)
3	Pierro Liatti/Fabrizia Pons	7th	N555 BAT (Gp.A)
1	Colin McRae/Derek Ringer	dnf	N1 WRC (Gp.A)
1000 Lakes (23-26 August)			
2	Kenneth Eriksson/Staffan Parmander	5th	N555 WRC (Gp.A)
1	Colin McRae/Derek Ringer	dnf	N1 WRC (Gp.A)
Australia (15-18 September)			
2	Kenneth Eriksson/Staffan Parmander	2nd	N555 WRC (Gp.A)
1	Colin McRae/Derek Ringer	4th	N1 WRC (Gp.A)
3	Pierro Liatti/Fabrizia Pons	7th	N555 BAT (Gp.A)
San Remo (13-16 October)			
1	Colin McRae/Derek Ringer	1st	N1 WRC (Gp.A)
2	Kenneth Eriksson/Staffan Parmander	5th	N555 WRC (Gp.A)
3	Pierro Liatti/Fabrizia Pons	dnf	N555 BAT (Gp.A)
Spain (4-6 November)			
1	Colin McRae/Derek Ringer	1st	N1 WRC (Gp.A)
3	Pierro Liatti/Fabrizia Pons	2nd	N555 BAT (Gp.A)
2	Kenneth Eriksson/Staffan Parmander	7th	N555 WRC (Gp.A)

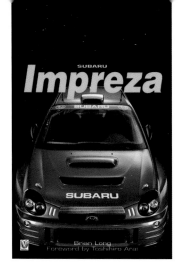

4

A 'brand new' car

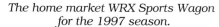

The home market WRX Sports Wagon
for the 1997 season.

The 1997 model year HX-20S, sporting facelifted bodywork. As part of an agreement made with Ta Ching Motors in Taiwan, the Impreza was built as a CKD unit in that country from 1997. Production figures were never that impressive (excuse the pun), but it is another angle in the model's history and part of its story.

September 9 1996 saw another round of revisions for the Impreza range. Described in publicity material as the 'Brand New' Impreza, the latest models - and the significantly different rally car it spawned - can be considered second generation vehicles, at least for the purposes of this book, although a minor change would probably be more accurate. It's probably quite significant that internal chassis codes were continued (the latest cars were given the Type D moniker), whereas the Impreza introduced in 2000 was designated Type A, implying a somewhat fresher start.

The reason for giving the 1997 model year range this 'Brand New' title was to demonstrate that the Impreza line had matured, acquiring a much more upmarket image, boosted by the marque's success in motorsport.

The latest engines - in 1.5, 1.8 and two-litre versions - incorporated technology learnt from the WRC series, and had the 'BOXER MASTER-4' designation (M standing for matured, A for advanced, S for sporty, T for torquey, E for economical, and R for reliable). Not only was power and torque enhanced, but the units were quieter and more fuel-efficient (normally-aspirated powerplants posted a 8.4 per cent improvement in economy, turbocharged engines 4.0 per cent). This was due to a combination of revised intake manifolds and adoption of molybdenum-coated pistons, which significantly reduced internal friction. Other detail changes included enhanced cylinder head cooling, and a return to mechanical valve lifters.

The two-litre WRX and WRX Type RA saloons were now rated at the Japanese voluntary limit of 280bhp, and the estate gained another 20 horses

Contemporary WRX interior, this one with automatic transmission and the Nardi steering wheel offered as an alternative to the standard four-spoke item with airbag.

under the bonnet (it was now listed with 240bhp). The gains were not so great for the STi cars, as they were already close to the maximum allowable output, although the STi sedans went from 275 to 280bhp, and the STi Sports Wagon peak shot up from 260 to 280bhp.

In addition, all manual WRX series models gained double-cone synchros and an uprated 'Quickshift' linkage to give shorter gearchange strokes and an improved shift feel; the automatic WRX Sports Wagon was now equipped with an AP Suretrac rear differential.

Subtle styling revisions gave the Impreza a more sporting appearance. All cars gained a new bonnet (still aluminium on the WRX series), mesh grille and sharper looking headlights. Turbocharged vehicles got new bonnet vents and a subtle splitter in the mouth of the central scoop, while normally-aspirated models received a revised front bumper/airdam (although the HX-20S continued to sport the WRX-style front bumper, which was deemed good enough to carry over from the previous generation).

Around the back, the rear bumper looked similar, but close inspection revealed a softer accent line, whilst the rear combination lights now incorporated a clear turn signal lens. The exterior facelift was completed via chunky new 16-inch alloys (the 15-inch ones used on the HX-20S were borrowed from the Gravel EX) and 14-inch wheel trim designs, plus some fresh body colours (including Lapis Blue Metallic, Flavone Green Metallic, and Royal Blue Mica).

In answer to the critics, the opportunity was taken to enhance the interior at the same time, although only as far as adopting better trim materials (a rather tasteful black/grey combination for all but the cheapest grades), a new four-spoke steering wheel (with standard airbag, although the HX-20S and WRX models could be specified with a Nardi three-spoke item which came without the SRS), and redesigned heater and air conditioning controls on some cars. Significantly, NVH levels were reduced, with extra sound deadening material being employed, and the estate gained improved utility via a different layout in the cargo area.

Front seats were made more comfortable, and safer, too,

The Hardtop Sedan range

Grade	Engine	Trans.	Price
2WD CF	1.5 litre	5-sp.Man.	1,199,000
2WD CS Extra	1.5 litre	5-sp.Man.	1,299,000
		4-sp.Auto.	1,392,000
2WD SX	1.5 litre	5-sp.Man.	1,399,000
		4-sp.Auto.	1,492,000
4WD CF	1.5 litre	5-sp.Man.	1,421,000
4WD CS Extra	1.5 litre	5-sp.Man.	1,524,000
		4-sp.Auto.	1,617,000
4WD HX-20S	2.0 litre	5-sp.Man.	1,859,000
		4-sp.Auto.	1,952,000
4WD WRX	2.0 Turbo	5-sp.Man.	2,555,000
4WD WRX Type RA	2.0 Turbo	5-sp.Man.	2,255,000

The Sports Wagon range

Grade	Engine	Trans.	Price
2WD C'z	1.5 litre	5-sp.Man.	1,370,000
		4-sp.Auto.	1,463,000
2WD GB	1.8 litre	5-sp.Man.	1,498,000
		4-sp.Auto.	1,591,000
4WD C'z	1.5 litre	5-sp.Man.	1,580,000
		4-sp.Auto.	1,673,000
4WD GB	1.8 litre	5-sp.Man.	1,706,000
		4-sp.Auto.	1,799,000
4WD HX-20S	2.0 litre	5-sp.Man.	1,906,000
		4-sp.Auto.	1,999,000
4WD WRX	2.0 Turbo	5-sp.Man.	2,399,000
		4-sp.Auto.	2,522,000

incorporating a pan frame to limit injury in the event of an accident. Combined with a stronger body and four-channel, four-sensor ABS coming as standard on all 4WD cars (except the WRX Type RA and Type RA STi Version III grades), the latest Impreza embodied some real advances in active and passive safety; braking efficiency on STi models was improved via four-pot caliper brakes up front.

Rounding off the changes, the steering was adjusted to give less free play (it was also a touch lighter than before, meaning less effort was needed for parking manoeuvres), and the suspension received some fine tuning, a task aided by the more rigid body.

For the time being at least, the two-door coupé was dropped from the line-up. The saloons became more upmarket, with the front-wheel drive CS Extra taking the place of the old CX, which was discontinued in favour of a new 102bhp, 1.5 litre SX grade. As for the four-wheel drive NA saloons, the 1.6 litre engine was replaced by the more powerful EJ15 unit, while the HX Edition S was superceded by the HX-20S announced earlier in the year,

albeit now with 135bhp from its two-litre engine.

In the Sports Wagon range, new grades - the 1.5 litre C'z and 120bhp 1.8 litre GB (both available with manual or automatic transmission, and in two- or four-wheel drive guise) - replaced the earlier entry level cars, while the HX-20S story was the same as that of the saloons.

The strict WRX continued, inheriting the same engine revisions as the nomally-aspirated cars to give a significant boost in power and torque, particularly in the case of the Sports Wagon models. Despite a drop in the compression ratio (from 8.5 to 8.0:1), the WRX saloon was listed with 280bhp at 6500rpm and 242lbft of torque at 4000rpm, while the standard WRX estate had 240bhp at 6000rpm and 224lbft at 4000rpm. This was mainly due to the new Mitsubishi TD04L turbocharger, although it should be noted that the STi cars had an IHI blower and the automatic version of the WRX Sports Wagon had different turbine blades.

Gearing was revised at the same time, with the normal WRX sporting

Colin McRae with the 1997 model year WRX. This photograph was used in the Japanese catalogue issued in September 1996.

Rear three-quarter view of the stock WRX Type RA for the 1997 season.

internal ratios of 3.166, 1.882, 1.296, 0.972 and 0.738 combined with a 4.444:1 final drive. The Type RA had the same final drive ratio, but closer gears (namely 3.083, 2.062, 1.545, 1.151 and 0.825); manual estate came with Type C WRX saloon gearing and 4.111:1 final drive. Naturally, the automatic WRX Sports Wagon was quite different. Although the 4.111:1 final drive was the same, internal ratios were listed as 2.785 on first, 1.545 on second, a direct third, and a seriously overdriven 0.694 top gear.

Wheel diameters stayed the same, but rim width was increased from 6.5J to 7J. The five-spoke alloys were shod with 205/50 VR16 Potenzas (type S01 on the run-of-the-mill WRX, with RE010s on the Type RA). The 15:1 steering ratio was carried over (the faster rack option was not listed, incidentally), giving 2.8 turns lock-to-lock.

The formula established on earlier cars was still much in evidence. The Type RA had to do without the side skirts, rear spoiler and valance extension, the colour-keyed door handles and mirrors, and a great deal of standard equipment found on the strict WRX. It was also only available in

a limited range of colours (in fact, Feather White only for 1997), while the more expensive cars could be Feather White (hardtop sedan only), Light Silver Metallic, Active Red, Royal Blue Mica or Black Mica.

There was just one major maker option - a steel tilt-and-slide electric sunroof for the WRX saloon, although interesting accessories included a so-called 'carbon kit' (with carbonfibre-style trim pieces for the centre console, air conditioning control panel, air vents and inner door handles, plus real carbonfibre for the handbrake and part-aluminium gearknob), auxiliary gauges (monitoring voltage, oil pressure and oil temperature), and a single meter for measuring turbo boost.

The WRX STi Version III saloons and estate made their debut alongside the rest of the 'Brand New' Impreza range, naturally inheriting the latest styling updates and a lot of the mechanical improvements. All STi vehicles were built on the same production line as standard cars from this point, with no restrictions whatsoever on numbers. Indeed, the three variations were listed in the catalogue, and could be purchased just as easily as a 1.5 litre Sports Wagon.

While most of the coachwork looked similar to that of the new WRX, the Version III cars could be distinguished by their signature front grille emblem (in pink, of course), WRC-

type foglight covers, small badges on the front fenders, and striking bootlid decals. Closer inspection revealed that the rear spoiler on the saloons (standard on both four-door STi cars, and incorporating a high mount brake light) was taller, while the two fitted to the station wagon were both slightly bigger. In addition, the Type RA STi featured a roof vent.

With a compression ratio of 8.0:1, both the saloons and the estate model were listed with 280bhp now (developed at 6500rpm, 1400rpm short of the red-line), although with a remapped ECU giving more turbo boost, the STi versions had more torque - 253lbft at 4000rpm - than the strict WRX on which they were based. Like the base car, the intercooler was now positioned flat underneath the bonnet scoop and, combined with dropping the direct ignition system, gave quite a different under-bonnet view.

Red induction manifolds became a regular feature on the Type RA STi, too, although there was no longer a badge on the fanbelt cover. Instead, there was a 'Tuned by STi' label on the large capacity, silver painted intercooler (the regular WRX intercooler had a black finish and different ducting); the intercooler sat snugly alongside a carbonfibre and die-cast aluminium strut brace. The Type RA gained an automatic water spray (plus a bigger reservoir to go with it) for the intercooler, with the traditional switch providing a manual override.

The engine had lightweight forged pistons with a molybdenum coating on the skirts, sodium-filled exhaust valves, and, to ensure a better seal, a metal instead of carbon cylinder head gasket; interestingly, with the HLA system gone, the valve shim adjuster was lighter on STi models.

At the same time, the EJ20K lost a lot of earlier STi features, like the oil jet directed onto the pistons, and all cylinder blocks (including the Type RA) were of open-deck construction. However, cooling was improved via a new radiator, and exhaust back-pressure was reduced with the adoption of a single, big-bore tailpipe (the strict WRX had twin pipes).

The gearbox design was refined in order for it to better handle the increased torque, and a stronger clutch was also specified. Naturally, an STi 'Quickshift' linkage was fitted, although

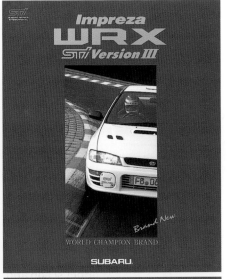

The STi Version III catalogue.

gearing was exactly the same as that listed on the non-STi WRXs, including the closer ratios for the Type RA version.

The chassis was also uprated to cope with the extra power, with four-pot brakes working on 294mm (11.6in.) front vented discs (the last STi model had 277mm, or 10.9in., diameter items), with ABS as standard on all cars except the Type RA. The Type RA was endowed with a different set-up to give the driver a more progressive brake, which incorporated bigger rear discs to replace the standard 266mm (10.5in.) items, although - strangely - it was possible to specify Version II

front brakes on this model.

The rear differential and axle components were uprated on the Type RA (which had a mechanical rear lsd rather than a viscous one, and also featured the latest generation of driver-controlled centre differential). Subtle changes in the spring, damper and anti-roll bar rates for STi cars improved high speed stability.

The wider wheels were the same design as those found on the run-of-the-mill WRX, but finished in gold instead of silver. Tyre choice was also carried over; beautiful, multi-spoke, forged BBS alloys were listed as a dealer option. As for the steering, the Type RA STi had the option of a quicker

13:1 rack, but otherwise was the same 15:1 ratio as the other WRXs.

Moving inside, although the seats were the same shape as the standard WRX items, they were unique to the STi cars. Whereas the saloons had grey highlights on the outer sections and the estate had grey inserts, STi models came with better quality grey inserts with stitching and the STi logo in red, as well as red panels beneath the head restraint.

There was a carbonfibre-style STi badge in the centre of the Nardi three-spoke wheel, with red rather than black stitching - a theme that continued on the leather gearknob. (The standard SRS wheel was available as an option on STi cars, by the way.) There was also a carbonfibre-type insert for the meter panel, except for the Type RA (although the latter had a centre diff position indicator). The Type RA was still sold without a lot of the sound deadening material found on other Imprezas, so it offered a different driving experience to the more civilized WRX.

Available in Black Mica, Feather White (the only shade listed for the Type RA STi), Royal Blue Mica (Sports Wagon only) or Light Silver Metallic, the Japanese press was in awe of the Version III model range. Praising almost every aspect of the car's dynamic ability, Hiromune Sano observed in *Car* that the Type RA was extremely rewarding to control but demanded complete concentration, even at town-type speed. In view of the vehicle's intended market position, I would say this was only natural, and would be more concerned if it was easy and relaxing to drive. Fuel consumption was heavy around town, but better whilst cruising at speed. As such, the average wasn't much different to that of a standard export Turbo.

Incidentally, the Alcyone SVX was discontinued at the end of 1996. A total of 24,379 had been built during its six-year reign as Subaru's flagship model. Compared to the 4000 units a month scheduled for the Impreza for home market consumption only, this was a very low figure, but, as a promotional tool, it did a magnificent job. Another era came to an end that year when President Isamu Kawai became Chairman, handing the Presidency to Takeshi Tanaka.

UK update
The facelifted 1997 model year cars

The STi range

Grade	Engine	Trans.	Price
WRX STi Ver.III	2.0 Turbo	5-sp.Man.	2,885,000
WRX Type RA STi Ver.III	2.0 Turbo	5-sp.Man.	2,785,000
WRX STi Ver.III (Wagon)	2.0 Turbo	5-sp.Man.	2,885,000

Press photograph of the facelifted Impreza 2.0 Sport AWD saloon. In addition to the bodywork changes, the Sport (a grade introduced to the UK market in spring 1996) had more supportive front seats for 1997, as well as new upholstery.

Interior of the 1997 model year Impreza Turbo.

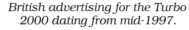

British advertising for the Turbo 2000 dating from mid-1997.

(including the Legacy, Justy and Impreza) made their debut at the 1996 British Motor Show, held at the NEC near Birmingham that year. The opportunity was taken to introduce the Legacy Outback and drop the less powerful Imprezas, with only the two-litre models surviving.

The two-litre, normally-aspirated engine received similar improvements to those outlined for the home market, bringing about enhanced torque characteristics and better fuel economy. With a higher 9.7:1 compression ratio, the NA unit was now listed with 114bhp at 5600rpm and 127lbft of torque at 4000rpm - enough to power the manual Sport saloon to a top speed of 118mph (189kph), with 0-60 coming up in a fraction under ten seconds.

The 2.0 GL 4WD model was listed at £13,584 OTR in saloon guise, with the estate (now coming with roof rails as standard) costing £500 more; the GL also had the option of an automatic gearbox. For those who wanted a WRX lookalike without the hefty insurance bill, the five-speed, 2.0 Sport AWD was available at £14,584 in four-door form, or £15,084 as a five-door. A high mount rear stoplight was fitted across the range and incorporated in the boot spoiler on the Sport and the turbocharged car.

However, it was the Turbo that attracted most attention, listed at £19,084 on the road, with the station wagon configuration adding a further £500. Major options, such as leather trim (£1140), a sunroof (£799), air conditioning (£1549) or a CD player (£327) soon sent the sticker price escalating, but there was no doubt that even a fully-loaded Impreza Turbo offered very good value for money, especially for a car capable of covering the 0-60 dash in 6.2 seconds before going on to a top speed of 143mph (229mph).

The Turbo was still listed with 208bhp which now developed at 5600rpm; 400rpm lower than before. The 214lbft of torque was also more accessible, peak output coming at 4000rpm instead of 4800. In a bid to further enhance driveability, the compression ratio was raised to reduce turbo lag, and there were modifications to the car's ignition, cylinder heads, the TD04L turbo, exhaust manifold and pistons.

Although the Turbo inherited the body revisions of the Japanese cars, it (and the Sport, for that matter) continued with the same 15-inch, five-spoke alloys as the 1996 models. It acquired a number of minor interior enhancements, too, including a new, albeit similar to the old one, four-spoke steering wheel (the same design as that fitted as standard on home market WRXs), complete with SRS airbag, and the same seats as those in the latest WRX saloons.

With subtle modifications to the suspension and braking, plus gearbox improvements carried over from Japan, *Complete Car* gave the latest Impreza Turbo 2000 AWD a brief test in the March 1997 issue, and noted: "Subaru's success in the 1995 World Rally Championship saw Turbo sales of the Impreza increase by 50%. Keen to maintain this momentum, Subaru has tweaked its 1997 Impreza range.

"With a re-sculptured bonnet air scoop and mesh-covered louvres, the front-end certainly looks mean and purposeful.

"A higher compression ratio helps reduce turbo lag and an improved turbo intake system increases boost torque. Torque has been upped to 214lbft and is now available at a more accessible 4000rpm.

"Show the Impreza a challenging road and it won't let you down. The all-wheel drive system, limited-slip differential and capable chassis cope with everything. Uprated springs and dampers can give a jittery ride, but ultimately the Impreza thrills.

"We recorded an average test consumption figure of 20.6mpg. Quite reasonable considering it was tanked almost everywhere it went - testament to the fun it gave us. There are some chinks in its armour, though; the interior is basic, the insurance high. Nevertheless, the Impreza could be placed in the same category as BMW's M3 - perhaps the ultimate Q-car."

Summing up, the magazine liked the fact that the car was "seriously rapid, [with] inspired handling. Great 'winged' front seats add to the rallying feel." It was also happy with the warranty and price, but "despite its macho stance it looks bland. [The] interior is dated and lacks equipment that its competitors have as standard." Insurance was also a problem in a land where - sadly - car crime is rife, and getting worse, despite what the politicians say. Acts of vandalism were recorded in many articles, including one by *Car Magazine*, which had a Turbo on long-term test.

After the initial run-in period (unusual nowadays, but something the author still adheres to whether the manufacturer says it's necessary or not), *CM*'s Hilton Holloway stated: "With 1500 miles on the clock, it was safe to open the Impreza up. The essence of its excellence doesn't take long to pin down. No one particular aspect of the performance and handling stands out, but the car works together impressively as a harmonious and well-integrated whole."

In another report, Holloway noted: "Pavement critics will find fault with the Impreza's combination of drab interior and garish seats. But once you're behind the wheel and experiencing the car's extraordinary performance, most picky criticisms are whipped away in the slipstream.

"As an all-round means of transport, this Impreza has to be close to a perfect compromise. It's compact, rides extraordinarily well, and is supercar-quick from A to B. Four-wheel drive puts a tin lid on my reverie. It completely quells understeer, puts all the power down all the time and makes the car fantastically secure in the pouring rain."

Fuel consumption was criticized, however, along with the seats and driving position for shorter drivers.

Ever noticed the Japanese fondness for 'limited edition' models? Special Imprezas were popping up all over Europe (some of them with the hallowed WRX designation), as well as on the home market, of course.

March 1997 saw the launch of the turbocharged Catalunya special edition in the UK. Limited to just 200 units, it featured black coachwork with gold 6J x 15, five-spoke alloys giving a dramatic contrast. There were discreet badges on the front wings and tail, but it was the interior that received the most attention.

The seats had red highlights where grey fabric was usually found on the standard cars, and door trims were black instead of grey. A carbonfibre-style dash insert, a different gearknob with red stitching, special black mats with red edging and 'Catalunya' logo, a numbered plaque on the centre console, and standard air conditioning rounded off the changes. The Catalunya carried a £21,610 price tag.

After a fascinating comparison test bringing together the ultimate evolution of the Lancia Delta Integrale and the Impreza Turbo 2000 - its modern-day equivalent - Andrew Frankel wrote for *MotorSport* : "Anyone could be fooled into thinking [of the Impreza as] a mildly warmed saloon, born to fight it out with tepid Vectras and Mondeos. And it is only when you have run it to the red-line in the early gears, looked in the mirror and seen just how far behind the Integrale lags that you realize that the Impreza, this Impreza at least, was born for rather greater things than it might at first suggest.

"Make no mistake, a Subaru Impreza Turbo 2000 is formidably fast, providing an urge that's not only stronger than that of this fastest of road-going Integrales but one which arrives earlier and lasts longer, too. Side-by-side you'd never think the

Subaru would be quicker but, in the event, it's not even a contest."

Despite having slightly less bhp, the power-to-weight ratio was stacked firmly in favour of the Japanese car, hence the difference in a straight line. The Impreza lacked the handling finesse of the Lancia, however, at least on tarmac, although the Subaru was quick to show its rally breeding on loose surfaces. Frankel continued: "The Impreza feels altogether more vague; a blunt instrument compared to Lancia's scalpel. Its smaller brakes may have less weight to control but, despite their undoubted powers of retardation, they never give quite the same air of breezy confidence boasted by the Integrale's fatter, wider discs.

"Even so, by the end of the day, it was the Impreza which had improved most upon my expectations. What I had approached imagining to be not much more that a conventional but crude hot saloon, I left with new respect. Quite apart from its undoubted dynamic abilities, it is also a credible family car with a big boot and a reasonable amount of space inside. More importantly, I discovered a car which was genuinely enjoyable to drive hard for reasons other than the punch it packed between the corners."

Against more contemporary competition, the Impreza left its mark. The turbocharged Subaru was compared to the Volvo S40 T4 in *What Car?* "The Impreza is the more satisfying to drive. Its four-wheel drive chassis is memorably reassuring through bends, so you'll attack unfamiliar roads with verve. Even in the wet, the worst it will do is run progressively wide of its line. If the steering was more precise, and had better weight and feel, you'd have little to wish for."

Another STi road car

22 January 1997 was the debut date of the spectacular WRX Type R STi Coupé, launched to celebrate the arrival of Subaru's new WRCar rally machine. Based on the WRX STi Version III, but employing the Retna two-door bodyshell, the 1240kg (2728lb) Coupé was built to order with a 2,985,000 yen sticker price.

Like all Ver.III cars, the Type R came with 280bhp and 253lbft of torque, but was closer to the Type RA in that in featured the same close-ratio gearbox, differentials (including a

The WRX STi Type R coupé. As well as the special rear quarter decals, the 'WRX' script (with 'Subaru Impreza' at the lower edge of the logo) on the bootlid was almost as big as a Japanese registration plate. It should be noted that the rear windows were actually much darker than they appear here.

The Version III V-Limited saloon, rather fittingly limited to 555 units. Note the roof vent and pink, six-star grille badge.

The Version III V-Limited in Sports Wagon guise. Like the Sedan, it was restricted to just 555 units, and featured a commemorative roundel and production number plaque near the rear lights.

Interior of the Version III V-Limited.

84

driver-controlled centre diff), automatic water spray button for the intercooler, and the same braking system with larger rear discs.

Of course, the body was very different. A colour-keyed lip spoiler was attached to the front airdam, and the side skirts and deeper rear valance were also finished in body colour (Feather White, Sonic Blue Mica or Chase Yellow could be specified); the door handles and power mirrors - with folding facility for tight parking situations - got the same treatment.

Alloy wheels were the familiar 7J x 16 items, finished in gold for blue cars, or black for yellow or white models. Other unique details included a 'Type R' badge and 1996 rally victory logo (similar to the 1995 one) on the tail, special rear quarter decals, and a dark tint on the back windows and rear screen.

Inside, the Type R came fully-equipped with automatic air conditioning, power-assisted steering (a 15:1 ratio was standard), power windows and central locking. Oxford blue-faced gauges were unique to the car, and seats had the '555 SWRT' logo. Like other STi seats, they were finished in grey/black with red accents, and came with a height adjustment facility.

At the same time as the Type R made its debut, another V-Limited was launched to commemorate Subaru's victory in the 1996 World Rally Championship (special versions of the Legacy estate and the Vivio were announced alongside the Impreza). This latest special edition was given the WRX STi Ver.III V-Limited tag. A total of 555 Sedans (priced at 2,935,000 yen apiece) plus 555 Sports Wagons (2,915,000 yen) were made available, finished in Sports Blue paintwork.

Based on the standard Version III cars (not the Type RA variant), the saloon featured a roof vent; all V-Limited models had a special logo on the seats, and a victory logo roundel on the bootlid (with a serial number plaque mounted directly underneath). Unlike the Type R, the V-Limited had a green tint on all window glass, although each of the Impreza variations launched in January featured a pink, six-star grille emblem.

The Forester off-roader was introduced in early 1997, by which time no less than 12 million Subarus

had been built, including the first million Legacy models. Legacy sales continued to grow, with the Legacy Lancaster further enhancing the appeal of the line. An official lowered suspension kit (with Bilstein and Eibach components) became available for the Impreza.

A couple of months later, in June 1997, the C'z White Edition was launched, featuring white paintwork (by far the most popular colour option in Japan), and a CD player as standard.

The Australian market

After remaining much the same for such a long time, the Australian Impreza line-up received a major reshuffle for the 1997 model year. In addition to the items carried over from the Japanese market facelift, the two-litre engine - introduced on the 1996 RX grade - replaced the 1.8 litre unit, although a basic 1.6 car was still available in the Antipodes.

There were a lot of happy Aussies during 1997. Despite the long list of improvements, the price of WRX motoring actually went down by the best part of 10 per cent. Not only that, but an automatic version was also listed, further expanding the model's appeal. At the start of the 1997 season, the range was as shown in the table.

Soon an automatic five-door WRX was added, priced at $44,490. By the end of 1997, this cost $500 more, but otherwise things stayed pretty much the same, except for a couple of limited edition models (including the first WRX Club Spec version).

The Impreza WRX certainly commanded a lot of respect in the Antipodes. In a comparison test to find the best handling car in Australia, the

hot little Subaru came a gallant second, beaten only by the BMW M3.

As *Wheels* stated in its April 1997 issue, it would use any excuse to test the car. Running out of options, it was decided to pitch a manual sedan against an automatic (equipped with the VTD system), but it made for interesting reading, nonetheless.

The improved performance of the 1997 cars - made possible through more boost for the TD04L turbocharger (a remapped ECU saw to that), a revised intake manifold design, and a larger air-to-air intercooler - was quickly apparent. The power was also more user-friendly, with the maximum 211bhp coming in 400rpm sooner (at 5600rpm); the torque curve was also meatier and flatter, with the 214lbft peak at 4000rpm - a full 800rpm lower down the 7200rpm rev range.

The gearing and 30kg (66lb) of extra weight did make a difference to the acceleration figures, but there wasn't that great a gap in real life, everyday situations. With the manual's ratios of 3.46, 1.95, 1.37, 0.97 and 0.74, plus a 3.90:1 final drive, the five-speed car covered 0-60 in 6.7 seconds, whilst the heavier automatic (2.78, 1.54, 1.00 and 0.69 mated to a 4.10 final drive) did it in 7.2 seconds. Significantly, there was only 0.5 of a second between the two over the standing-quarter, and average fuel consumption was the same. The main difference was with throttle response, which was better on the manual car. For this reason, it was the five-speed model that won testers' hearts.

Incidentally, although Australian WRXs had the latest bodywork, they still used the old-style, five-spoke alloys shod with 205/55 VR15 Bridgestones.

The Australian range

Grade	Engine	Trans.	Price
LX Sedan	1.6 litre	5-sp.Man.	$19,990
LX Five-Door	1.6 litre	5-sp.Man.	$20,490
GX Sedan	2.0 litre	5-sp.Man.	$24,990
GX Sedan	2.0 litre	4-sp.Auto.	$26,790
GX Five-Door	2.0 litre	5-sp.Man.	$25,490
GX Five-Door	2.0 litre	4-sp.Auto.	$27,290
GX Five-Door (4WD)	2.0 litre	5-sp.Man.	$27,490
GX Five-Door (4WD)	2.0 litre	4-sp.Auto.	$29,290
RX Sedan	2.0 litre	5-sp.Man.	$29,990
RX Five-Door	2.0 litre	5-sp.Man.	$30,490
WRX Sedan	2.0 Turbo	5-sp.Man.	$40,990
WRX Sedan	2.0 Turbo	4-sp.Auto.	$44,490
WRX Five-Door	2.0 Turbo	5-sp.Man.	$41,490

Manual cars came with a conventional three-spoke Momo steering wheel (2.8 turns lock-to-lock), and automatics were fitted with a driver's airbag.

The US market

Naturally, the American 1997 MY Impreza range inherited all of the changes introduced in Japan, although the US market still had its own 2.2 litre engine, and the two-door body was continued as a standard catalogue model.

The engine was refined with a hike in the compression ratio (via modified pistons), adoption of mechanical lifters (new valves and valve seats were introduced in order to keep adjustment to a minimum), and improvements in the cooling system. The changes added up to 137bhp at 5400rpm and 145lbft of torque at 4000rpm - increases of around 5 per cent on the previous year - and fuel consumption was improved a little.

The Outback Sport was the flagship of the range, with ABS brakes, power-assisted steering, air conditioning, central locking, power windows and mirrors, two-tone paint, mudguards, and a radio/cassette as part of the $18,490 package. This most sporting of station wagons now had a WRX-style bonnet, a restyled front end, slightly more ground clearance, and larger 15-inch wheel and tyre combination.

Bradley Nevin at *Car & Driver* noted: "The few gripes we have about the Impreza Outback Sport include a coarse-sounding road noise from the tyres and a wind howl from the roof-rack that enters the passenger cabin at highway speeds.

"Aside from these quibbles, we like the Impreza Outback Sport. It rides, handles, and looks great. All it really needs is the WRX's 280 horsepower engine to justify those hood scoops."

But a more powerful Impreza was on its way, and in spring 1997 the 2.5 RS Coupé was introduced as an early 1998 car. Shortly after the New York Show launch, Sam Mitani said in *Road & Track*: "One look and I was hooked ... In my opinion it possesses the most character of all the compact coupés out there today." So what was so special?

The fuel-injected, 2.5 litre engine was borrowed from the Legacy and

A couple of pieces of US advertising linking the Impreza to its success in the WRC arena, even though rallying is not that popular in the States compared to Europe. Both adverts date from the latter half of 1997.

Forester range. With a bore and stroke of 99.5 x 79mm, cubic capacity was listed at 2457cc. Four valves per cylinder and 9.7:1 compression ratio gave the flat-four 165bhp at 5600rpm, and 162lbft of torque at 4000rpm (the red-line was marked at 6500rpm).

So there was extra power for starters, and, as a consequence, a stronger synchromesh on second gear (internal ratios were listed at 3.55, 2.11, 1.45, 1.09 and 0.78 on the manual gearbox, incidentally, matched to a 4.11:1 final drive; an automatic transmission was optional).

However, the RS, weighing in at 1287kg (2832lb), was also fairly heavy, so disc brakes all-round were specified, with ABS fitted as standard. Vented, 277mm (10.9in.) discs with twin-pot calipers were used up front, with solid 266mm (10.5in.) diameter items at the rear.

Body modifications included a different front bumper with integrated airdam (actually, it was the same as that on the contemporary Japanese SX and CS Extra sedan grades), projector foglights, side skirts, a WRX-type bonnet, rear spoiler, and colour-keyed power door mirrors and side mouldings (black on lesser cars).

Ironically, with all of these 'aerodynamic' appendages, the RS had more drag than the standard coupé, recording a Cd of 0.35 instead of 0.32. But that wasn't the point - it looked good, and in a country with relatively low speed limits, such a small difference would fade into insignificance.

The RS came with air conditioning, electric windows, a power sunroof, sports seats covered in unique cloth, a leather-trimmed steering wheel (the 16.5:1 ratio on the power-assisted steering gave 3.2 turns lock-to-lock), an uprated suspension, 7J x 16 gold-coloured alloys shod with 205/55 HR16 rubber, and exhaust trim, so it was certainly a nice package.

After recording a standing-quarter time of 16.4 seconds and a top speed of 124mph (198kph), John Phillips at *Car & Driver* stated: "I love this car. A short-throw shifter. A fat, leather-covered wheel connected to quick-witted steering. An engine that emits a coquettish growl beyond 4000rpm. A firmly damped suspension that isn't flinty. Aggressively grippy seats. In fact, except for that hideous rear wing this Impreza is a worthy successor to the original [Nissan] Sentra SE-R: frill-free playfulness that in no way negates the car's essential practicality."

Road & Track later compared the RS with the Acura Integra GS-R and Nissan 200SX SE-R, and declared the Honda the winner on superior speed. However, Joe Rusz picked the Subaru, stating: "To me, practicality and comfort win out over sheer performance. That's why I'd take the Subaru Impreza, even though I believe that the Acura is by far

the sportiest and most exciting car of the lot. The Subaru's flat-four is more workhorse than thoroughbred but it gets the job done with a minimum of fuss. And the Impreza's all-wheel drive forgives the occasional trespass when that apex isn't where it was supposed to me. Think of it as the comfort food of compact sports coupés."

With exchange rates standing at around 130 yen to the dollar, the RS was launched at $19,195 in manual form, or $19,995 for those who wanted a more relaxed drive forwarded by an automatic transmission. With the SVX discontinued at the end of 1997, Subaru needed this fresh injection of glamour: the timing was perfect. To give the car added kudos, availability was limited, with initial press releases quoting just 600 units.

Other US Imprezas at this time

included the Outback Sport (now with prices starting at $17,995, or about $1700 more than the standard five-speed estate), the Coupé, and the Sedan. All except the RS and Outback came with the same level of equipment, listed as the L grade.

The Coupé was priced at $15,895 in manual guise, with automatic transmission adding $800. ABS braking (still disc/drum on 2.2 litre cars), 15-inch wheels and tyres, front and rear anti-roll bars, power-assisted steering, air conditioning, cloth trim, power windows and mirrors, central locking, a four-speaker radio/cassette, rear spoiler, body side rubbing strips, wheel covers, and a digital clock all came as standard.

The Sedan (with the same sticker price as the Coupé) and Sport Wagon had an almost identical level of

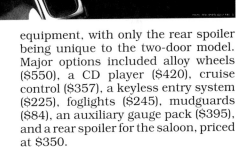

This page & next three: The 1998 model year WRX catalogue, including the STi Version IV cars.

equipment, with only the rear spoiler being unique to the two-door model. Major options included alloy wheels ($550), a CD player ($420), cruise control ($357), a keyless entry system ($225), foglights ($245), mudguards ($84), an auxiliary gauge pack ($395), and a rear spoiler for the saloon, priced at $350.

The STi Version IV

The Type E changes announced on the first day of September 1997 were nearly as significant as those introduced a year earlier. The instrument gauges - previously arranged in a semi-circle (the speedo and tachometer in the centre, with smaller dials for engine

temperature and fuel tucked into each corner) - were redesigned. There was now a central speedometer, with a smaller tachometer to the right and minor gauges on the left. While the gauges of most vehicles retained white on black markings, the WRX series had white-faced meters with black calibrations.

In addition to instrument panel revisions, the rest of the dashboard got a long overdue facelift. Lines were less rounded, but the overall image was of

higher quality, with new switchgear, heater controls and vents, centre console, and a couple of useful cubbies; one incorporated in the middle of the top roll, and another between the front seats.

Door trim and furniture was also updated, and there was fresh upholstery for the seats (including a new insert arrangement on most grades) to give the car a sportier feel. Actual seating was also improved, and there were other detail changes like

the addition of seatbelt pockets.

The steering wheel design was revised yet again, although it looked similar to that of lesser grades. The WRX series saw the biggest change, with adoption of a four-spoke Momo wheel (the same leather-trimmed wheel was used on the new STi and HX-20S models, too). All cars came with a driver's airbag, and dual airbags listed as a maker option.

Still on the safety theme, four-channel ABS was listed as standard on

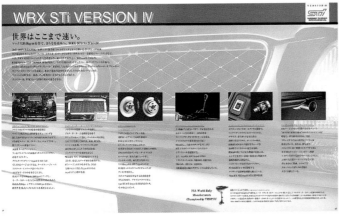

all but the front-wheel drive C'z, the WRX Type RA, and Type R and RA STi cars; high pressure brake hoses were specified across the board to increase braking efficiency.

The C'z and GB wagons got UV-cut glass at this stage, plus the option of Pure White and Rose Red Mica paint. The C'z Sports Wagon could also be specified with the so-called 'Sporty Pack' option, including projector foglights and a roof spoiler.

Generally speaking, the normally-aspirated line-up and prices were much the same as the previous season, despite the various improvements, although the basic CF grade disappeared, the C'z estates were a fraction cheaper, and the HX-20S was a touch more expensive (the manual saloon was now 1,873,000 yen), probably because of the Momo steering wheel and new, six-spoke alloys.

In addition to the fascia and steering wheel revisions already mentioned, the WRX also gained a six-speaker stereo with CD player (only the Type R and RA versions missed out on this), while the strict WRX Sports Wagon received a keyless entry system as part of the package. WRX and STi seat trim patterns were carried over (although new door panels were adopted to fit around the latest handle/armrest arrangements, and the rear seats in the estate were modified slightly to give occupants more support), and it was pretty difficult from the outside to tell a 1997 model from a 1998.

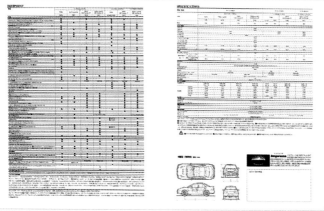

The standard WRX Sports Wagon was given a touch more power at this point, now up to a healthy 250bhp (developed at 6000rpm, and the same for manual or automatic versions); maximum torque was quoted as 225lbft. Meanwhile, the strict WRX hardtop sedan and Type RA continued with 280bhp and 242lbft of torque.

With all WRX models (except the STi Type R and RA) now fitted with the more responsive Suretrac rear limited-slip differential, the list price increased slightly. The WRX Pure Sports Sedan

Dashboard of the HX-20S for the 1998 season. Note the black-faced gauges compared to those of the WRX models.

(manual only) was now 2,569,000 yen, with the Type RA version at 2,269,000 yen. The manual WRX Sports Wagon was 2,413,000 yen, and the automatic commanded a still very reasonable 2,536,000 yen.

Official accessories were the same as those for 1997, although there was a new, satin-finish meter panel (as fitted to 1998 STi models), along with kneepads for the driver. And, of course, the auxiliary gauge faces were now white rather than black.

With the facelift came the launch of the latest STi cars - the WRX STi Version IV saloons, coupé (after a good reception, the STi Coupé now became a proper catalogue model) and estate. Like the strict WRX, the Ver.IV range looked very similar to its immediate predecessor, although there were a number of detail changes under the skin.

Turbo internals were changed to achieve better response and longevity, and, combined with revised valve timing, enhanced low- to mid-range torque. Whilst peak power remained at the voluntary limit of 280bhp (at 6500rpm), maximum torque increased by 7lbft; the catalogue now stated 260lbft at 4000rpm.

The Type R and RA gained an improved rear braking system, employing two-pot calipers on oversized vented discs, and, naturally, all the

other Type E improvements were carried over to the flagship models. There was one minor difference between the STi cars and the strict WRX models with regard to the Momo steering wheel; the STi version had red stitching (complete with matching gearknob) instead of black, although the horn ring and centre disc were now the same across the turbocharged line-up.

The STi Version IV Sedan had a 2,899,000 yen sticker price, with the Type RA 100,000 yen less. The Type R STi Version IV Coupé was listed at 2,999,000 yen, and the STi Sports Wagon at 2,899,000 yen. Accessories included uprated suspension and clutch kits, foglights, mudflaps, the coupé-style front lip spoiler (supplied in black only), and BBS alloys carried over from the previous year.

Testing the Version IV saloon for *Navi*, Paul Frere noted that the engine was remarkably smooth for a two-litre turbocharged unit, with instantaneous response from the turbo from just under 3000rpm. He was also impressed with the neutral handling, the "brilliant" brakes and the comfortable ride, although was a little concerned with the gearchange, as the spring defining the fifth to third/fourth planes was rather weak. Nevertheless, in his summary, Frere described the car as a "practical and enjoyable homologation special. A very rare combination."

The standard WRX saloon and estate were available in Feather White, Light Silver Metallic, Active Red, Royal Blue Mica or Black Mica; the Type RA was available in white only. The colour range was restricted on the STi models, too, with the station wagon having four options (all but the red shade), the sedan and Type R coming in white,

Publicity shots showing the front, rear and dashboard of the Impreza WRCar.

silver or black, and the Type RA white only. The STi cars (except the Type RA, that is) gained colour-keyed underskirts at this time, incidentally.

The WRC challenge continues

With two consecutive World Rally Championship titles secured, the pressure was on for Subaru to score a hat trick. The FIA's new World Rally Car rules allowed a little more freedom in vehicle design in that the minimum 2500 homologation run was no longer necessary. Specialist machines could be built by outside concerns, as long as they were based on a production model.

Subaru announced its WRCar just before the 1996 Catalunya Rally, and it received homologation papers on the first day of 1997. In line with the FIA regulations, the engine was moved an

inch (25mm) back towards the bulkhead to improve weight distribution, the track measurements were increased (although, ironically, McRae ran a narrow track car in NZ due to the conditions on that particular rally), dictating bodywork changes that included aerodynamic refinements.

The styling element of the project started in March 1996. Based on the two-door Retna coupé, the bodywork was designed by Peter Stevens (the ex-Lotus man who was heavily involved with the McLaren F1 GT project). As well as a lack of two rear doors and beefier wheelarches, the Impreza WRC could also be quickly distinguished from the front by the angled mouth in the grille and airdam (earlier cars had apertures that were square in shape). At first glance, the rear end was very similar, but close scrutiny revealed

that the exhaust exits were on the right-hand side instead of the left, and there was a much bigger rear wing. The prime objective was to convert lift into a degree of downforce.

Stevens looked after the bodywork; engineering was David Lapworth's responsibility. In the engine department was a significant improvement in the cooling system and a lighter crankshaft. A larger intercooler (relocated at the front of the engine) and revised turbo and manifold design combined to extract more torque from the powerplant - its 1994cc displacement giving 300bhp at 5500rpm, and 347lbft of torque at 4000rpm. This was transmitted to the road via a Prodrive six-speed gearbox linked to 'active' front and centre differentials, and a mechanical one at the rear.

After pioneering the semi-automatic transmission for rallying, it was, perhaps, ironic that the Subaru was one of the few leading cars to have a manual six-speed gearbox, as the Mitsubishi Lancer Evolution (the only model not to take advantage of the WRCar regulations, but still competitive nonetheless), Ford Escort WRC, and Toyota Corolla WRC, which made its debut later in the season, each had sequential shifts: McRae hardly ever used the clutch, however, so his gearchanges were still very fast.

Finally, the interior was brought up-to-date, featuring a heavily revised dashboard that incorporated a small monitor in place of traditional analogue instruments (permitted under the new regulations), and the extensive use of lightweight carbonfibre.

Testing took place at the MIRA facility in the Midlands at the end of October, overseen by Lapworth and

1997 Monte Carlo Rally (Liatti).

1997 Swedish Rally (Eriksson).

A service halt in Sweden.

his colleague, Tom Hunt, with McRae also involved in the evaluation process towards the end. More trials took place in Spain, where it was possible to compare the new car with the 1996 version in more realistic surroundings.

Talking to Keith Oswin at *Autosport*, Colin McRae observed: "It feels good right away. There's a lot more suspension travel and so the car doesn't get airborne in the same way as the old one. It's a lot wider and so that makes it very much more stable in the corners. The aerodynamics also mean it's not as nervous as the old car and I can go a lot deeper into corners without the tail getting really sideways. Although the engine isn't much different to the current one, its response is much better. I can't wait to get this car to Monte Carlo next January."

Weighing in at 2706lb (1230kg, the FIA minimum), the Subaru Impreza WRC made its World Rally

1997 Safari Rally (McRae).

Championship debut on the 1997 Monte Carlo Rally.

The 1997 rally season

The controversial 'event rotation' system was no longer employed, so the 1997 season took in a total of 14 rounds (to qualify, manufacturers had to enter all of them) with a new F1-style points system which placed the emphasis on winning. In addition, this was the first year of the new WRCar regulations, so no-one knew what to expect from the leading manufacturers. As it was, the Monte Carlo Rally proved just how close the top teams were in terms of competitiveness.

The 555 SWRT driver line-up was unchanged, although after a decade of racing together, Derek Ringer gave up his seat next to Colin McRae to Nicky Grist - Juha Kankkunen's regular co-driver in the TTE camp. Grist was impressed with McRae's driving style, stating: "It's absolutely natural, nothing is forced at all. One thing I've noticed is that Colin has a knack of setting up a car well before a corner, so that from the first possible moment he is already accelerating down the next straight."

1997 rally record

As already mentioned, the works teams were very evenly matched in the Monte Carlo Rally. Indeed, Freddy Loix led for Toyota on the first day, Carlos Sainz for Ford on the second, and Tommi Makinen (Mitsubishi) on the third, but it was Pierro Liatti who finished ahead on the one that really mattered - the final one! This was Liatti's first WRC win, and also marked a great achievement for Subaru; victory on the world's most prestigious rally with a brand new machine. McRae was running in the top five before black ice caused him to crash out of the event, although privateer, Olivier Burri, took an amazing seventh place with his Impreza.

In Sweden, Eriksson led on the first day, and was still leading on the second until a gearbox problem slowed him. A spin on the last day ruined McRae's chances of victory, but his Swedish teammate fought his way back to win the event by 16 seconds.

Going into Kenya, Subaru led the Championship with 23 points to Ford's 16, while Sainz was narrowly ahead of

1997 Tour de Corse (McRae).

1997 New Zealand Rally (Eriksson).

Kenneth Eriksson and Staffan Parmander after winning in NZ.

Liatti and Eriksson. McRae had an eventful Safari, overcoming various problems to claim a well-deserved victory (Pirelli's 100th, incidentally); Eriksson retired after losing one of his rear wheels, although Frederic Dor came sixth in a privately-entered Impreza. Subaru also won the Group N category once again (in general, Mitsubishi dominated the Class, but the Safari was always kind to Subaru), this time via Johnny Hellier in a WRX-RA model.

McRae was now leading in the Drivers' title chase, but engine failure for both works Impreza pilots in Portugal slowed both his and Subaru's charge. At least the Japanese privateer, Masao Kamioka, put in a good performance (in M555 STE) to take sixth.

Things got better across the border in Spain, with McRae and Liatti running one-two at the end of day one. A puncture cost McRae dear on the second day (he finished fourth, eventually), while Liatti came out second best in a head-to-head battle with reigning World Champion, Tommi Makinen. It was a good performance, though, and Imprezas also filled fifth and sixth places.

On the twisty roads of Corsica, where it has been said that the only straight piece of tarmac is at the airport, McRae was stunning, taking victory ahead of Sainz's Ford and the rapid Peugeots; Liatti came fifth.

The next round was a different story, however, as McRae suffered setbacks from transmission and power steering problems, and Eriksson's lack of testing in the unique conditions of Argentina showed in the early stages. The Swede also experienced gearbox problems, which made his third place all the more creditable.

Both works Imprezas were going well before retiring early with steering problems in Greece. However, private entries came eighth and ninth, and the 555 SWRT held onto its lead in the Championship, albeit reduced to 11 points.

Both McRae and Makinen (the Championship leader) went out early in New Zealand, retiring after engine failure (McRae) and an excursion into the countryside (Makinen). This left Kenneth Eriksson to fend off the Ford challenge, which he did admirably (helped by Sainz's encounter with a

1997 Rally of Australia (McRae).

Colin McRae flying high in Australia.

1997 RAC Rally (McRae).

Colin McRae and co-driver Nicky Grist after winning the 1997 RAC.

suicidal sheep!), while 'Possum' Bourne came fifth in another Impreza entered by Subaru Australia.

Toyota was back! However, Makinen increased his WRC lead on his home event, the Flying Finn able to make the most of the retirements of McRae, Eriksson and Sainz. The Subaru drivers went out on the second day with engine troubles, found to be caused by camshaft belt pulley failure. At least Subaru managed to stay in front in the Championship, though Mitsubishi was getting very close: Subaru was on 74 points, and Mitsubishi had 66, five ahead of Ford.

After Indonesia, Ford moved into second place, just one point behind Subaru. McRae led after the first day and looked unstoppable, but an accident on the second day caused so

much damage that it ended his rally. Eriksson fought hard, but just couldn't match the pace of the Escorts. He came third, which helped his APC points tally no end.

The 555 SWRT team was back in top form on the San Remo, finishing one-two. McRae - who'd been on the receiving end of team orders in the past - now found himself the beneficiary, with Liatti pulling over on the last stage to let the Scot through. Subaru extended its lead to 13 points, whilst McRae reduced the gap between him and Makinen from 20 to 14.

McRae won again in Australia, handing Subaru its third World Championship, and keeping his hopes of the Drivers' title alive in the process (Makinen needed one more point to be safe). Meanwhile, although Eriksson failed to finish, so did his main rivals in the APC, so the Swede secured his third consecutive Asia-Pacific title. Mention should also be made of 'Possum' Bourne, who came fifth in the Subaru Australia car.

On the RAC Rally, despite McRae's crushing victory, in coming sixth Makinen did just enough to take the Drivers' crown. Eriksson failed to finish again (with engine trouble this time), although Liatti came seventh in a third vehicle entered by the 555 SWRT, which was actually one of the two original test cars (chassis no.97.002, and later registered P200 ALL after it was released to the private All Stars team). Unfortunately, Eriksson was the other nominated driver alongside McRae.

As already mentioned, Subaru won its third consecutive World Rally Championship in 1997 - the first Japanese manufacturer to do so. With a total of 114 points, Subaru finished the season 23 points clear of Ford, and 28 ahead of Mitsubishi.

Following his late charge, Colin McRae was beaten in the Drivers' Championship by just one point, whilst Eriksson came fifth and Liatti sixth. Kenneth Eriksson retained his Asia-Pacific title, although his only win came in New Zealand (part of the WRC as well). With four out of six rounds going to Impreza drivers, Subaru took the maker's title with ease.

Interestingly, Krzysztof Holowczyc won the European Championship driving a Prodrive-prepared Subaru Impreza (he was originally going to campaign a Ford), and Satwant Singh claimed the African series with an Impreza WRX Type RA.

The UK 1998 model year

European cars received the same interior facelift as did their home market counterparts, and actually became more similar in terms of specification in the process. The new fascia had dual airbags as standard, whilst the Turbo gained the latest, white-faced gauges (with black calibrations by day, glowing

1997 rally record

No.	Driver/Co-driver	Position	Reg. No. (Group)
Monte Carlo (19-22 January)			
4	Pierro Liatti/Fabrizia Pons	1st	P3 WRC (Gp.A)
3	Colin McRae/Nicky Grist	dnf	P2 WRC (Gp.A)
Sweden (7-10 February)			
4	Kenneth Eriksson/Staffan Parmander	1st	P5 WRC (Gp.A)
3	Colin McRae/Nicky Grist	4th	P4 WRC (Gp.A)
Safari (1-3 March)			
3	Colin McRae/Nicky Grist	1st	P8 WRC (Gp.A)
4	Kenneth Eriksson/Staffan Parmander	dnf	P16 WRC (Gp.A)
Portugal (23-26 March)			
3	Colin McRae/Nicky Grist	dnf	P4 WRC (Gp.A)
4	Kenneth Eriksson/Staffan Parmander	dnf	P5 WRC (Gp.A)
Spain (14-16 April)			
4	Pierro Liatti/Fabrizia Pons	2nd	P10 WRC (Gp.A)
3	Colin McRae/Nicky Grist	4th	P9 WRC (Gp.A)
Tour de Corse (5-7 May)			
3	Colin McRae/Nicky Grist	1st	P9 WRC (Gp.A)
4	Pierro Liatti/Fabrizia Pons	5th	P10 WRC (Gp.A)
Argentina (22-24 May)			
3	Colin McRae/Nicky Grist	2nd	P8 WRC (Gp.A)
4	Kenneth Eriksson/Staffan Parmander	3rd	P16 WRC (Gp.A)
Acropolis (8-10 June)			
3	Colin McRae/Nicky Grist	dnf	P12 WRC (Gp.A)
4	Kenneth Eriksson/Staffan Parmander	dnf	P11 WRC (Gp.A)
New Zealand (2-5 August)			
4	Kenneth Eriksson/Staffan Parmander	1st	P11 WRC (Gp.A)
3	Colin McRae/Nicky Grist	dnf	P4 WRC (Gp.A)
1000 Lakes (29-31 August)			
3	Colin McRae/Nicky Grist	dnf	P12 WRC (Gp.A)
4	Kenneth Eriksson/Staffan Parmander	dnf	P19 WRC (Gp.A)
Indonesia (19-21 September)			
4	Kenneth Eriksson/Staffan Parmander	3rd	P16 WRC (Gp.A)
3	Colin McRae/Nicky Grist	dnf	P8 WRC (Gp.A)
San Remo (12-15 October)			
3	Colin McRae/Nicky Grist	1st	P7 WRC (Gp.A)
4	Pierro Liatti/Fabrizia Pons	2nd	P14 WRC (Gp.A)
Australia (30 October-2 November)			
3	Colin McRae/Nicky Grist	1st	P18 WRC (Gp.A)
4	Kenneth Eriksson/Staffan Parmander	dnf	P17 WRC (Gp.A)
RAC (23-25 November)			
3	Colin McRae/Nicky Grist	1st	P12 WRC (Gp.A)
8	Pierro Liatti/Fabrizia Pons	7th	P982 YWL (Gp.A)
4	Kenneth Eriksson/Staffan Parmander	dnf	P19 WRC (Gp.A)

yellow on black with the lights switched on) and the same four-spoke Momo steering wheel as Japanese WRX models, complete with matching leather handbrake grip and gearknob.

The turbocharged car's stereo radio/cassette was given a removable panel to make it less attractive to thieves, and the WRX sedan-style seats were carried over (unlike Japanese turbocharged cars, the saloon and estate had the same front seats); the latest door trim and furniture was also much in evidence, housing controls for the electric windows.

Another move towards bringing British and Japanese market cars closer in terms of specification was enhanced low-down torque for the turbocharged engine, and the larger, 7J x 16 five-spoke alloys found on Japan's WRX (finished in silver and shod with 205/50 VR-rated rubber) were adopted for the European Turbo. Strangely, though, UK cars continued with black door handles and mirrors.

Autocar tested the £20,215 Impreza Turbo five-door in February 1998, and noted: "For 1998 the focus on high performance has become sharper than ever, though not at the expense of refinement or comfort, Subaru is quick to point out. Outwardly, the differences range from the fitment of larger, 16-inch wheels and tyres and new side skirts to, most obviously, a super-aggressive front-end restyle.

"Inside, there's a new look fascia that features reasonably discreet white dials, as well as an ingenious, Forester-inspired cubby on top of the dash. The

UN VRAI TOUR DE FORCE.

Sièges baquets à l'avant.

Pommeau du levier de vitesses gaîné de cuir.

IMPREZA 4WD GT TURBO «555»

Carrosserie bleu rallye, 4 portes, 155 kW (211 ch), 16 soupapes, turbo à échangeur thermique, 4 x 4 permanent, 2 airbags, ABS, renforts de protection sur le pourtour de la voiture, direction assistée, freins à disques ventilés de l'intérieur à l'avant, châssis sport, sièges baquets sport, revêtement des sièges noir, jantes alu dorées, spoilers AV et AR, phares antibrouillard, verrouillage central, lève-glaces él., radio-cassettes stéréo, toit ouvrant él. coulissant et inclinable, 3e feu de stop, antidémarrage, différentiel à glissement limité, 5 vitesses, consommation moyenne 10,2 l/100 km (mixte), Fr. 37 380.-, équipement «555» compris.

ÉQUIPEMENT «555»:

• Sièges en tissu noir et alcantara gris
• Jantes alu dorées
• Set de décoration «555» (non monté)
• Contre-portes revêtues d'alcantara
• Pommeau du levier de vitesses gaîné de cuir noir

Part of the French catalogue for the Impreza 4WD GT Turbo 555, one of several limited edition models sold in France in recent years.

steering wheel and gearlever now come wrapped in leather, albeit of rather thin gauge, while the deep bucket seats remain some of the finest you will find in any sporting car.

"Just as Subaru claims, turbo lag has been all but eliminated from the throttle response, which is now as sharp as any blown car's. It also sounds a good deal fruitier than before, emitting a series of purposeful whistles and rasps that belie the car's civilized

motorway gait."

The Impreza's brakes - coming with 294mm (11.6in.) diameter ventilated discs up front and 266mm (10.5in.) items at the back, with ABS as standard, were said to be just fine, and it was quick, too. With the same gearing as Japan's strict WRX models, the standing-quarter was dealt with in 14.2 seconds, recording a terminal speed of 87mph (139kph).

Autocar's people described the

The highly desirable WR Sport by Prodrive.

vehicle as well-equipped, and then went on to say: "The fast Impreza benefits from the same quirky practicality that all versions boast. Namely, more than generous cabin room for four adults, terrific all-round visibility (thanks to the frameless doors and big glass areas), good rather than top drawer build quality and, post-revamp, a perfectly decent fascia with a well resolved driving position."

The testers loved the "blinding performance, fabulous handling, seats, and steering feel," but were not too happy with the "frightening thirst, and fidgety low-speed ride." Ultimately, the Impreza was given a rare five-star rating.

By the way, as well as a works rally car, a silver Prodrive saloon was also on display at the 1997 Earls Court Show, priced at £26,990. The *Autocar* noted: "[This] conversion for McRae pretenders will be the centerpiece for Prodrive's new WR Sport range. Based on the Turbo 2000, expect performance upgrades soon."

The same magazine later carried out a road test on the WR model which, as an approved conversion, retained the full maker's warranty; a real bonus to counter the flood of grey imports landing on British shores. It was noted: "There are four elements to the Prodrive treatment: a body kit (£2467), a chassis tweak (£3231), an interior rethink (£2820) and an engine tune-up which raises power to 240bhp (£1968). Our test car had the lot, upping its price by a wincing £10,163 to £30,169.

"The now familiar 1994cc flat-four is mildly tuned with a revised ECU, Ramair air filter and a new exhaust ... Our test car was also fitted with a quickshift (£260), which shortens and tightens the gearlever throws.

"It may sound wonderful, but ultimately the WR proved no quicker than the standard Impreza Turbo. Make no mistake, the Prodrive machine is plenty fast. Any saloon that is capable of reaching 60mph from a standstill in 5.6 seconds and 100mph in 15.9 is not disappointing. But the fact is, the standard five-door Impreza reached both increments 0.1 sec. faster when we tested it [earlier in the year]. The result is the same between 30 and 70mph (WR 5.7 seconds, regular hatch 5.6). And the Prodrive car is 2mph slower flat out (141mph against 143mph). Weight isn't an issue either;

the WR saloon weighs 1283kg [2822lb] to the standard five-door's 1306kg [2873lb].

"Fitted with uprated springs and dampers and 17-inch Speedline wheels, the WR is an inspiration over a challenging road, with levels of composure, adjustability and feel that few cars can match. And the ride was less harsh than the regular car's."

The Prodrive conversion was certainly an interesting alternative which had all the right associations with the Subaru marque (like AMG with Mercedes-Benz, or Alpina with BMW), and yet the car remained affordable and practical in everyday use.

The standard leather-trimmed Momo steering wheel was retained (and therefore the dual airbags), but Prodrive Recaro Sport seats provided extra support during hard cornering. The main instruments were augmented by an extra row of three gauges (with matching white faces) situated above the dashboard's central air vents. The latter modification meant losing the cubby, but at least it gave the driver more information on what was happening under the bonnet.

The brakes were given high performance Prodrive pads. Six-spoke, 7J x 17 cast alloy wheels, shod with 205/45 VR17 Pirelli P-Zeros, were fitted to give the car extra presence, along with colour-keyed skirts and mirrors (but not door handles), plus a taller rear wing. Otherwise, things were left well alone, with all the standard luxuries - such as a radio/cassette unit, electric windows, central locking and alarm - carried over. Like the catalogue Impreza Turbo, major options included metallic paint (£241), a CD player (£298), air conditioning (£1550), and an electric sunroof (£799).

The highly tuned engine developed 240bhp at 5600rpm and 240lbft of torque at 4000rpm. With standard gearing, this combined to give a standing-quarter time of 14.4 seconds in the *Autocar* test. The magazine summed up the Prodrive conversion as: "Sensational, but [the] standard car is better."

The normally-aspirated Impreza line-up remained the same as far as grades were concerned, with prices now starting at £13,915 and going up to £20,215. In reality, Impreza prices were not all that different to those

listed for the bigger Legacy, although at least they would be held over until the 1999 season.

Later in the year, *Autocar* compared the Impreza Turbo with the new Honda Accord Type R and the Vauxhall Vectra GSi. It concluded: "As good as [the Type R] is, the Honda can't match the Subaru for all-round brilliance. Or for value. The Subaru Impreza Turbo is still the greatest performance car bargain in the world." And it was set to get better ...

STi Celebration models

Not surprisingly, in January 1998 another batch of V-Limited models was launched to commemorate Subaru's victory in the World Rally Championship. There were three in all, all finished in Sonic Blue Mica with gold alloys: the WRX Type RA STi Version IV V-Limited sedan, and the WRX Type R STi Version IV V-Limited and WRX Type R V-Limited coupés.

In addition to the standard features found on the Type RA, the latest V-Limited had a helical front lsd, a quick ratio steering rack, bootlid logo (by now a very familiar design), a numbered plaque on the centre console, cherry red, six-star grille emblem, colour-keyed door handles and power mirrors, automatic air conditioning, electric windows, central locking, and special seat monograms. A total of 555 were available, listed at 2,950,000 yen apiece.

The Type R STi was not all that different to the base car in reality, with the paintwork and rear roundel being the main differences. Priced at 2,999,000 yen, it was limited only inasmuch as sales ceased in March.

On the other hand, the 2,499,000 yen Type R V-Limited was a 1000-off oddity. Although it looked similar to the other coupé, with gold alloys and rear victory badge, it featured a roof vent, a lower boot spoiler (with high mount rear stoplight), foglights, an export version of the grille emblem, unique seat trim and logos, black stitching on the steering wheel and gearknob (the other two cars had red stitching), and a console-mounted serial number plaque. Equipped with luxuries like automatic air conditioning, power colour-keyed folding mirrors, electric windows and central locking, this was a very desirable package.

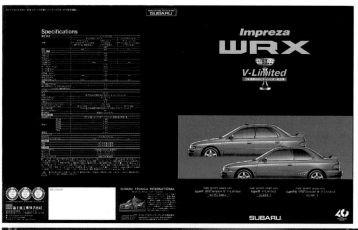

Photograph of the WRCar-STi contained in the 1997 Tokyo Show press pack.

Brochure for the STi Version IV V-Limited models.

Even more desirable was the 22B-STi coupé. Launched on 16 March 1998, the 22B had made its debut at the 1997 Tokyo Show, badged as the 'WRCar-STi' at that time. Sharing the same E-GC8 chassis code as the other two- and four-door WRX series models,

the car was never homologated, so was for street use only. But what a machine!

Although it bore more than a passing resemblance to the rally warrior, there were a number of significant differences, too. The wheelarches had a slightly different

profile to those of the pukka WRC car, as they were shaped to match the 17-inch BBS wheels specified for the model. The rear wing stood taller, and the front and rear valances were similar, but not exact replicas. The bonnet vents were also a touch smaller to enable Subaru to use a stock aluminium hood (although the actual vents were unique to the 22B). And, naturally, most of the panelwork was steel, rather than ridiculously expensive carbonfibre.

The coachwork was based on standard Retna panels, but with some metal cut out, new welded in and then loaded to give a good finish before Sonic Blue Mica paint was applied. It featured deep side skirts and aggressive fenders, making the car some 80mm (3.1in.) wider, which meant a hefty increase in local tax. The rear wing adjusted up to 17 degrees for enhanced downforce, and the lower wicker (incorporating a high mount LED stoplight) gave the effect of twin blades.

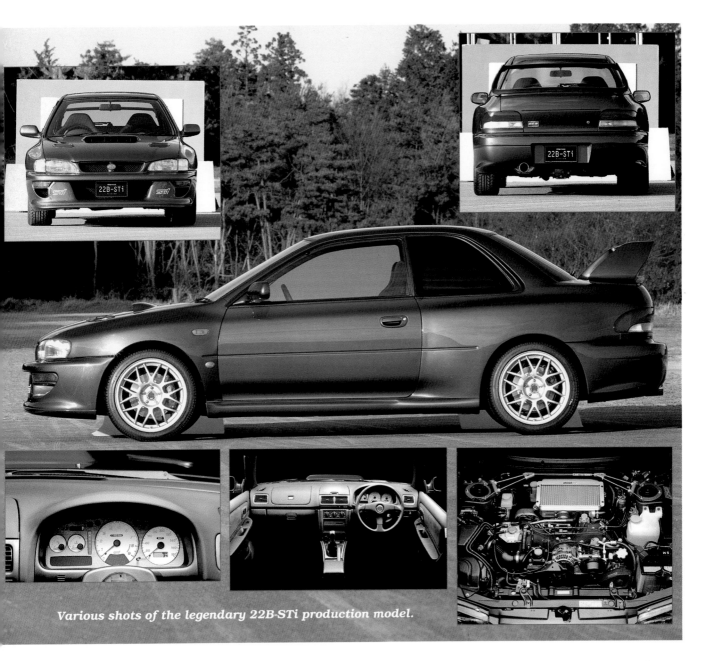

Various shots of the legendary 22B-STi production model.

The gold-painted alloys, single, chrome-tipped exhaust, STi emblem on the front wings, and pink grille badge completed the picture outside.

However, the key component in the 22B was its larger engine. With a bore and stroke measurement of 96.9 x 75mm, the bigger bore took capacity up from 1994cc to 2212cc. Combined with an IHI RHF5HB turbocharger (the same as that used on the 1996 and 1997 STi Imprezas), intercooler, fuel-injection and an 8.0:1 compression ratio, the flat-four gave 280bhp at 6000rpm (the red-line was marked at 7900rpm), but torque was now listed at 267lbft at 3200rpm. A wide power band, spreading from 2800rpm to 5200rpm, and virtually no turbo lag made for easy cross-country progress.

Like a pure racer, the EJ22 engine featured a closed deck cylinder block for greater rigidity, a metal head gasket, forged pistons, sodium-filled exhaust valves, and hollow stem inlet valves. In addition, there was the now-familiar water spray for the intercooler to keep intake air temperatures lower if the car was used hard for long periods of time.

Like the V-Limited cars, the 22B came with WRX Type RA gearing (3.083 on first, 2.062 on second, 1.545 on third, 1.151 on fourth and 0.825 on top, with a 4.444:1 final drive). However, the cogs were given a special treatment to make them harder, driveshafts were uprated, and there was a competition twin plate clutch, with one of the plates being ceramic. It was lightweight but very sharp and excellent at transmitting drive - the 0-60 dash could be dismissed in just 4.3 seconds.

The wider body allowed the track to be increased, with the front 10mm (0.39in.) wider than standard and the rear up by 40mm (1.57in.). All suspension bushes were uprated, forged aluminium lower control arms and special inverted Bilstein shock absorbers were employed, combined with Eibach springs, and rose-joints were fitted on the lateral suspension links at the front and rear. With help from the carbonfibre strut brace and 235/40 ZR17 Pirelli P-Zeros mounted on 8.5J BBS forged aluminium alloys, the 22B would happily pull 0.93g on the skidpan.

Keeping performance in check was achieved by ventilated discs on all four corners. Up front, four-pot calipers were put to work on 294mm (11.6in) rotors, while 290mm (11.4in.) items were employed at the back with two-pot calipers. ABS was not offered, but the brake calipers were painted red to add a little kudos and the VTD system, allowing the driver to select torque distribution from 35:65 to a locked 50:50, was part of the package.

The interior was much the same as a regular STi model, but had a numbered, limited edition plaque on the centre console and a special, anti-reflection coating on the dash. Trim was in blue and black to match the exterior, with a red STi logo stitched into the seatbacks. The quicker 13.0:1 steering was controlled via a three-spoke Nardi wheel with red stitching: no airbag, of course.

Although there wasn't a stereo (just an aerial), power windows, central locking, and air conditioning were standard, helping to take the kerb weight to 1270kg (2794lb), distributed 57 per cent front, 43 per cent rear. Just 400 were built. With a 5,000,000 yen price tag, the entire run was allocated in just 24 hours ...

Later, Subaru built an additional 25 units for export. Although none of these went to the USA, a total of 16 were shipped to the UK, made possible through the use of Single Vehicle Approval legislation. Badged the '22B-STi Type UK,' it had a miles per hour speedo (linked to an mph odometer), self-levelling headlights, better anti-corrosion measures to contend with the British climate, a different fuel filler neck to suit UK pumps (the 22B had a 60 litre, or 13.2 gallon tank), a rear foglight, the 180kph speed limiter

removed, and a host of other minor differences to make the car road legal. Officially priced at £39,950, it made its debut at the 1998 NEC Show.

Five cars made it to Australia, priced at $132,000 apiece ($125,000 plus the $7000 needed for the necessary documents to put the car on the road). One 22B was kept by the importer, and this vehicle was duly tested in a number of magazines. Impressed but not overwhelmed by the performance figures on paper, the effervescent Bob Hall wrote in *Wheels* magazine: "What the numbers don't relay is the 22B's intensity. It's almost violent. If you don't get a rush when the hammer's dropped in this car, you should visit your local mortuary. Now. But what's most impressive is the throttle response; astonishingly rapid for a turbocharged car. Not quite instantaneous, mind, but perceptible turbo lag is pegged to an impressively low level. And this enhanced engine reaction time makes for a nicer car in the real world.

"When it comes to chassis competence, we've been favourably impressed by previous STis, so there were high expectations for the 22B. Still, *nobody* who drove it was quite ready for its adhesion and cornering competence. In dynamics alone, the 22B comes awfully close to matching the classic Porsche 928 for chassis balance. It really is that good."

US update

24,242 Imprezas were sold in the States during 1997, representing about 20 per cent of Subaru's total sales for the year (the Legacy accounted for most). The 1998 model year cars inherited the latest instrument panel design and revised door trim, with prices ranging from $16,390 to $19,690.

The Forester arrived in the States at this time, and the Impreza 2.5 RX coupé did the rounds on the American show circuit to gauge reaction. Nearer to the Type R STi - or even the 22B-STi model - in its chassis and body modifications, sadly, it failed to make its way into dealerships.

Australian news

Due to helpful exchange rates, the 1998 model year cars were reduced in price by around $3000. A few new grades were added, including automatic versions of the RX saloon and estate, and the five-door 1.6 LX. A two-litre Sportswagon also joined the line-up, priced at $22,990 with a manual gearbox, or $24,790 with automatic.

Wheels tried the front-wheel drive GX sedan at the start of the 1998 season and noted: "Not having to turn all the 4WD parts leaves this model feeling initially more alert than the 4WD GX, and acceleration is palpably improved. A similar, if not identical, suspension set-up means this GX loses little of the four-paw's composure, and in the dry it handles just as well. The flat-four, good for 88kW [120bhp], performs strongly once the revs are off the floor and pulls with fairly meaty

Australia's WRX Club Spec Evo 2 limited edition.

torque most of the way to the top. While not the quietest powerplant, the Subaru's flat growl is kept at an appreciable distance until it passes through a couple of resonant pitches on its way to the red-line.

"For some reason, snatchiness is never far away: clutches can be harsh and the drivetrain's character is such that footwork has to be gentle and the revs matched closely to avoid shunting under acceleration or engine braking. But get it right and this is one fine-handling, lusty, valueful car."

The GX came with luxury trim, and whilst the RX - with 15-inch alloy wheels and body kit - was, perhaps, the model more suited to enthusiasts, it was the WRX that continued to be the darling of the motoring press.

The latest WRX models inherited the five-spoke alloys with 16-inch rubber and white-faced gauges of the Japanese cars. Fitted with air conditioning, ABS, power-assisted steering, central locking, electric windows, remote control mirror adjustment, a radio/cassette and an immobilizer, the discount applied to the WRX was not as great as that for lesser Imprezas. The manual cars went down in price by only $1000 (the five-speed WRX sedan was now $39,990), although the automatic saloon was $2700 less than the previous season, while the five-door version was reduced by $1200.

The two-litre WRX Club Spec Evo 2 limited edition was launched at the end of May 1998. Like the first Club Spec model, the $41,490 Evo 2 was finished in blue with gold alloys. There was suede trim on the seats and door inserts, and red stitching on the Nardi steering wheel and gearknob. The press release read: "Based on last year's successful model which sold out in eight days, the All-Wheel Drive Impreza WRX is resplendent in its unique blue and gold colours of the all-conquering factory rally cars. Only 230 examples will be coming to Australia."

All Club Spec models came with manual transmission only, and, whilst they gave a taste of STi motoring (the gold-coloured alloys, red detailing on the Nardi wheel, and so on), proper STi models were starting to trickle into New Zealand at about this time.

The Impreza Turbo Terzo

Spring 1998 saw the launch in the UK

Promotional brochure for the limited edition Terzo model.

of the limited edition Impreza Turbo Terzo. Priced at £22,995 and limited to 333 units, it was finished in Terzo Blue Mica with gold alloys (the standard 16-inch items painted and shod with Potenza rubber). The Terzo had unique badges ('3 terzo' logos on the front wings and tail), predominantly black trim with grey Alcantara highlights, special carpets, a numbered plaque, alarm and air conditioning.

Interestingly, the Impreza came first in the 1998 JD Power Survey, run in conjunction with *Top Gear* magazine in the UK. Knocking the Toyota Corolla off the top spot, the Impreza was a popular winner: "A storming performance from this year's top car. Build, performance and dealers can't be faulted, but it's rather thirsty." said the magazine.

Fuel consumption was the only quibble again in the 1999 survey, when the Impreza scored an even more impressive victory, with 99 points out of a possible 100! There was more good news for the Japanese company, too, as the Legacy came second! The following year, the Impreza had to make do with second place, as the Legacy was declared the top car on that occasion. Subaru certainly had a fine reputation in the British Isles.

The *Autocar* carried out an interesting comparison test in its 23 September 1998 issue, looking at the way in which a number of sporting machines handled the Silverstone race track. The Caterham Superlight R was the fastest around the circuit, clocking 1min. 06.26secs.; the Ferrari 550M was next, followed by the Lotus Esprit

V8 GT and the Mitsubishi Evolution V. The Prodrive Impreza WR lapped at 1min. 14.52, this relatively poor time blamed on typical 4WD understeer on tarmac, although Prodrive did state that a lot of this could be taken out according to customer preference. On the plus side, the Impreza's braking and stability were highly praised.

News update

1998 was an important year for Subaru. The 'New Century' Legacy was introduced, along with the Legacy B4 and Pleo. Both the Legacy and Pleo (the replacement for the Vivio) received RJC 'Car of the Year' awards, and the larger car set a new world record for a production estate car over one kilometre, averaging 169.1mph (270.5kph) at Salt Lake City, Utah. The Legacy Wagon had previously held the record, set in 1993.

On the Impreza front, in May 1998 the 1.8 litre GB Sport grade was launched. The main differences to the run-of-the-mill GB included colour-keyed door handles, a Momo leather-trimmed steering wheel, a leather gearshift and handbrake handle, new fabric trim, and the three-dial air conditioning controls fitted to more expensive models. Available in Sonic Blue Mica, Light Silver Metallic, Rose Red Mica or Pure White, prices started at 1,591,000 yen.

Early September 1998 witnessed the usual round of changes, this time brought together under the Type F designation. The main change was the introduction of the Boxer Phase II engine, as employed on the Legacy and

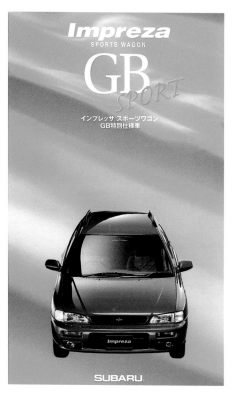

Cover from the GB Sport catalogue.

The 1999 model year SRX grade for the domestic market.

Forester a few months earlier. The Phase II power units were modified to give better low- to mid-range torque characteristics, thus improving response, off-the-line performance, and providing a better match for the automatic transmission. At the same time, the crankshaft thrust bearing location was changed for quieter running.

The manual shift feeling was improved on WRX, WRX Type RA and STi models, with smoother gearchanges as a result of better synchros. The automatic gearbox was also refined, and the transmission to engine joint made more rigid by using eight bolts to mate the components instead of the previous four.

All cars got a honeycomb grille, multi-reflector headlights, new upholstery for the seats and door panels, and new wheel covers for the grades that didn't come with alloy wheels. Fresh exterior colours were also introduced, including Arctic Silver Metallic and Cool Grey Metallic.

The SX and HX-20S grades were dropped, leaving only the 1.5 litre CS Extra in the saloon line-up (prices started at 1,298,000 yen for this 95bhp

model). However, the two-litre car was replaced by the 4WD SRX in sedan and Sports Wagon guises. With the cheapest model costing 1,943,000 yen, the SRX was basically a normally-aspirated WRX. It had AVCS (Subaru's Active Valve Control System), a variable valve timing and intake system that gave stronger bottom-end torque and better fuel economy. With a 10.8:1 compression ratio, this latest EJ20 unit produced 155bhp at 6400rpm and 144lbft of torque at 3200rpm.

The braking system consisted of two-pot calipers working on vented discs up front, with solid discs at the back. Anti-roll bars were fitted at both ends - 19mm (0.75in.) at the front, 17mm (0.67in.) at the rear - and there was 195/60 rubber on the HX-20's old 15-inch alloys.

The new, multi-reflector lights were augmented by matching foglights in the latest WRX front airdam. A rear spoiler (roof and waist on the Wagon version) came as standard, as did the WRX-style side and rear skirts. Inside, there was a CD/radio, white-faced gauges, a WRX-type steering wheel, and special seat trim.

As well as inheriting the Phase II EJ20 engine (manual WRXs had the EJ207 and automatics the EJ205), and gaining 7lbft of torque in the process (at least in the case of the saloons), the WRX suspension was modified, becoming like that found on the 22B, with inverted struts. This arrangement, whilst heavier, was substantially stronger and improved cornering performance.

Oddly, power was reduced down to 240bhp on the Sports Wagon again, although peak torque went up to 227lbft; the strict WRX estate continued to be the only car in the series to have

a 9.0:1 compression ratio (very high for a turbocharged engine), as all other machines had an 8.0:1 c/r. Gearing continued to be the same across the entire range, incidentally.

Visible changes for 1999 included a stylish new front bumper and grille, giving better cooling and enhanced aerodynamics; multi-reflector foglamps matched the latest headlights. Inside, there was a new, albeit very similar, Momo steering wheel, and different seat fabrics - saloons had black seats with yellow highlights, while the estate came with two-tone grey upholstery.

An electric sunroof was listed as an option for the WRX saloon and estate (not available on the Type RA, as it came with a roof vent). Meanwhile, the RA could be specified with ABS, dual airbags and automatic air conditioning, which took the price to within 22,000 yen of the standard WRX, and lost the intercooler water spray in the process.

Weighing in at 1270kg (2794lb), the WRX saloon (manual only) was priced at 2,579,000 yen, and the Type RA, which weighed 60kg (132lb) less, commanded 2,279,000 yen. The WRX estate cost 2,423,000 yen in 1300kg (2860lb) manual guise, or 2,546,000 yen as an automatic.

Colours for 1999 WRX Sports Wagon included Cool Grey Metallic, Rose Red Mica, Pure White, Arctic Silver Metallic and Black Mica. The standard saloon came with four coachwork colour options: the same as those offered on the estates but without the red shade, while the Type RA came in white only.

As had become traditional, the latest STi cars were announced at the same time (3 September 1998). Naturally, the Version V models

Japan's strict GB estate (as opposed to the GB Sport), as it appeared in the 1999 model year catalogue, and the fascia of the same vehicle.

inherited the new front grille, bumper and headlights, and the foglight cover design was revised to suit. The two saloons and the coupé got a bigger rear spoiler, although the estate kept the same wings, and the 16-inch, gold-coloured alloy wheels were also carried over. In the author's humble opinion, the Ver.V was the best looking Impreza of them all, especially in two-door form.

The STi Version V saloons, coupé and estate, had the same power and torque as the Version IV models, but with subtle engine differences. There

was a thinner water jacket, the piston rings were made thinner in a bid to reduce friction, and the intake port design was revised. Better low- to mid-range torque answered critics, and there were detail changes in electrical and cooling systems.

The transmission casing was reinforced, and the centre differential lsd was made smaller and lighter. The Type RA came with a mechanical rear limited-slip differential, with others equipped with the Suretrac diff from Automotive Products. All STi cars had manual transmission only, with

gearing carried over from the Ver.IV models.

As for the chassis, there was a new Sports ABS braking system for the sedan and estate, with a G-sensor and individual control on the rear wheels. The Type RA damper rates were made 10 per cent harder than those of the normal WRX (with Bilstein shocks listed as an option), and could be bought with the two-pot front brakes, allowing the customer to fit his own aftermarket system. It was also the only model to get the quicker 13:1 rack as standard.

There were no major changes inside, although the latest Momo

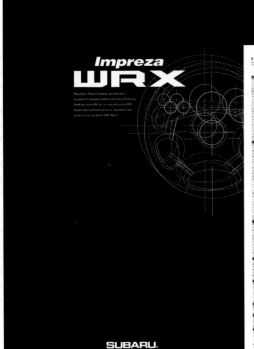

The WRX catalogue for 1999, including the STi cars (and following three pages).

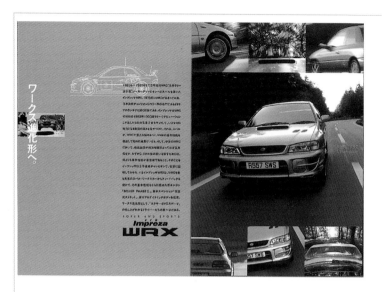

ワークス進化形へ。

BOXER 4WD SPORTS
Impreza
WRX

ダウンヒルを愉しめる、天性の運動バランス。

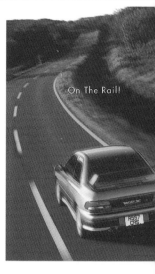

BOXER SYMMETRY 4WD SYSTEM

On The Rail!

スポーツ・ドライビングに余裕を与える、ボクサーエンジン。

BOXER PHASE II

Over 6000rpm!

速いシャシーをつくる、高剛性ボディ＆ロングストロークサス。

INVERTED-STRUT SUSPENSION

Dancing!

ドライバーとクルマのインターフェイス。

集中力とリラックスを自在に包む空間。

TECHNICAL NOTE 3 ENGINE

BOXER PHASE II 搭載。力強い低・中速トルクと高信頼性が走りを変える。

TECHNICAL NOTE 4 4WD

ボクサー・シンメトリー4WD。速さとアクティブセイフティを両立する。

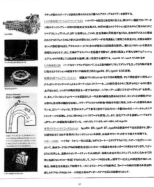

TECHNICAL NOTE 5 SUSPENSION

高剛性倒立式ストラットが走りのキレをパワーアップする。

TECHNICAL NOTE 6 BODY&SAFETY

高剛性＆衝撃吸収ボディが走りと安全を支える。

PURE SPORTS COUPE
WRX type R STi Version V

WRCワークスからのフィードバックを結集。

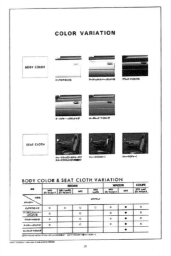

COLOR VARIATION

BODY COLOR

SEAT CLOTH

BODY COLOR & SEAT CLOTH VARIATION

EQUIPMENT

ACCESSORIES

SPORTS EDITION INTERIOR

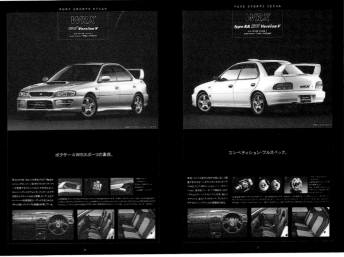

PURE SPORTS SEDAN
WRX STi Version V
WRX type RA STi Version V

ボクサー4WDスポーツの真価。

コンペティション・フルスペック。

WRX
2.0ℓ BOXER PHASE II
4cam16valve TURBO 4WD(5MT)

PHOTO: ブラック・マイカ

ピュアスポーツセダンの進化。

最高出力280PS、最大トルク34.5kg-m。低中速トルクを高めたBOXER PHASE II 搭載。サスペンションには輪高剛性倒立式ストラット採用。リヤデフにはシュアトラックLSDを装備、水平対向エンジンとシンメトリー4WDによる圧倒的なパワーと絶対的な走行安定性を誇るピュアスポーツセダンが進化した。

【主要装備】大径マフラー／マルチリフレクター／電動格納式リモコンドアミラー／サイド&リヤアンダースカート／リヤスポイラー／アルミ製フロントロアアーム／本革巻きシフトブーツ&ハンドブレーキレバー／パワーアンテナ／間欠付フロント／クイックシフトレバー／6センサー4チャンネルABS／リヤ・シュアトラックLSD／オートエアコン

① 倒立式ストラットサスペンション
② MONO3型ヒルダウンオーディオ本革巻きステアリングホイール
③ CDプレーヤー付高性能オーディオ&4スピーカー[ADDZEST]

WRX
type RA
2.0ℓ BOXER PHASE II
4cam16valve TURBO 4WD(5MT)

PHOTO: ピュアホワイト

コンペティション・ベーシック。

シンプルな装備による軽量ボディ。インタークーラー・ウォータースプレイ、クロスミッション、ハードサスペンション、リヤ・シュアトラックLSD、ボタンザRED10、ハイウォッテージバルブヘッドライトと実戦で役に立つ機能装備を搭載。オーディオレス、エアコンもオプションのスパルタンモデルである。

【主要装備】パワーウォッシュバルブ付ハロゲンヘッドライト／H4インチ&ホイール／アルミ型フロントロアアーム／MONO3型ヒルダウンエアバッグ内蔵本革巻きステアリングホイール／本革巻きシフトブーツ&ハンドブレーキレバー／クイックシフトレバー／クロスミッション／倒立式ストラットサスペンション[ハードタイプ]／リヤ・シュアトラックLSD

① インタークーラー
ウォータースプレイ
② アルミ型フロントロアアーム
③ 16インチホイール／タイヤ
[ボタンザRED10]

STi/Version V
2.0ℓ BOXER PHASE II
4cam16valve TURBO 4WD(5MT)

PHOTO: クール・グレー・メタリック

280psのピュアスポーツワゴン。

機能的なワゴンパッケージに280psのSTiチューンエンジンを搭載し、ピュアスポーツワゴンという稀有な存在を主張する。強力なロストッピングパワーを発揮するフロント4ポットキャリパーディスクブレーキ、スポーツABSをはじめピュアスポーツセダンと同等の機能パーツが与えられている。

【主要装備】カラードサイド&リヤアンダースカート／205/50R16タイヤ[ボタンザ501]／CDプレーヤー付高性能オーディオ[KENWOOD]／STi仕様付チューニングエンジン／スーパークイックシフトレバー／スポーツABS／倒立式ストラットサスペンション／本革巻きステアリングホイール／リヤ・シュアトラックLSD／フロント4ポット&リヤ2ポットキャリパーベンチレーテッドディスクブレーキ／オートエアコン

① 大型ルーフ
ウエストスポイラー
② STi仕様キー
ストラッドタワーバー
③ 一体型インタークーラーダクト

2.0ℓ BOXER PHASE II
4cam16valve TURBO 4WD(5MT/E-4AT)

PHOTO: ブラック・マイカ

ピュアスポーツを愉しむワゴン。

低・中速域を高めた新世代水平対向エンジンBOXER PHASE II 搭載。ATには前後のトルク配分が35：65から直結まで、可変&不等トルク配分にするVTD-4WD伝達。サスペンションは輪高剛性倒立式ストラット、リヤデフにはシュアトラックLSDを装備。スポーツワゴンの真価がここにある。

【主要装備】ルーフウエストスポイラー／電動格納式リモコンドアミラー／サイド&リヤアンダースカート／アルミ型フロントロアアーム／MONO3型ヒルダウンエアバッグ内蔵本革巻きステアリングホイール／本革巻きシフトブーツ&ハンドブレーキレバー／クイックシフトレバー[5MT]／倒立式ストラットサスペンション／6センサー4チャンネルABS／リヤ・シュアトラックLSD／オートエアコン

① 大径フォグランプ
[マルチリフレクター]
② CDプレーヤー付高性能オーディオ&4スピーカー[KENWOOD]
③ VTD-4WD[AT車]

22　23　24　25

Brochure for the STi Version V Limited models.

steering wheel was adopted, and the front seat trim was revised once again (rear seats remained the same, finished in black and grey). Featuring suede inserts, the STi front buckets were the same shape with essentially the same upholstery, but there was now more red fabric on the bolsters. Although the Momo wheel incorporated an airbag, dual airbags were still an option on the entire WRX series range.

All STi cars (except the white-only Type RA version) came with the same four paintwork options as the standard WRX saloon. The STi Version V saloon was priced at 2,919,000 yen, and the Type RA variant 60,000 yen less. The Type R coupé was the most expensive car at 3,009,000 yen, with the WRX STi Version V estate costing the same as the sedan.

Interesting accessories included last year's auxiliary gauges and driver's kneepads, and there was now a so-called 'Sports Edition' interior which had rather OTT red trim for part of the steering wheel, gearknob, centre console, instrument binnacle, fresh air vents and door release surrounds.

At the end of November, three new cars were released, making up the WRX Limited series. There were two STi Limited models (a saloon and a coupé), plus a Type RA Limited sedan, all finished in Sonic Blue Mica with gold alloys.

The 2,999,000 yen WRX Type RA STi Version V Limited came with a front helical lsd, a pink, six-star grille badge, titanium shift knob, serial number plaque, special seats (entirely blue up front with STi and Subaru

logos stitched into the backs, with black seats in the rear), automatic air conditioning, colour-keyed door handles and power mirrors, electric windows and central locking. Just 1000 were made available.

The WRX Type R STi Version V Limited was much closer to standard, although it did gain a WRC-type roof vent and a pink, six-star grille badge. On sale until March 1999, it was priced at 3,009,000 yen.

The final car went under the WRX Type RA Limited moniker. It featured ABS brakes, multi-reflector foglights, an STi Version IV-type rear spoiler (incorporating a high mount stoplight), a serial number plate on the console, special seats (the same as those fitted to the Type RA STi Version V Limited), automatic air con, power mirrors (in blue, as were the door handles), power windows and central locking. This car was also restricted to 1000 units and priced at 2,399,000 yen.

The 1998 rally season

The season was contested with WRC98 cars (the earlier models, 19 of which were built, were known by the WRC97 moniker). With 300bhp driven through a Prodrive six-speed gearbox, like all the top runners, they weighed in at 1230kg (2706lb). Only 11 WRC98s were produced, carrying the chassis numbers 98.021 to 98.033 (like the WRC97 series, not all numbers were allocated).

While the driver line-up remained unchanged, at the end of 1997 David Lapworth moved up the Prodrive ladder to become Competitions Chief, as Dave Richards wanted to concentrate his efforts on the Benetton F1 programme (he has since changed allegiance to the BAR-Honda camp).

1998 rally record

The weather caused a great deal of drama in the opening round of the season, but McRae came through the snow and ice (not to mention an early excursion into a field) to take third - the best Monte result recorded by a British driver for three decades. Liatti was seriously quick on the dry tarmac and led the rally for part of the first day; he came fourth. Another Impreza came eighth, making the Monte Carlo Rally a great success for the Subaru camp, despite not being able to hoist the winner's trophy.

With Liatti not expected to do well in the snow, Kenneth Eriksson was drafted in for the Swedish Rally. The Swede was actually leading with only a few stages to go, but then encountered gearbox problems which slowed his charge. Still, he was the top finisher in the Subaru camp, as McRae retired with electrical trouble halfway through the event, whilst Liatti struggled in an experimental car fitted with electronically-controlled dampers.

On the Safari, all the Subarus went out with engine maladies. The Frederic Dor and Kevin Gormley pairing retired on SS5, Liatti on SS10 (driving car no.98.020 on its only works outing; it was later registered P2 WRC - an old Prodrive plate that used to belong to 97.003, which was subsequently given the P100 ALL number - and used by

1998 Rally of Portugal (McRae).

Achim Mortl), and McRae fell by the wayside on the next stage due to overheating. Mitsubishi led the Championship on 22, with Ford on 21, Toyota 19, and Subaru behind on 10.

It was a different story in Portugal, where Colin McRae held on to take victory by the narrowest of margins after a late charge from Sainz (TTE). Having led from the third stage all the way to the end, the win gave a substantial boost to the title hopes for both the Scot and Subaru.

However, across the border in Spain, the Subaru team was never really in the running. Most observers put this down to a lack of grip on the high speed tarmac, but, in any case, the rear differential of McRae's car failed, and Liatti crashed out of the event.

Thankfully, Subaru more than made up for this disappointment in Spain with a fine victory for McRae in Corsica. Although there was a chance of disqualification early on (the Scot rolled in with bald tyres at the end of SS2), he led almost from start to finish. Liatti had a puncture early on, and this almost certainly cost him second. Nevertheless, Subaru led the Manufacturers' title chase, and McRae

1998 Tour de Corse (McRae).

1998 rally record

No.	Driver/Co-driver	Position	Reg. No. (Group)
Monte Carlo (18-21 January)			
3	Colin McRae/Nicky Grist	3rd	P7 WRC (Gp.A)
4	Pierro Liatti/Fabrizia Pons	4th	P14 WRC (Gp.A)
Sweden (5-8 February)			
4	K. Eriksson/S. Parmander	4th	R19 WRC (Gp.A)
10	Pierro Liatti/Fabrizia Pons	9th	P7 WRC (Gp.A)
3	Colin McRae/Nicky Grist	dnf	R17 WRC (Gp.A)
Safari (27 February-2 March)			
3	Colin McRae/Nicky Grist	dnf	R7 WRC (Gp.A)
4	Pierro Liatti/Fabrizia Pons	dnf	R8 WRC (Gp.A)
Portugal (22-25 March)			
3	Colin McRae/Nicky Grist	1st	R19 WRC (Gp.A)
4	Pierro Liatti/Fabrizia Pons	6th	P7 WRC (Gp.A)
Spain (19-22 April)			
3	Colin McRae/Nicky Grist	dnf	R9 WRC (Gp.A)
4	Pierro Liatti/Fabrizia Pons	dnf	R10 WRC (Gp.A)
Tour de Corse (3-6 May)			
3	Colin McRae/Nicky Grist	1st	R11 WRC (Gp.A)
4	Pierro Liatti/Fabrizia Pons	3rd	R12 WRC (Gp.A)
Argentina (20-23 May)			
3	Colin McRae/Nicky Grist	5th	R9 WRC (Gp.A)
4	Pierro Liatti/Fabrizia Pons	6th	R10 WRC (Gp.A)
Acropolis (5-9 June)			
3	Colin McRae/Nicky Grist	1st	R11 WRC (Gp.A)
4	Pierro Liatti/Fabrizia Pons	6th	R12 WRC (Gp.A)
New Zealand (25-28 July)			
3	Colin McRae/Nicky Grist	5th	R11 WRC (Gp.A)
4	Pierro Liatti/Fabrizia Pons	6th	R19 WRC (Gp.A)
1000 Lakes (21-23 August)			
4	Jarmo Kytolehto/Arto Kapanen	8th	R12 WRC (Gp.A)
3	Colin McRae/Nicky Grist	dnf	R10 WRC (Gp.A)
San Remo (10-14 October)			
4	Pierro Liatti/Fabrizia Pons	2nd	R15 WRC (Gp.A)
3	Colin McRae/Nicky Grist	3rd	R14 WRC (Gp.A)
Australia (5-8 November)			
3	Colin McRae/Nicky Grist	4th	R10 WRC (Gp.A)
4	Pierro Liatti/Fabrizia Pons	dnf	R12 WRC (Gp.A)
RAC (21-23 November)			
3	Colin McRae/Nicky Grist	dnf	R14 WRC (Gp.A)
4	Alister McRae/David Senior	dnf	R15 WRC (Gp.A)
12	Ari Vatanen/ Fabrizia Pons	dnf	P7 WRC (Gp.A)

consistent event, Subaru in the picture. The Acropolis was another punishing round, but, after battling with Richard Burns and Didier Auriol, McRae came through to take the victor's laurels, putting both himself and Subaru back at the top of the Championship tables. Liatti had been holding third place until a mistake took him off the road and he had to dig his way out; he finished sixth.

McRae was third in New Zealand until a puncture towards the end cost him dearly. As it was, the TTE team dominated the NZ event. Meanwhile, Jarmo Kytolehto was drafted in to campaign a works car in Finland. Ultimately, the Finnish pairing came eighth on their home rally, despite a brief excursion into a ditch. Colin hit a tree, and with the rear offside wheel pointing any which way but straight, that was the end of his challenge.

An early puncture cost McRae his chance of victory in San Remo, but third (just ahead of Sainz - his main rival in the title chase) was a good finish. Team orders weren't an option with the Spaniard so close, so Liatti took a well-deserved second, beaten only by Makinen in the Mitsubishi Lancer.

In Australia, Liatti crashed out on SS5 while McRae fought for the lead; he was running in first with only two stages to go, but his turbo blew, ending his chance of lifting the winner's trophy and, more importantly, any hope of claiming the Championship crown. He finished the event in fourth, four places ahead of Possum Bourne in another Subaru.

The RAC saw the brothers McRae and Ari Vatanen campaigning the works cars. Sadly, Colin and Ari went out with engine trouble, and Alister had an accident on SS22 whilst lying in second place. Incidentally, the older McRae had been leading for most of the rally before a piston gave way.

Following the disappointment on his home event, Colin McRae finished the season in third place, 13 points behind Tommi Makinen, and 11 down on Carlos Sainz. Subaru also finished in third, unfortunately, trailing Mitsubishi and Toyota by quite some margin.

The Asia-Pacific Championship lost a lot of its sparkle in 1998, as the FIA decreed that works drivers would not be allowed to score points. As a

held top slot in the Drivers' Championship.

In Argentina, McRae had been leading before he hit a boulder in the road. His improvised repairs kept him in the rally and, with Liatti running a result, there was no longer any reason to field top runners from the WRC, although Subaru did make an effort in China (555 was the main sponsor of the event) and came away with a one-two victory.

Australia In 1999

The 1999 model year cars were announced at the end of August 1998. Actually, Australia was the first country to get the 1999 Imprezas, even before the home market.

The 1.6 litre cars were discontinued at this stage, and the remaining Impreza range (boasting no less than 16 grades) went four-wheel drive. The two-litre, normally-aspirated engine was now rated at 125bhp with 135lbft of torque, mated to an improved transmission. New trim materials were also a feature.

As with all other export markets, the WRX received more power (now up to 218bhp, giving an improvement in performance of around 10 per cent in the higher gears), and the cosmetic upgrades found on Japanese spec cars: the restyled front end and taller rear spoiler being easy to spot. Bigger brakes (with four-pot calipers up front) kept the additional power in check, while the interior acquired dual airbags, and red stitching on the leather steering wheel and gearknob.

Manual and automatic versions of the 2.0 LX five-door, 2.0 GX four- and five-door, 2.0 Sportswagon, 2.0 RX four- and five-door, and 2.0 WRX four- and five-door were available, with prices ranging from $21,990 to $42,290.

In February 1999 the special edition WRX Classic was launched. Limited to 150 units, it was available in Green Mica, Dark Blue Mica or Black Mica, with colour-coded door handles and mirrors. It had beige leather seats, a leather and wood Momo steering wheel with matching gearknob, plus a chrome gate for the manual cars. In addition to the usual WRX equipment, the meter panel had a metallic finish, there was a keyless entry system with alarm, and a CD player as standard. At $42,990 for the five-speed car (or $44,990 for the automatic), it was ultimately so successful that the Australian importers did it again, selling a similar car a little while later.

On June 21 1999, the 150-off WRX Club Spec Evo 3 made its debut. Based on the standard five-speed WRX,

The WRX Classic, launched in Australia in early 1999.

it was finished in a new Blue Steel Mica shade, with colour-keyed skirts, door handles and mirrors, gold alloys, and special badging. Inside, there was blue Alcantara seat trim, similar to that of the 22B. With a keyless entry system included, the Evo 3 was priced at $41,690.

Having imported a Version III Type R STi Coupé for evaluation and display purposes (it was exhibited at the Sydney Show), the hot Subaru received a lot of good press from enthusiast publications. STi models slowly started to filter through to the Australian market shortly after, although in strictly limited quantities. Initially, a total of 399 different two-door cars (Version V Type Rs) were shipped in 1999, and sold within weeks of arriving on Australian shores.

Corporate news

First displayed at the 1997 Tokyo Show as a concept, 14 months later, in December 1998, the Casa Blanca estate was launched as a 5000-off limited edition. Featuring a retro-look front-end and detailing, it had a 1.5 litre engine, automatic transmission (only),

the option of front- or four-wheel drive, and Minilite alloys. Finished in either Dark Purple Mica, Arctic Silver Metallic or Royal Blue Mica, prices started at 1,536,000 yen. Perhaps not surprisingly, it was still available a year later.

Subaru had an interesting Impreza on its stand at the 1999 Auto Salon. Painted white, the car featured deeper spoilers all-round, a twin-blade wing at the back, gold six-spoke RAYS alloys, a pillow-bush suspension upgrade (with ride height adjustment and four damper rate settings), roll-cage, and red interior trim (including Recaro competition seats with racing harnesses, and red-faced gauges).

Cumulative production of four-wheel drive vehicles reached a staggering 5,000,000 units in 1999. In April that year, the C'z Sport was launched. Featuring 14-inch Minilite alloy wheels, a leather-trimmed Momo steering wheel, Kenwood stereo, roof spoiler, special seat trim, and off-white meters, it came in Sonic Blue Mica, Pure White or Arctic Silver Metallic.

However, for enthusiasts the big news on 6 September 1999 was the

The Impreza Club Spec Evo 3 of 1999 vintage.

The rather unusual Casa Blanca model, introduced at the end of 1998.

EXHIBITION CAR [出展車]

スバルインプレッサ STi 改

インプレッサSTiバージョンをベースに、ハイパワーエンジンを搭載し、
内外装にコンペティションイメージのモディファイを加えた、最速コー
ナリングクーペを提案。

エンジン：●2000エンジン：●高出力対応カムシャフト ●大口径フッ素ゴム製エアインテークダクト
●赤チヂミ塗装ベルトカバー ●セラメタツインクラッチ ●2000ハイパワーECU
●キンコ丸大型高効率エアクリーナー ●大口径バスーカ型・シングルエキゾーストマフラー
トランスミッション：●軽量変更＆ハードショットピーニング処理・強化トランスミッションギヤ
エアロパーツ：●WRカータイプ・フロントバンパー ●固定式大型リヤスポイラー
●大型エアインテークダクト ●WRカータイプ・フードプレスグリル
●チタン製STiエンブレム ●カーボン製ドアミラー
足回り：●RAYS製オリジナル軽量鍛造競技用アルミホイール（7JJ×16"）
●車高調整＆減衰力4段可変式スポーツストラット＆スプリングサスペンション
●ピロー式フロントストラットアッパーマウント ●強化足廻りブッシュ
●強化ピローブッシュ式トレーリングリンク ●強化ピローブッシュ式ラテラルリンク
●軽量高剛性品目のアルミ製フロントストラットタワーバー
●軽量高剛性品目のアルミ製リヤストラットタワーバー
●赤色ブレーキキャリパー（フロント：4ポット／リヤ：2ポット） ●スポーツブレーキパッド
●ステンメッシュブレード・テフロンチューブ製ブレーキホース
インテリア：●競技用レカロ・フルバケットシートSP-GN ●赤色表皮リヤシート
●赤色表皮アトリム ●ステンレス製サイドシルプレート ●アルミ製シフトノブ
●ステンレス製ABCペダルカバー ●カーボン製センターパネル
●レッドカラースピードメーター ●6点式ロールバー ●タカタ製競技用フルハーネス

● 大型エアインテークダクト   ● レッドカラースピードメーター
● WRカータイプ・フードプレスグリル   ● 競技用レカロ・フルバケットシート (SP-GN 各)
● 車高調整＆減衰力4段可変式   ● ステンレス製ABCペダルカバー
● 強化ピローブッシュ式トレーリングリンク   ● タカタ製競技用フルハーネス

※本ページの商品は開発中の商品が多数含まれています。

Specification of one of the cars on display at the 1999 Tokyo Auto Salon.

Japanese advertising from spring 1999.

announcement of the Impreza Type G revisions, and the debut of the WRX STi Version VI models. Normally-aspirated cars with ABS had the system uprated via Brake Assist, an inhibitor was fitted on the clutch (the pedal had to be depressed before the starter would engage), and there was new, special glass which dispersed rain more efficiently.

C'z Sport standard equipment was modified slightly (mainly a new wheel and tyre combination) and added as a catalogue model (the only NA one available in yellow), while the SRX could now be ordered with blue paintwork.

While the mechanical specification and interior was left untouched, the WRX series (except the Type RA versions, that is) had a deeper front lip spoiler, and the strict WRX models now had the same colour-coded underskirts as the STi cars. Bullet-shape door mirrors could be specified as a no-cost option on Type RA variants (finished in black, like the door handles), and new six-spoke, 16-inch alloys and coachwork colours were introduced to give the range a fresh look.

The WRX saloon (2,579,000 yen) was available in Pure White, Arctic

Silver Metallic, Black Mica, Cool Grey Metallic or the new Gran Blue Mica shade, while the Type RA, priced at 2,279,000 yen, came in white only. As for the estate, this had the same five coachwork colour options as the saloon, and retained its unique two-tone grey interior. The WRX estate cost 2,423,000 yen as a manual, or 2,546,000 yen with an automatic transmission.

Like the strict WRXs, the 280bhp STi Version VI saloons, coupé and estate all had exactly the same mechanical specification as their immediate predecessors. The STi cars inherited the latest front spoiler attachment, and the two- and four-door models were given an even more dramatic rear wing.

Oddly, the new six-spoke wheel design was only used on the Sports

Wagon (painted gold for the STi vehicle), while the other cars continued with the older - but probably more attractive - five-spoke alloys. The only other change was adoption of thinner rear quarter glass for the Type R coupé.

Prices were held over, so the Version VI cost the same as the Version V models, although the exterior colour chart included a few revisions (the interior was unchanged, incidentally, although a carbonfibre-style trim kit was listed in the accessories section). With the black hue dropped from the list, the sedan and estate were available in Pure White, Arctic Silver Metallic, Cool Grey Metallic or Cashmere Yellow; the RA in white or yellow, and the Type R coupé in white, silver, grey or Gran Blue Mica.

By the end of 1999, no fewer than 373,862 Imprezas had been exported. The bulk of these went to the USA, which accounted for 172,885 units (Canada took the North American figure to 182,734). Europe was next in line; Britain provided Subaru with its biggest market for the model, taking 23,806 of the 104,171 sold.

The Impreza was particularly popular in Australia, which took 30,905 units between 1992 and 1999, about the same amount as all of the Middle East and African countries put together, and almost twice as many as the South American continent.

In December a business alliance was established between General Motors and Suzuki (the long-standing agreement with Nissan came to an end four months later). The American giant bought a 20 per cent stake in Subaru, resulting in GM members joining the FHI board the following spring, and the issue of a new five-year business plan. The SIA factory in America was not really affected, as Isuzu already had established links with General Motors.

UK update

In the UK, no fewer than six regional police forces used a Prodrive Impreza for chasing stolen cars. It was a sign of the times, and a good choice, given the model's turn of speed and all-weather grip, thanks to the four-wheel drive system. Other law enforcement bodies in other countries followed suit, most notably the Australian police force.

Meanwhile, the main news stories emanating from the NEC in 1998 centred on the latest Legacy and

September 1999 saw the debut of the STi Version VI cars.

Outback estates, but Subaru's stand also featured a 320bhp 22B-STi model. It was said at the time that only a dozen or so of the two-door coupés would be sold in the UK; ultimately, 16 made the journey from Japan from a total run of 25 export units.

Like the Australians, Europeans gained more power for the 1999 model year (the Phase II turbocharged engine now developed 218bhp at 5600rpm, along with 214lbft of torque at 4000rpm). The Turbo also got the latest front grille, bumper and airdam arrangement, reflector headlights, and a taller rear spoiler; four-pot front brakes with bigger discs (vented all-

A 1999 model year Impreza Turbo fitted out as a Police demonstrator. No fewer than six UK regional Police constabularies had adopted the car by 2000, as well as the MoD and a number of foreign forces.

round) were another welcome improvement carried over to UK machines. The new Momo steering wheel graced the interior, and the seats were given height adjustment. An alarm and immobilizer was a good safeguard (fitted as standard), and fresh coachwork colours were introduced at the same time.

The Impreza range was still the same in early 1999, although prices now started at £14,250. The turbocharged saloon had a £20,950 sticker price, with the estate version commanding a further £500.

Car magazine compared a Turbo saloon with the Audi TT at around this time. The German car came close, but not close enough to knock the Subaru off its perch. One enthralled staffer wrote: "It had been a few months since I'd driven one, and I was enraptured anew by that engine, the speed, the balance, the steering. No wonder this car is considered one of the greatest of the 90s, no wonder it's had so much praise heaped upon it. No wonder it is now much more than a Japanese saloon car; it's a cult."

The Subaru marque has an unrivalled reputation in Britain, as witnessed by the JD Power Survey results. In addition to the Impreza, UK dealerships also listed the Justy, Legacy and Forester. The Impreza Turbo continued to dismiss rivals as soon as they arrived on the scene. Following a tough comparison test, the *Autocar* declared: "The Audi S3 is a fine all-rounder, but Subaru wins on fun and value-for-money."

For those seeking something a little different, 1999 saw Prodrive introduce the RB5 and P1 models in the UK. *Top Gear* introduced the RB5 with the following words: "You might not have Richard Burns' driving talent but at least you can have his car. Well, nearly. The Subaru Impreza RB5 gains Blue Steel Metallic paint and matching Alcantara trim, plus rally lights, 17-inch Speedline alloys and a short-throw gearshift. Subaru's genetic modification expert, Prodrive, is also getting in on things with a 250bhp RB5 offering 20 per cent more torque, said to provide 'startling' mid-range grunt. On sale in April, the standard 218bhp RB5 will cost £24,995 and its Prodrive cousin £27,545."

The same magazine eventually tested the RB5, listed with 237bhp at

World rally success is written all over it.

RB 5

Catalogue pages from the RB5 brochure.

6000rpm and 258lbft of torque at 3500rpm thanks to the latest Prodrive Performance Pack: "The engine redlines at 7000rpm and, whereas some gearboxes change ratios smoothly at low revs only to get clumsy at high engine speeds, the Prodrive version's short-throw 'box remains snickily accurate throughout ... The fun and games happen anywhere from 3500 revs upwards. That's when 258lbft of torque makes its presence felt."

Completely colour-keyed in its own unique shade (at least in UK terms - it was actually the same as Japan's Cool Grey), even down to the plastic foglight covers (finished with 'RB5' decals, which also appeared on the front wings and tail), the RB5 had an STi-type rear spoiler and solid rear bulkhead, adding to the vehicle's rigidity.

The latest disc brakes were said to possess good feel, and there was certainly nothing wrong with the handling, aided by the 205/45 ZR17 P-Zeros mounted on six-spoke titanium-effect alloys. The 0-60 dash could be covered in 5.2 seconds before going on to a top speed of 145mph (232kph). One test quoted an average fuel consumption figure of 27.3mpg, which seems remarkable given the performance.

Comfort was not forgotten, though. In addition to the usual equipment, air conditioning came as standard, and the black and blue bucket seats had part suede upholstery. The centre console got a special finish, along with a plaque declaring which car of the 444 built you were driving.

The 1999 rally season

Ten cars were built to WRC99 spec (a new series of chassis numbers was allocated, running in sequence from 99.001 to 99.010). Power and weight was officially the same as the previous season. Cars came with Prodrive's ATM (Automated Manual Transmission) system - a normal six-speed gearbox with an electronically-controlled sequential system activated by oil pressure. The driver could opt to make changes via a lever to the right of the steering wheel, or with traditional gearbox movements.

A new roof vent arrangement for 1999 increased the car's top speed by 2mph (just over 3kph), and with 555 sponsorship gone, a new paint scheme based on the marque badge was adopted. Gravel events used 205/65 Pirelli rubber on 15-inch OZ rims, while bigger diameter alloys were adopted for asphalt rallies.

With McRae going to Ford, and both Liatti and Eriksson finding new teams, there was a completely new driver line-up for 1999. Richard Burns came back to the Subaru camp after a successful spell with Mitsubishi, where he'd shown a great deal of promise alongside Tommi Makinen. Born in Reading, England, in 1971, Burns had already donned blue overalls on a number of occasions between 1993 and 1995.

Juha Kankkunen, as four times World Champion, brought maturity and experience. Born in 1959, the Flying Finn had spent most of his career with Toyota and Lancia,

Juha Kankkunen.
Richard Burns.

113

although he'd been contracted to Ford the previous season. In addition, the Belgian driver, Bruno Thiry, made an occasional appearance for Subaru, having made his name with Opel and Ford.

1999 rally record

Surprisingly, the hero in the Subaru camp for much of the Monte Carlo Rally was Gilles Panizzi in a Prodrive-supported WRC98 model. He led from SS4 to SS7 and was running second until an accident on the last leg put him out of the event. Kankkunen ran a calculated race to take second place after Panizzi's retirement, with Thiry fifth and Burns eighth following Colin McRae's exclusion.

Tyre trouble hindered the progress of the Subaru drivers in Sweden, although Burns and Kankkunen had an intense battle, ultimately settled in favour of the Brit (by just over five seconds). Thiry, who finished tenth, was trying out a new gearbox in the third works car.

The Safari was unkind to Subaru again, with electrical problems causing the early retirement of Kankkunen and Thiry, although Burns did a sterling job, leading until his suspension failed halfway through. He duly retired, meaning Frederic Dor was the top Subaru finisher (he came seventh in a privately-entered Impreza).

Kankkunen's engine blew for no apparent reason in Portugal but, despite complaining bitterly about his tyres, Burns came fourth, with Thiry sixth; Rui Madeira and Luis Climent were ninth and tenth respectively in privately-entered Group A Imprezas.

The Subaru team failed to shine in Spain: the works cars came fifth, sixth and seventh. Now on 18, the SWRT trailed Toyota by 25, with Mitsubishi and Ford also quite a way ahead. In the Drivers' Championship, the men in blue overalls seemed to be out of the running completely. Corsica was even worse, though, with Pirelli coming under fire again. Although Burns held on to seventh, Thiry crashed at the end whilst lying ninth.

In Argentina, Burns had led for most of the rally, but was pipped to the post by his Finnish teammate on the last stage. This added further bad blood to a troubled relationship, as Burns was convinced that Prodrive's management had requested

1999 Monte Carlo Rally (Kankkunen).

High-speed action from the 1999 Monte.

Kankkunen to hold his position. Anyway, it was a good result for Subaru, elevating the team to third in the WRC league table, ahead of Ford and only five points down on Mitsubishi.

In Greece, Kankkunen suffered a broken subframe which put his suspension out of action, but Burns won his first rally for Subaru after most of the other top runners either retired or had problems. His win helped Subaru to stay in touch in the Manufacturers' title chase, however,

and did his own points tally no harm in the process - he was now lying joint fourth in the Championship with Colin McRae.

The WRC circus moved on to the Antipodes. Kankkunen recorded a solid second place in NZ, while Possum Bourne came fifth in last year's car. Burns retired with gearbox trouble early on, but was never in a position to bother Makinen's Mitsubishi.

Kankkunen was incredibly quick on home ground, and took a stunning

Burns and the Impreza came good in Australia, taking the victor's laurels after having led the event from the halfway point. While Kankkunen dropped out quickly, Toshihiro Arai claimed eighth and Group N honours in a WRX.

The RAC was Prodrive's 100th rally win. An oil filter came loose, causing a fire on Burns' car, but, fortunately, no damage was done (or time lost). Between them, the two Subaru men had hogged the top spot since the second stage, but it was Burns who came out ahead at the end, giving him

victory that few would begrudge him, except Burns, perhaps, who came second to the Finn once again. Still, the SWRT was now in second place, albeit 20 points down on TTE.

China was included in the calendar for 1999. Kankkunen (driving S8 SRT, although unique number plates were issued for the event) was beating Burns (in T14 SRT) until the front differential

1999 Rally of Argentina (Kankkunen)

1999 Acropolis Rally (Burns).

Richard Burns and Robert Reid celebrating after a fine victory in Greece.

played up, although the Reading man led the rally from SS7 to SS13. Ultimately, he was overhauled by Auriol in the Corolla, but his second place was highly creditable, especially given the appalling conditions in the wake of a major storm. Kankkunen came

fourth, but, with Sainz third, Toyota increased its lead to 22 points.

In San Remo, transmission troubles put paid to Subaru's chances early on. Kankkunen had to fight back after his clutch failed, and Burns retired with gearbox trouble. Fortunately,

1999 1000 Lakes Rally (Kankkunen).

second place in the Championship. With a one-two victory, Subaru was unbelievably close to claiming the spoils, but TTE had done enough in Australia to secure the title for Toyota once more.

Tommi Makinen won the WRC crown yet again, although Burns came second, seven points down on the Finn, but three ahead of Auriol and 11 ahead of Kankkunen. Toyota won the Manufacturers' battle, claiming 109 points; Subaru came second on 105 and Mitsubishi third (83 points).

Possum Bourne was the top Subaru driver in the Asia-Pacific Championship, but he failed to compete in every round, handing the APC title to a Mitsubishi driver. The Asia-Pacific series was a shadow of its former self.

News from the USA

All leading specifications, equipment levels and prices were carried over for 1999, although introduction of the Phase II engines meant a touch more power. The 2.2 litre flat-four was now listed with 142bhp at 5600rpm and 149lbft at 3600rpm. The 2.5 litre unit still had 165bhp, but 4lbft more torque, taking the total to 166lbft at 4000rpm. At the same time, improvements in the transmissions made for smoother shifts.

The 2.5 RS had the biggest changes, with the paint on the alloy wheels going from gold to silver (the tyres also gained a VR rating), and new front-end styling; the RS's frontal aspect was now similar to the Japanese WRX, with large foglights. Inside, there was leather trim on the steering wheel and gearknob, and white-faced gauges.

With the arrival of the 2000 model year, Impreza prices ranged from $15,895 to $20,095. The 2.5 RS Sedan was introduced to augment the existing hot coupé, and, whilst its rear spoiler was more discreet than the two-door model, both RS models had better low- to mid-range response, a viscous limited-slip rear differential, cruise control, and the latest 16-inch six-spoke alloys used on the Japanese WRX. Two- and four-door RSs were priced the same - $19,295 for manual cars with automatic transmission adding a further $800.

The $18,095 Outback now had cruise control as standard, and a waist spoiler was added to complement the roof-mounted one. Otherwise, prices and basic specifications were the same for all L grade machines.

Apart from the addition of the Popular Equipment Package for the L grade (including exhaust trim, carpets and mudguards, plus roof rails for the estate), the Premium Sound Package (featuring a CD player, upgraded speakers and an amplifier) and the Security Package (with keyless entry system), options were pretty much the same, too.

The British scene

The respected *Car* magazine voted the Impreza 'Car of the Decade' at the end of 1999, with a similar accolade bestowed upon the well-loved Subaru by *Performance Car*. And things were due to get better, too.

The 2000 model year Turbo was at last given colour-keyed door handles and mirrors, as well as the latest WRX-style, 16-inch, six-spoke alloys, a new gearknob, a graphite finish on the centre console (first seen on the RB5 model) and some fresh paint options, including a rather attractive Red Mica hue.

The Impreza range and prices were carried over for 2000, except for the launch of the two-door P1 at the 1999 Earls Court Show. As Prodrive's Hugh Chambers said: "We wanted P1 to be a car you could drive quickly to Scotland from London, and arrive fresh and relaxed. I think that's what we've produced." It took around a year to

The prototype Subaru Impreza P1, introduced at the 1999 Earls Court Show.

1999 rally record

No.	Driver/Co-driver	Position	Reg. No. (Group)
Monte Carlo (17-21 January)			
6	Juha Kankkunen/Juha Repo	2nd	S8 SRT (Gp.A)
16	Bruno Thiry/Stephane Prevot	5th	S7 SRT (Gp.A)
5	Richard Burns/Robert Reid	8th	S6 SRT (Gp.A)
Sweden (11-14 February)			
5	Richard Burns/Robert Reid	5th	S9 SRT (Gp.A)
6	Juha Kankkunen/Juha Repo	6th	S8 SRT (Gp.A)
11	Bruno Thiry/Stephane Prevot	10th	S7 SRT (Gp.A)
Safari (25-28 February)			
5	Richard Burns/Robert Reid	dnf	R15 WRC (Gp.A)
6	Juha Kankkunen/Juha Repo	dnf	R9 WRC (Gp.A)
11	Bruno Thiry/Stephane Prevot	dnf	P7 WRC (Gp.A)
Portugal (23-26 March)			
5	Richard Burns/Robert Reid	4th	S9 SRT (Gp.A)
14	Bruno Thiry/Stephane Prevot	6th	S7 SRT (Gp.A)
6	Juha Kankkunen/Juha Repo	dnf	S8 SRT (Gp.A)
Spain (19-21 April)			
5	Richard Burns/Robert Reid	5th	T12 SRT (Gp.A)
14	Juha Kankkunen/Juha Repo	6th	S10 SRT (Gp.A)
6	Bruno Thiry/Stephane Prevot	7th	T11 SRT (Gp.A)
Tour de Corse (7-9 May)			
5	Richard Burns/Robert Reid	7th	T12 SRT (Gp.A)
6	Bruno Thiry/Stephane Prevot	dnf	T11 SRT (Gp.A)
Argentina (22-25 May)			
6	Juha Kankkunen/Juha Repo	1st	S8 SRT (Gp.A)
5	Richard Burns/Robert Reid	2nd	S9 SRT (Gp.A)
Acropolis (6-9 June)			
5	Richard Burns/Robert Reid	1st	T12 SRT (Gp.A)
6	Juha Kankkunen/Juha Repo	dnf	T11 SRT (Gp.A)
New Zealand (15-18 July)			
6	Juha Kankkunen/Juha Repo	2nd	S7 SRT (Gp.A)
5	Richard Burns/Robert Reid	dnf	T14 SRT (Gp.A)
1000 Lakes (20-22 August)			
6	Juha Kankkunen/Juha Repo	1st	T11 SRT (Gp.A)
5	Richard Burns/Robert Reid	2nd	T12 SRT (Gp.A)
China (16-19 September)			
5	Richard Burns/Robert Reid	2nd	-005 (Gp.A)
6	Juha Kankkunen/Juha Repo	4th	-006 (Gp.A)
San Remo (11-13 October)			
6	Juha Kankkunen/Juha Repo	6th	S10 SRT (Gp.A)
5	Richard Burns/Robert Reid	dnf	T15 SRT (Gp.A)
Australia (4-7 November)			
5	Richard Burns/Robert Reid	1st	T12 SRT (Gp.A)
6	Juha Kankkunen/Juha Repo	dnf	T11 SRT (Gp.A)
RAC (21-23 November)			
5	Richard Burns/Robert Reid	1st	T14 SRT (Gp.A)
6	Juha Kankkunen/Juha Repo	2nd	S10 SRT (Gp.A)

develop the car. Peter Stevens did the bodywork revisions, keeping looks familiar but incorporating unique front and rear spoilers. (Available with two different settings, the lipped front spoiler housed Hella driving lights instead of foglamps and directed air to the brakes, whilst the rear had inserts with the 'P1' logo.) Finished in Sonic Blue Mica, with colour-keyed door mirrors, handles and side skirts, not to mention the gunmetal grey, ten-spoke 7J x 17 OZ alloys and hefty 'Impreza P1' badge on the bootlid, it really did look the business.

And it's a good thing. As *Autocar* observed: "Merely import an existing model and you end up competing with hundreds of independent car traders doing exactly the same thing. A unique UK flagship based on the WRX was needed. A car developed and type approved on our roads to be sold as a model in its own right through Subaru's regular dealerships.

"That's exactly what the P1 is. A machine created out of the WRX, but shorn of many rough edges to maximize its potential as everyday transport.

"The biggest hurdle for Prodrive was modifying the 1994cc horizontally-opposed turbo engine to comply with European noise and emissions requirements, whilst retaining the standard WRX's 277bhp. Top of the list of changes was a reprogrammed electronic control unit designed and manufactured by Fuji. A new catalytic converter has been fitted, the standard twin catalysts being ditched for a larger single item.

"The result is a cleaner and quieter engine, but one that loses none of the WRX's outright poke. [With an 8.2:1 compression ratio], maximum power is an identical 277bhp at 6500rpm, while peak torque stays at 253lbft at 4000rpm."

Testers said they liked the engine, and continued: "The gearshift - STi rather than Prodrive-derived - is also excellent and the ratios are well suited to UK roads." The internal ratios were 3.17 on first, 1.88 on second, 1.30 on third, 0.97 on fourth and 0.74 for top gear, with the final drive listed as 4.44:1.

Despite weighing 1283kg (2823lb), the Prodrive P1 was capable of dismissing the 0-60 yardstick in 4.7 seconds, and the standing-quarter in 13.9. Top speed was listed at 155mph (248kph), so this was a very quick machine. Fortunately, Subaru's ABS brakes with hefty vented discs came as standard, but even these were not up to the job, according to a number of contemporary articles, and fuel consumption was said to be heavy.

The suspension consisted of WRX rear springs, with softer ones at the front and harder shocks all-round; the anti-roll bars were carried over from the standard European Turbo. Revised geometry combined with a carbonfibre strut brace, a solid rear bulkhead and 205/45 ZR-rated Pirelli P-Zeros on 17-inch rims, which added up to some very impressive skidpan figures.

The steering wheel was the standard four-spoke Momo with red stitching (but only adjustable for rake, and with the standard 2.7 turns lock-to-lock rack, not the quick rack as first published in a number of preview articles - a disappointment for some) to match the gearknob. The white-faced gauges were said to be difficult to see at night, but the seats (Prodrive buckets with black, red and blue fabric highlighted by grey Alcantara) and driving position were highly praised.

The P1 was well-equipped, too, with air conditioning, electric windows (with green tinted glass), central locking, dual airbags, a rear wiper and CD player fitted as standard. Despite the big STi tailpipe, NVH levels were well controlled, so, unlike some sporting machines, it was actually possible to listen to music. Prodrive carpets and grey Alcantara on the door trims finished the cockpit nicely.

The *Autocar* summary said: "In isolation the P1 is a shatteringly impressive car, one whose body control and suspension composure set new hot saloon standards. But it is not the mould-breaker we had expected. Perhaps we expected too much."

Nevertheless, Prodrive originally planned to build 500 P1s, but actually produced twice that number. Sales began in spring 2000, with a list price of £31,495, complete with full three-year warranty.

In answer to the critics, it was possible to upgrade the brakes (for £1527) to a racing-type system: the fronts with 326mm (12.8in.) discs and Alcon four-pot calipers. It was also possible to go for a larger wheel and tyre combination (available in either gold or gunmetal; although they looked similar, they were actually 18-inch rims

Subaru UK's MD, Ed Swatman, celebrating in style the marque's runaway victory in the 2000 JD Power Survey.

The Impreza Sport Special marked the end of an era in the UK. On sale from June 2000, it was the final limited edition model based on the second generation cars.

with 225/35 ZR rubber and cost the best part of £2000 for a set of four), as well as a big bore exhaust system, the latter adding another £350 to the price. Hella gas discharge spotlights could be specified for £470, with Recaro buckets at £1995 (although most felt the standard P1 seats were fine) and leather trim (another £1995). However, with the various options fitted, *Car* magazine gave the P1 a five-star rating without any quibbles whatsoever.

The UK bid farewell to this Impreza generation with a two-litre, normally-aspirated 'Sport Special' saloon. In addition to the usual Sport goodies, such as ABS brakes, electric windows, alloy wheels and front foglamps, the limited edition 125bhp model also featured air conditioning, Turbo-style seats, a Momo leather-trimmed steering wheel, white-faced instruments, and the taller rear spoiler off the Turbo. With sales starting in June 2000, 200 cars were available in Black Mica, with a further 200 in Cashmere Yellow,

priced at £16,500 apiece.

Australian farewell

Whilst Australian sales have always been relatively low, the level of enthusiasm for the Impreza most definitely is not. All 2000 model year cars gained dual airbags, but the big news for the 2000 season (announced in early August 1999) was the official introduction of the WRX STi Version VI saloon to the Australian market. Making its debut on 14 October at the Sydney Show, the STi model came in White or Blue Steel Mica, although only 400 of the $62,500 machines were made available.

Thanks to the full 280bhp and 260lbft, while not much quicker off the line than the standard Aussie WRX, the in-gear performance was significantly enhanced - this was one seriously fast motor car. Adam Porter at *Wheels* noted: "This is where the true strength of the STi lies. On any given piece of winding tarmac, playing

Australia's striking Club Spec Evo 4 model, launched in March 2000.

with the STi's mammoth torque curve is bound to leave you with a grin from ear to ear."

In another article, the STi car was compared with the Holden HSV GTS 300 and Mercedes-Benz AMG E55. Amazingly, the little Subaru came out at the front of the group, as it was not only quicker, but easier to control and by far the best value.

Prices were up slightly for 2000, ranging from $22,790 to $42,990. However, like the UK Turbos, the 2000 model year WRXs came with colour-keyed door mirrors and handles, the new six-spoke alloys, and a few subtle changes to the interior.

Wheels compared a $39,990 manual WRX saloon with the Audi S3, priced at over $70,000, in its January 2000 issue, and concluded: "Many have rivalled the WRX, but none have been victorious. That doesn't make the Audi S3 a lesser car. You could say that with its many luxury and safety features as well as impressive quality, it's more car than the WRX. But let's face it, the WRX's performance is one-dimensional - and that one thing happens to be everything."

Meanwhile, on 29 December 1999, the WRX Special Edition saloon was launched. It was identical to the WRX Classic launched ten months earlier, even down to pricing. As for the standard range, there was a further price increase in the spring but, with the new cars coming, they were reduced to just below 1999 levels in a bid to clear stocks at the end of 2000. The top WRX model represented the greatest saving, dropping from $43,760 to a more than reasonable $41,100.

The highly desirable WRX Club Spec Evo 4 was launched at the 2000 Adelaide Show in March. Available as a saloon or estate, it was limited to 300 units, priced just $1000 over the standard car. Yellow paintwork was set off by black five-spoke alloys, and inside was an upgraded stereo system (including CD player), a Momo steering wheel with SRS airbag, and an STi-style metal finish dash panel; the sedan also got yellow trim inserts, apeing those of the Japanese cars. Limited edition badges were applied on the rear doors and bootlid, with a numbered plaque mounted on the centre console.

A month later came the 200-off RX Special Edition in black, the second limited version based on the RX. Available as a saloon or estate (with manual or automatic transmission), it featured a Momo leather-trimmed steering wheel, CD player, white-faced gauges, and special decals. Prices started at $27,900.

More Japanese specials

Surprise, surprise, in November 1999, four cars in the WRX Limited series were launched, all finished in Sonic Blue Mica with 16-inch, gold-coloured, six-spoke RAYS forged alloy wheels. There were two Type RA sedans (a strict model and an STi version), an STi coupé, and an STi Sports Wagon.

The WRX Type RA STi-based Version VI Limited saloon was restricted to 2000 units, priced at 2,999,000 yen apiece. Special features included a front helical lsd, a pink, six-star grille badge, aluminium pedal blocks, a blue dash insert panel, a numbered plaque on the blue centre console, last year's blue seats (with a different logo), and an STi titanium shift knob. Colour-keyed power door mirrors and handles, air conditioning, electric windows and central locking came as part of the package, and an STi double-wing rear spoiler (developed by the FHI Aerospace Division) was listed as an option.

Only 1000 WRX Type RA Limited saloons were made available, priced at 2,429,000 yen. It received the same blue interior treatment (including the blue front seats, but minus the STi part of the logo), aluminium pedals, a serial number plate, convenience package (automatic air conditioning, etc.) as the more expensive version, but with ABS brakes, a lower rear spoiler, multi-reflector foglights, and a black, six-star insignia on the nose.

The 3,039,000 yen WRX Type R STi Version VI Limited coupé had the blue dash and console inserts (with numbered plaque), aluminium pedals and blue front seats, plus an STi titanium shift knob. Limited to 1000 cars, it also featured a WRC-type roof vent and pink, six-star grille badge.

The final special was the 500-off WRX STi Version VI Limited estate. Priced at 2,949,000 yen, it had the pedals and fascia modifications, a plate carrying the car's serial number, Kenwood CD/MD combination audio, and an STi titanium shift knob. Standard seats had blue accents on the front pair (with SWRT and STi logos stitched in), and a pink, six-star emblem adorned the grille.

While other cars in the home market line-up remained the same, January 2000 saw the debut of the C'z Sport II estate. Based on the C'z Sport, this special edition came with a WRX-type front bumper, foglamp covers, the slightly more pronounced WRX-type front grille, an STi-type roof spoiler, a Kenwood CD/MD unit and special seat trim. Prices started at a remarkably low 1,399,000 yen.

Based on the Electra One concept vehicle displayed at the 1999 Tokyo Show and the 2000 Tokyo Auto Salon, the dramatic S201 STi model was announced on April 3 2000. Limited to just 300 cars (with a list price of 3,900,000 yen), such was its nature -

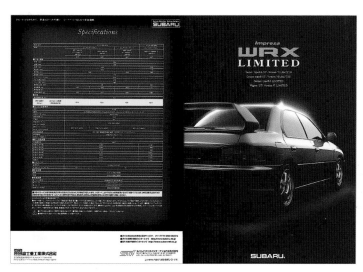

Brochure for the Limited series launched in Japan at the end of 1999.

120

Japanese advertising for the whacky S201.

wheels almost looked too small in relation to all of the aerodynamic appendages.

The inside was very similar to that of the Limited series, with aluminium pedals, a titanium shift, blue-painted dash insert and centre panel, blue front seats with the STi logo stitched in, and a numbered plaque on the centre console. Air conditioning, power windows, central locking, and an electric aerial were part of the package.

Interestingly, power was enhanced, listed at 300bhp at 6500rpm (the 260lbft peak torque figure remained unchanged, however). The extra 20bhp was due to an STi sports ECU, which increased turbo boost, larger intercooler ducting, and a big bore exhaust (120mm, or 4.7in., at the exit) with reduced back pressure.

The suspension was given height adjustment, and the rear trailing and lateral links had pillow-ball bushes for greater location accuracy. A helical lsd was adopted up front, and the 7J x 17 RS-Zero wheels, although different to the five-spoke ones fitted on the Electra One, were also quite special. Jointly developed by RAYS and STi, they were lightweight forged aluminium items (usually priced at 59,000 yen a set), and gave a good view of the red-painted brake calipers.

Production of the 'Brand New' Impreza range ended in the summer to make way for the 'New Age' model, launched on 23 August 2000. This latest version promptly received a special award from the Japanese COTY committee, and was declared undisputed 2000 'Car of the Year' by *Wheels* magazine in Australia.

Meanwhile, not surprisingly, there were no major changes for the start of the American 2001 model year. Prices of L grade and Outback models went up by $100, while the cost of RS motoring increased by $200.

With its 2.5 litre engine, the RS gained carbonfibre-style interior trim, red stitching on the steering wheel and gearshift, a CD player and embroidered mats, so the $200 was a negligible increase. To finish off, an owner could opt for a $1295 leather trim package.

US Impreza coachwork colours, introduced for the 2000 season, included Blue Ridge Pearl, Sedona Red

especially compared to the fairly restrained styling of the WRX - that one Japanese magazine portrayed it as a plastic model kit.

The body resembled something with which to tackle the Pike's Peak hillclimb in Colorado rather than a Tokyo traffic jam, but styling kits have always been big business in Japan. The S201 featured a deep integrated front grille and bumper (with standard headlights rather than those used on the show car), a massive air scoop on the bonnet, original side skirts and rear door spats, and what was termed a 'rear aero-bumper.' The FHI Aerospace Division double-wing rear spoiler, offered as an option on the Limited series a few months earlier, was a standard fitment, with an LED high mount rear stoplight incorporated in a novel bootlid attachment. Finished in Arctic Silver Metallic with dark grey detailing, the six-spoke, gold alloy

The Impreza L is equipped with a powerful 142-horsepower 2.2-liter SOHC horizontally opposed engine, AM/FM stereo with cassette, a dash storage compartment, air conditioning and power mirrors, windows and door locks.

IMPREZA L COUPE IN SEDONA RED PEARL

The Subaru All-Wheel Driving System makes the Impreza a sporty choice for driving fun. The versatile Impreza model line is designed to satisfy with many standard conveniences. If the rally spirit calls to you, answer it with the Impreza 2.5 RS. Featuring a muscular 165-horsepower

IMPREZA L SEDAN IN ASPEN WHITE

2.5-liter horizontally opposed engine and a sport-tuned suspension, the Impreza 2.5 RS provides exhilarating performance and satisfying road feel. Extras include 16-inch aluminum-alloy wheels, a hood scoop, rear spoiler, aerodynamic ground effects, a sport tailpipe, exclusive 2.5 RS sport-style

Peace of mind is built right into every Impreza with safety features like height-adjustable 3-point front seatbelts, 3-point rear outboard seatbelts with rear center lap belt, side-impact door beams, dual front air bags* and energy-absorbing front and rear crumple zones.

interior, 4-channel/4-sensor anti-lock braking system (ABS), large diameter multi-reflector fog lights, white meter gauges, a single-disc CD player and a power sunroof with tilt-up and retract ventilation features. A multitude of quality components in every Impreza model help to re-energize a basic love of driving.

Easy to load with lots of room for gear, the Impreza L Sport Wagon offers a cargo area cover, grocery bag hooks and a 60/40 split fold-down rear seatback that easily makes room for long items.

IMPREZA L SPORT WAGON IN ACADIA GREEN METALLIC

* Seatbelts must be worn at all times. Children should always be properly restrained in the rear seat.

DRIVING CONFIDENCE FOR A
Go-Anywhere Lifestyle

Impreza

IMPREZA 2.5 RS SEDAN SHOWN IN SEDONA RED PEARL

"The bottom line is that while other vehicles are spinning out, or getting stuck in the snow and mud, the Impreza RS keeps moving with confidence."
— Washington Post, February 2000

Double-page spread from the American 2001 model year catalogue.

Pearl, Aspen White, Acadia Green Metallic, Silverthorn Metallic and Black Diamond Pearl; trim was available in beige or grey, or a black/grey mix for the RS. Interesting options included the STi 'Quickshift,' carbonfibre trim pieces, an auxiliary gauge pack, sports exhaust, strut tower bars (including the lightweight STi version), a titanium gearknob, and decals carrying the 'Subaru Performance Tuning' logo. The six-spoke, 15-inch alloy wheel option for the smaller-engined models now had a painted or brushed finish, incidentally.

The 2000 rally season

Last year's cars were campaigned for the opening rounds of the 2000 WRC season, but Portugal witnessed the debut of the latest weapon in Subaru's armoury. Although it looked similar to last year's model (aerodynamic revisions were kept to a minimum), it had better weight balance, improved cooling, and a number of revisions to the powerplant (including new conrods and a heavier flywheel, and a new

location for the IHI turbo in a bid to improve performance and weight distribution) and differentials. In fact, with around 80 per cent of the car redesigned, it was practically the 2001 model in disguise.

2000 Safari Rally (Burns)

Stunning shot from the Safari Rally - perhaps the ultimate challenge.

Power was quoted as 300bhp at 5250rpm, with maximum torque a whopping 346lbft, developed at a fairly lazy 3500rpm. Drive was taken through a six-speed Prodrive electro-hydraulic unit to active differentials at the front, centre and rear, then transmitted to the road via Pirelli rubber mounted on OZ alloys.

Richard Burns and Juha Kankkunen continued as Subaru's main drivers, with occasional appearances from Simon Jean-Joseph (Prodrive's test driver, and a tarmac specialist), Petter Solberg and Markko Martin.

2000 rally record

As noted earlier, the 1999 series cars were used during the early part of the new season. Even so, Burns was right on the pace in Monte Carlo, winning one stage and not dropping lower than third on the others. Sadly, his engine wouldn't start in Parc Ferme on the second day, bringing his rally to a premature end. Meanwhile, Kankkunen won two stages, and ran a consistent race to hold on to a podium finish.

The WRC then moved to an unusually warm Sweden, making tyre choice much more critical. Interestingly, five manufacturers finished in the points, but no-one could match the pace set by Gronholm's Peugeot. Burns came fifth (his charge was blunted after hitting a rock), whilst Kankkunen overcame problems caused by a broken rear suspension to take sixth.

The Safari saw a reversal of fortunes for Subaru with the Japanese company completely dominating the African event. Burns led from the front to take a splendid victory, followed home by Kankkunen (the STi management was quick to give credit to Pirelli, as the top Michelin runners suffered with far more punctures than the Impreza drivers). Toshihiro Arai (born in Japan in 1966 and on his first Safari outing) finished a superb sixth in another works-supported car (S7 SRT), and Roberto Sanchez came tenth in a Group N WRX Type RA - the first of a gaggle of RAs to complete the toughest rally on the WRC calendar.

With the 2000 car at his disposal, Burns won over half of the stages in Portugal, despite having to run four of them without power-assisted steering after the pump pulley gave way. It was his second convincing win of the season, although his Finnish teammate went off the road early on, hitting a

tree. At least Subaru and Burns were leading their respective Championships.

Moving across the border into Spain brought little more luck for Kankkunen; a broken alternator pulley cost him valuable time at the start of the rally while repairs were made, leading him to throw in the towel on the second day. Burns led the rally in the early stages, but was overhauled by former SWRT pilot, Colin McRae, after the Englishman had gear selection problems. McRae's clutch played up on the third day, but it was the Scot that ultimately lifted the winner's trophy.

Burns overcame numerous minor problems in Argentina to claim top slot in over half of the stages, thus securing a well-deserved victory and extending his lead in the Championship. However, he'd been pressed hard by Gronholm (who finished second) and Sainz, up until the latter's retirement. Makinen came third, less than a minute ahead of the second Subaru. Burns' win and Kankkunen's fourth place increased the gap between Subaru and Ford, which was lying in second.

In Greece, Burns had been running well until his turbo packed up (a problem that led to the adoption of new filters), but it was probably Solberg that impressed the most, winning the most stages before mechanical failure sidelined his Ford; soon he would don the blue overalls of the SWRT. Arai came fourth, only one place behind Kankkunen, who'd had to overcome a gearbox fire (leaving him with only one gear for part of the rally), and damaged front suspension and steering during the event. Whilst the Acropolis claimed a lot of victims, five Imprezas finished in the top ten.

New Zealand was best forgotten, as steering fluid loss put both Burns and Kankkunen out on SS20. Arai had an accident, so it was left to the highly experienced 'Possum' Bourne to restore Subaru's honour - he finished sixth.

No-one could match the pace of

2000 Rally of Argentina (Burns).

Gronholm on the 1000 Lakes, although Burns did win four stages before an excursion into the Finnish countryside put him out. Kankkunen had won three stages, but a puncture cost him four minutes, and naturally dropped him down the leaderboard; he finished his home event in eighth. This disappointing run of results meant Ford moved ahead of Subaru and Gronholm leapfrogged Burns, but the title chase was still close at this point.

Sainz (Ford) led in Cyprus from start to finish; not good news for Subaru's Championship hopes. Although Burns was equally fast, a number of minor problems ruined his chances of a podium finish. Kankkunen's 150th rally (he'd won 23 of them, giving him four WRC crowns along the way) was not one to celebrate, as he, too, had more than his fair share of trouble. Arai finished ninth, and Simon Jean-Joseph came tenth.

Jean-Joseph took Kankkunen's place on the Tour de Corse, but the Frenchman was unlucky to have an oil cooler pipe come adrift and start a fire. Thankfully, he was able to carry on, finishing in seventh. The twisty asphalt suited the Peugeots, although Sainz pipped Burns to third place, costing both the SWRT and the British driver valuable points. Solberg's Subaru debut was not the best as his gearbox played up just after the start.

Not surprisingly, Peugeot set the pace again in San Remo. Burns damaged his sump, causing engine problems that led to his retirement. Jean-Joseph took fastest time on a couple of stages, finishing seventh overall, while Solberg came ninth.

Burns came good in Australia, robbed of victory by a puncture after a consistent drive, but the other works cars all failed to finish (although Bourne came sixth and Arai 13th in works-supported machines). Kankkunen was doing well until a coming together with a tree deranged his steering to the extent that he couldn't go on. Markko Martin, the Estonian driver with a SWRT contract already signed for 2001, had an oil leak which caused a fire, ending his rally, and Solberg had an accident on stage eight.

Burns was still in the running for the WRC crown, assuming he could win his home event, and Gronholm either failed to finish or come outside the top six, but Subaru's chances had

2000 RAC Rally (Burns).

long since expired. And so, to the final round.

Solberg was impressive in Britain until an accident put him out of the event, and Arai's car caught fire. Kankkunen ran a mature race to finish fifth, less than two minutes down on Burns, who won in style, coming back from 12th after his rear suspension collapsed. Unfortunately for the Englishman, Gronholm was right behind him to take the Championship

2000 rally record

No.	Driver/Co-driver	Position	Reg. No. (Group)
Monte Carlo (20-22 January)			
4	Juha Kankkunen/Juha Repo	3rd	T16 SRT (Gp.A)
3	Richard Burns/Robert Reid	dnf	T15 SRT (Gp.A)
Sweden (10-13 February)			
3	Richard Burns/Robert Reid	5th	R20 WRC (Gp.A)
4	Juha Kankkunen/Juha Repo	6th	T16 SRT (Gp.A)
Safari (25-27 February)			
3	Richard Burns/Robert Reid	1st	T14 SRT (Gp.A)
4	Juha Kankkunen/Juha Repo	2nd	S10 SRT (Gp.A)
Portugal (16-19 March)			
3	Richard Burns/Robert Reid	1st	W18 SRT (Gp.A)
4	Juha Kankkunen/Juha Repo	dnf	W17 SRT (Gp.A)
Spain (31 March-2 April)			
3	Richard Burns/Robert Reid	2nd	W20 SRT (Gp.A)
4	Juha Kankkunen/Juha Repo	dnf	W19 SRT (Gp.A)
Argentina (11-14 May)			
3	Richard Burns/Robert Reid	1st	W18 SRT (Gp.A)
4	Juha Kankkunen/Juha Repo	4th	W17 SRT (Gp.A)
Acropolis (9-11 June)			
4	Juha Kankkunen/Juha Repo	3rd	W19 SRT (Gp.A)
3	Richard Burns/Robert Reid	dnf	W20 SRT (Gp.A)
New Zealand (13-16 July)			
3	Richard Burns/Robert Reid	dnf	W21 SRT (Gp.A)
4	Juha Kankkunen/Juha Repo	dnf	W22 SRT (Gp.A)
1000 Lakes (18-20 August)			
4	Juha Kankkunen/Juha Repo	8th	W23 SRT (Gp.A)
3	Richard Burns/Robert Reid	dnf	W20 SRT (Gp.A)
Cyprus (8-10 September)			
3	Richard Burns/Robert Reid	4th	W21 SRT (Gp.A)
4	Juha Kankkunen/Juha Repo	7th	W22 SRT (Gp.A)
Tour de Corse (29 September-1 October)			
3	Richard Burns/Robert Reid	4th	W25 SRT (Gp.A)
4	S. Jean-Joseph/J. Boyere	7th	W24 SRT (Gp.A)
18	Petter Solberg/Philip Mills	dnf	W17 SRT (Gp.A)
San Remo (20-22 October)			
4	S. Jean-Joseph/J. Boyere	7th	W24 SRT (Gp.A)
19	Petter Solberg/Philip Mills	9th	W17 SRT (Gp.A)
3	Richard Burns/Robert Reid	dnf	W25 SRT (Gp.A)
Australia (9-12 November)			
3	Richard Burns/Robert Reid	2nd	W19 SRT (Gp.A)
4	Juha Kankkunen/Juha Repo	dnf	W23 SRT (Gp.A)
17	Petter Solberg/Philip Mills	dnf	W22 SRT (Gp.A)
18	Markko Martin/Michael Park	dnf	W21 SRT (Gp.A)
RAC (23-26 November)			
3	Richard Burns/Robert Reid	1st	W25 SRT Gp.A)
4	Juha Kankkunen/Juha Repo	5th	W24 SRT (Gp.A)
17	Petter Solberg/Philip Mills	dnf	W18 SRT (Gp.A)

by just five points.

After a hard-fought season, Subaru finished the 2000 WRC in third place (on 88 points against the 91 of Ford and 111 of Peugeot), while Richard Burns came second in the Drivers' Championship, narrowly beaten by Marcus Gronholm.

'Possum' Bourne took the spoils in the Asia-Pacific series, winning three of the six rounds and scoring enough points along the way to easily secure the Manufacturers' title for Subaru; Proton came second, with Mitsubishi third.

Peter 'Possum' Bourne - Subaru stalwart and multiple winner of the Asia-Pacific Championship.

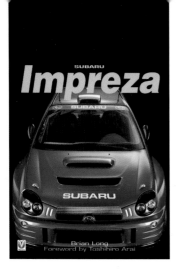

5

The New Age
Impreza

The Legacy was given a minor facelift in 2000, but the Impreza was to be all-new. A number of high profile celebrities have featured in Subaru's domestic advertising over the years. Currently, Jennifer Lopez is the chosen star to represent the marque, but Mel Gibson, Winona Ryder, Bruce Willis, Kevin Costner and Rod Stewart have also appeared.

The Legacy underwent a minor change in spring 2000, including the introduction of the three-litre Lancaster Six. A few months later, on 23 August, the 'New Age' Impreza - the third generation, as far as this book is concerned, but the true second generation of the model - was launched.

The press introduction took place in the centre of Tokyo. I remember it was quite a spectacle, with commentary by TV announcer and keen motorist Annette Kodaira, and a massive selection of cars on display following the customary briefing.

Having become used to the

Takeshi Ito, Project Leader for the 'New Age' Impreza.

An interview with the project leader

Miho Long: By the time of the new car's launch, the Impreza had become legendary. Were you aiming to give the customer more of the same in a different package, or were you hoping to produce something really special, particularly in the case of the WRX?

Takeshi Ito: During development, I was well aware of the worldwide enthusiasm for the WRX, and, it has to be said, this made me a little nervous in the beginning. However, I could see that the older model had reached the peak of its development - a completely new design was called for to keep the Impreza competitive. To enhance the vehicle's potential, we introduced the six-speed transmission, made the body much stronger, and adopted a package that would allow larger wheel and tyre combinations to be fitted. Of course, weight was a major concern, but we increased performance to counter this, and quickly proved the machine's worth in competition. I'm sure that some day in the future, another increase in performance will be required, but the platform should be more than capable of handling it.

Miho Long: Car makers are particularly worried about pricing nowadays. Were there any features you wanted to add but couldn't because the 'bean counters' said no?

Takeshi Ito: There were a few things, sure. But in terms of the vehicle's efficiency, there were no shortcuts or compromises.

Miho Long: There was criticism from some quarters regarding the styling. What do you have to say to the doubters?

Takeshi Ito: I feel that a small company like Subaru has to produce cars that stand out from the crowd. If one created a mainstream, conservative vehicle, it would compete head-on with cars produced by the larger concerns, which is pointless. We need products that display originality in order to appeal to a different clientele.

Miho Long: How much of the car's design was influenced by the need for it to become a competitive rally machine?

Takeshi Ito: The Impreza has a reputation to uphold, so it's very important for us to bear in mind the needs of the SWRT as well as normal road users.

Miho Long: What was the most pleasing aspect of the new vehicle in your opinion?

Takeshi Ito: I have a WRX STi which I drive at the weekends. I love the feeling of oneness with the car - its chassis response and efficiency on winding roads, and the power delivery from the engine. And, of course, I like the styling, especially the front mask!!

conservative styling of earlier Imprezas, the new lines were quite a shock. The reaction in the room was rather muted, even by subdued Japanese standards. My particular problem was not with the headlights *per se*, but with the cheaper estates, which appeared far too heavy on their tiny wheel and tyre combinations, which was not helped by the large lights at both ends; the top Sports Wagon and the WRX saloon (and later STi models) looked fine.

There's no doubt that the new styling was controversial. In essence, the design team took all engineering requirements and the latest world safety considerations into account (Subaru was striving for a European NCAP four-star rating for the vehicle), added a touch of individuality, and the new Impreza is what popped out the other end of the supercomputer. If nothing else, it was bold, and, without doubt, met the criteria of standing out from the crowd (there was a concerted effort to distance the car from the Mitsubishi Lancer). And those headlights - which incorporated the front indicators - certainly worked well.

Not only was the new body safer, with large glass areas giving good visibility, thanks to carefully designed pillars, it was also substantially stronger. The sedan was some 185 per cent better in terms of resistance to twisting, and there was a staggering 250 per cent improvement with regard to resistance to bending. The figures posted for the five-door shell, without the benefit of a solid bulkhead behind the rear seats, were not quite as good, but very impressive, nonetheless.

The saloon and estate designs were actually quite different, sharing only the basic floorpan, bonnet (aluminium on all cars; even the 1.5 litre station wagons, with an air scoop on turbocharged models), front doors and bodywork behind the bumper areas (the bumpers were slightly different). In reality, the new styling represented quite an investment, as, apart from minor components (door handles, lights, mirrors, and so on), everything else was unique. With sales projections predicting that the sedan would sell in

small numbers, it was also quite a gamble ...

The saloons had bulging Audi Quattro-esque wings to allow for the wider track of the four-door models, although this did increase local taxes for the new sedan: the estate continued to sport a fairly narrow body, so benefited from the cheaper rates of the outgoing range. However, in order to improve handling, the wider stance was a must.

Overall length was 4405mm (173.4in.) on all cars, and the 2525mm (99.4in.) wheelbase dimension was, of course, shared. After that, the saloon was lower, wider (despite the same 150mm (5.9in.) ground clearance). Sedans were listed at 1435mm (56.5in.) tall and 1730mm (68.1in.) wide at the body sides, while the same measurements were 1460mm (57.5in.)

A small selection of the design proposals put forward for the third generation Impreza. Note that one of them gives a hint of a coupé, although a two-door body was never on the cards.

and 1695mm (66.7in.) on the estates.

Subaru management realized there had been too many grades in the past, so the new line-up (early cars were classified as Type A vehicles, by the way) boasted fewer models, but each had a distinct character and sporting nature. Perhaps the most significant move was to list only two saloons, both of which received the hallowed WRX badge. The range in Japan is shown in the accompanying table.

While the bodywork, executed by Chief Designer, Mamoru Ishii, may have been *avant garde*, Project Leader, Takeshi Ito (who had been in charge of the new Impreza's development since its inception in early 1997), chose evolution rather than revolution for

The Sedan range

Grade	Engine	Transmission	Price
4WD WRX NA	2.0 litre	5-sp.Man.	2,033,000
		4-sp.Auto.	2,156,000
4WD WRX NB	2.0 Turbo	5-sp.Man.	2,383,000
		4-sp.Auto.	2,536,000

The Sports Wagon range

Grade	Engine	Transmission	Price
2WD I's	1.5 litre	5-sp.Man.	1,363,000
		4-sp.Auto.	1,456,000
2WD I's Sport	1.5 litre	5-sp.Man.	1,363,000
		4-sp.Auto.	1,456,000
4WD I's	1.5 litre	5-sp.Man.	1,543,000
		4-sp.Auto.	1,636,000
4WD I's Sport	1.5 litre	5-sp.Man.	1,660,000
		4-sp.Auto.	1,753,000
4WD 20N	2.0 litre	5-sp.Man.	1,998,000
		4-sp.Auto.	2,121,000
4WD 20K	2.0 Turbo	5-sp.Man.	2,348,000
		4-sp.Auto.	2,501,000

Overhead view of the turbocharged Impreza chassis.

Cutaway drawing of the EJ20 Turbo engine.

the mechanical and chassis components.

Starting with the familiar 1.5 litre EJ15 unit - despite retaining the 10.0:1 compression ratio - the engineers managed to squeeze a few more horses from it, thanks to a new intake manifold, so it was now listed with 100bhp at 5200rpm, and 105lbft of torque at 4000rpm. The 1493cc flat-four could be mated to either a five-speed manual or a conventional four-speed, electronically-controlled automatic gearbox with a new Mercedes-Benz-style selector gate.

The normally-aspirated EJ20 was carried over, developing 155bhp and 144lbft of torque. However, while the five-speed transmission was still listed (with a dual mass flywheel and a lighter clutch than before, and internal ratios of 3.454, 2.062, 1.448, 1.088 and 0.825, combined with a 3.90:1 final drive), the automatic option was now the Sport Shift type with a +/- gate on the selector and change buttons on the steering wheel. All two-pedal cars shared the same gearing, although two-litre models had a 4.11:1 final drive instead of the 4.44:1 specified on the 1.5 litre range.

The turbocharged 1994cc engine was slightly different, giving more power and torque over a wider rev-range, smoother running and better fuel economy (the latter courtesy of a new catalytic converter arrangement, multi-perforated fuel-injectors and the TGV system). With a modified Mitsubishi

TD04H turbo (the turbine and compressor received attention), larger wastegate port and intercooler, AVCS and a 9.0:1 c/r, it gave 250bhp at 6000rpm, along with 245lbft of torque at 3600rpm.

The internal ratios on the five-speed gearbox were unique: 3.166 on first, 1.882 on second, 1.296 on third, 0.972 on fourth and a 0.738 top, combined with a 4.44:1 final drive, although the Sport Shift automatic had the same 2.785, 1.545, 1.000 and 0.694 cogs, and a 4.11:1 final drive. There was a gear indicator panel in the lower part of the tachometer, and another, more traditional, one in the left-hand meter (covering fuel level and engine temperature).

Methods of transmitting drive to the wheels were quite different from car-to-car. With a manual gearbox, all 4WD vehicles had a viscous limited-slip centre differential. However, automatic naturally-aspirated models came with an active torque split 4WD system (employing electronics, sensors and a multi-plate hydraulic transfer clutch), while the two-pedal NB and 20K had the VTD-4WD set-up. Turbocharged cars also had a Suretrac lsd at the back and a double offset joint (DOJ) propshaft.

The chassis was developed under Masao Kurihara. Suspension was via MacPherson struts all-round, with dual links at the rear, plus anti-roll bars fore and aft; the front suspension was mounted on a subframe to increase rigidity and isolate sources of NVH. Although all components and their geometry were revised, simplicity was the key, in consideration of the Impreza's role in motorsport. As Mitsubishi's rally boss once told the author, multi-link systems may be better on a pure road car, but when it comes to executing repairs in the heat of competition, simple is best.

Both saloons had forged aluminium lower A-arms, incidentally, and the suspension as a whole was able to work better due to reduced friction, in addition to the stiffer body and stronger mounting points. As mentioned earlier, the saloons had a wider track - 1485mm (58.5in.) at the front, and 1475mm (58.1in.) at the rear - some 20mm (0.78in.) bigger than that of the two-litre estates.

All cars had PAS and alloy wheels included in the price. Behind the

Tasteful publicity shot of the WRX NA sedan.

wheels, both saloons and two-litre estates had vented discs and two-pot calipers up front, with solid discs at the rear: ABS was listed as standard, the NA and 20N grades being given Brake Assist at the same time. The 1.5 litre cars had a disc/drum set-up.

Paramount in the development team's list of goals was driving pleasure, but attention to detail in the interior ran a close second. Driving position, ease of entry and exit, all-round vision (the tops of the wings were bulbous so that the driver could see them), reduced NVH levels and better packaging - in order to make a compact car feel roomy

Rear view of the purposeful WRX NB saloon, with the dashboard of the same car seen here in automatic guise.

132

The I's Sport pictured in Paris, with the interior of the same car.

- were all key areas to be tackled.

Trim materials were revised, even in the luggage area, where softer panels were used to give the vehicle an air of quality rather than workmanlike practicality. Ergonomics were improved, with better seating, a completely new fascia, and a fresh instrument panel; the gauges were set in three main dials, with white on black markings, yellow needles, and a central tachometer on the two-litre models.

Equipment levels were very high on the new Impreza. Even the entry level I's estate (carrying the LA-GG2 chassis code for front-wheel drive and LA-GG3 for 4WD) boasted 14-inch, eight-spoke alloy wheels, ABS with

Rear three-quarter shot of the 20N estate.

Brake Assist, dual airbags, air conditioning, power-assisted steering (with tilt adjustment and a 16.5:1 ratio), rear wash/wipe, a keyless entry system, colour-keyed door handles and power mirrors (with folding facility), electric windows with UV-cut glass, driver's seat height adjuster, a split rear seat, and four speakers and an aerial pre-installed ready to accept one of the optional stereo units. The I's came in five colours, with grey fabric trim.

Moving up to the I's Sport brought a different front bumper (featuring brake cooling vents and a lower front lip), a rear roof spoiler, a leather Momo four-spoke steering wheel to replace the basic four-spoke item on the I's, a CD/radio/cassette combination unit, and two-tone grey trim to complement the six exterior colours.

The 20N (chassis type TA-GG9) added seven-spoke, 15-inch alloys (shod with 195/60 rubber), four-wheel disc brakes with ABS and Brake Assist, front foglamps (mounted in the I's Sport bumper), colour-keyed side skirts, exhaust trim, automatic air conditioning, a CD/radio unit with glass inlayed aerial, slightly deeper bolsters on the front seats, and black patterned cloth trim; automatic vehicles had the selector buttons on the Momo steering wheel.

The turbocharged 20K (TA-GGA) had new, 16-inch, five-spoke alloys (with 205/50 tyres), twin exhaust finishers, a quicker 15.0:1 steering rack, Suretrac lsd at the back, and front bucket seats trimmed in two-tone grey fabric; automatic cars were equipped with the VTD-4WD system, and, of course, the different steering wheel. Like the 20N, coachwork colours included Pure White, Premium Silver Metallic, Gran Blue Mica, Rose Metallic and WR Blue Mica.

Maker options included the Clear View Pack (described earlier in the book), navigation systems with combined stereo, and the so-called Safety Pack (side airbags, three-point seatbelts for all rear passengers, and a third head restraint on the back seat) for all cars. The basic I's could be upgraded via a rear roof spoiler and foglights (the latter being a different design to that found on the other models), while the 20N and 20K had the option of a glass sunroof, a six-speaker audio system, and HID headlights (strangely, combined with

tinted window glass).

Dealers were able to offer a number of aerodynamic and styling appendages, seat covers (including a beige or black leather-look set), a rear parcel shelf-cum-luggage cover, and coloured trim inserts for the console and dash binnacle. A few months after the launch, a 'Grade Up Package' was offered for the front-wheel drive I's Sport, including 15-inch alloys and tinted glass.

The saloons had a similar specification to the 20N and 20K, with front foglights, colour-keyed side skirts, exhaust trim pieces, a rear wash/wipe, Momo leather-trimmed steering wheel (with selector buttons on two-pedal cars), leather sports gearknob and handbrake handle, keyless entry system, automatic air conditioning, power windows and mirrors, a CD/radio with four speakers, driver's seat height adjustment and dual SRS airbags.

As well as mechanical differences, the NA and NB differed in equipment levels, too. The NA had 15-inch, seven-spoke alloys (the same as those fitted to the 20N) with 195/60 rubber, while the NB had 16-inch, five-spoke items. Shod with 205/50 VR-rated tyres, these were actually last year's wheels carried over and therefore of a different design to those on the 20K.

Other detail differences included 20N-type seats and trim for the NA (chassis code TA-GD9) and 20K-style seats and fabrics for the NB, and, whilst both cars had PAS, the turbocharged model had the quicker 15:1 rack, giving 2.6 turns lock-to-lock; the NB (TA-GDA) also featured an outside temperature gauge, and, like the 20K, a larger 60 litre (13.2 gallon) fuel tank; normally-aspirated cars had to make do with one 20 per cent smaller.

Of course, additional weight was the price for enhanced safety and extra electrical goodies, with the manual NA weighing in at 1290kg (2838lb) and the equivalent NB some 50kg (110lb) more than that: the last turbocharged WRX sedan had been 1270kg (2794lb), so the difference was quite substantial.

Sedan colour choices included Premium Silver Metallic, WR Blue Mica, Rose Metallic, Pure White and, for the NB only, Midnight Black Mica. Maker options were much the same as those for the estates, with the HID lights, navigation system, Clear View Pack,

Safety Pack and six-speaker stereo upgrade listed, although the rear spoiler and tinted glass for the rear screen and rear doors were unique to the saloon.

BBS alloy wheels were listed in the accessories catalogue, with 15-, 16- and 17-inch rim sizes (the latter would require new tyres as well, of course), and a number of STi parts were also available, including an uprated and lowered suspension, front strut braces, red detailing on the steering wheel and gearknob, auxiliary gauges, aero mirror covers, and a rather OTT rear spoiler.

The STi cars

The STi range was launched separately at the New Pier Hall overlooking Tokyo Bay. Taking place on 24 October, it was much more low-key than the August launch, but nonetheless important, especially for enthusiasts.

At the heart of any STi model is the engine. For the new STi cars, the engineering team chose a semi-closed deck cylinder block, increasing unit rigidity. Inside, the forged piston heads were modified and given new, lightweight conrods with big-ends secured by Allen screws rather than traditional nuts and bolts.

This latest fuel-injected four had the Active Valve Control System (AVCS) looking after the lightweight valves, four for each cylinder as usual, and with the twin-camshafts per bank operating on shimless lifters to allow higher engine speeds. The head gasket was metal to ensure a better seal; exhaust valves were sodium filled (to dissipate heat better) whilst inlet valves were hollow to reduce valvetrain inertia.

The intercooler (finished in silver like the standard WRX, but with the STi logo sprayed onto the vanes) was slightly bigger, as was the air scoop feeding it on the bonnet. An intercooler water spray was fitted, with automatic mode and manual override buttons, and the reservoir was enlarged to allow for longer periods of usage. The IHI RHF55 turbocharger and ECU also received attention in a bid to boost performance.

In its latest guise, with an 8.0:1 compression ratio, the EJ20 engine developed 280bhp at 6400rpm, along with 274lbft of torque. At the same time, emissions from the single big bore exhaust were cut and economy was enhanced via adoption of an air-fuel ratio sensor, multi-perforated fuel-

Two pieces of Japanese advertising from the time of the launch - one for the 1.5 litre estates, and the other for the latest WRX saloon. Ito-san devoted a lot of attention to the Sports Wagon. This was an interesting ploy, but perhaps not so surprising given recent fashion trends and previous sales records, especially for the domestic market.

Invitation to the launch of the 'New Age' Impreza STi range.

Engine and chassis of the high performance STi model.

injectors, and a new catalyst. The powerplant, with its trademark red induction manifolds, was protected internally by an oil cooler and from underneath by a substantial STi sumpguard.

A close-ratio, six-speed gearbox really set the STi models apart. There was greater rigidity in the casing, internal components and the linkage, lubrication and cooling were improved, and the clutch was suitably uprated to cope with the extra torque. Gearing was the same on all STi cars, with 3.636 on first, 2.375 on second, 1.761 on third, 1.346 on fourth, 1.062 on fifth and 0.842 on top; a 3.90:1 final drive was specified. There were double synchronizers on first and third and a triple one on second, and, in a bid to stop accidental changes into reverse (to the far right and down, outside a double-H pattern), a pull-up slider ring was fitted between the gearknob and gaiter.

A viscous limited-slip centre differential was specified (usually splitting torque equally between front and rear until wheels at one end or the other started to slip), combined with a Suretrac lsd at the back of the vehicle. However, the standard Type RA (with 16-inch wheels and tyres) featured the familiar, driver-controlled centre diff (with basic 45:55 distribution setting) with a Suretrac diff up front (optional on the other saloon) and a mechanical rear lsd. If the optional 17-inch rims were chosen, the Type RA came with Brembo brakes and ABS instead.

On the subject of brakes, the WRX STi saloon had Brembo brakes, with ventilated discs all-round, and four-pot calipers up front and two-pot items at the rear. Coming with Super Sports ABS (incorporating a lateral G sensor and EBD), the brake calipers were

painted gold with this set-up, which could also be specified as an option on the Type RA. The standard Type RA and STi Sports Wagon also had vented discs at both ends, but they were smaller in diameter, and came with Subaru's own calipers (four-pot/two-pot), finished in black; the estate was equipped with an ABS system.

Power-assisted steering was standard on all cars. Uprated suspension (with 30 per cent stiffer spring rates and a higher roll centre at the rear to reduce understeer) featured inverted dampers. With an aluminium and titanium front strut brace (again, designed by the FHI Aerospace Division), the layout was an elegant piece of engineering. With the coupé gone, there were three basic grades in the STi line-up:

The STi range

Grade	Engine	Transmission	Price
4WD WRX Sedan	2.0 Turbo	6-sp.Man.	3,198,000
4WD WRX Type RA	2.0 Turbo	6-sp.Man.	2,968,000
4WD WRX Sp. Wagon	2.0 Turbo	6-sp.Man.	2,998,000

From the outside, at first glance, the WRX STi Sedan didn't look all that different to the NB model. Careful inspection revealed that the air intake on the hood was slightly bigger, the badging was unique (including a signature pink grille emblem), there were STi foglamp covers instead of actual lights, the WRX's optional rear spoiler came as standard, and, most obviously, the wheels were different - gold-coloured, five-spoke, 7.5J x 17 alloys shod with 225/45 ZR-rated Potenza RE040s.

Inside, the steering wheel was the same as that fitted to the manual WRX NA/NB, but with red stitching instead of black. There was an aluminium frame around the gearshift (also fitted on the estate, but not the RA), and an aluminium pedal set for all cars.

A nice touch was the adjustable shift light - a warning system that informed the driver to change gear as the pre-set rev limit (capable of being set in 100rpm increments from 2000rpm all the way up to the 8000rpm red-line) was reached. Otherwise, the instruments were largely similar to those of the WRX NB (with a fuel/temperature combination gauge on the left, a central tachometer, and the

speedometer to the right), although the NB had a red zone starting at 7000rpm.

Bucket seats with suede-like blue seating surfaces and black outer sections finished the interior (complete with matching rear seats and door trim panels). A CD/MD/radio combination unit, special ignition key and remote control central locking added a touch of luxury; dual airbags were standard on all cars.

The Type RA (carrying the same GH-GDB chassis code as the more civilized STi saloon) had basic black door mirrors and different, shallower sill extensions compared to the other STi cars. It also had a roof vent, an A-post mounted aerial instead of a glass inlayed one, and smaller diameter wheels and tyres. Standard fare was last year's 16-inch rims, although, as mentioned earlier, the regular STi saloon's 17-inch combination with uprated brakes could be specified as an option (the Type RA with this specification cost 3,068,000 yen, and had a fractionally wider track).

Although the air conditioner, power window operation, stereo equipment, maplights, rear wash/wipe and keyless entry system were missing (the aluminium surround on the gearshift was missing as well), the Type RA at least came with the same seats as its more expensive counterpart, and had a quicker 13:1 steering rack, too (the other two STi variants had a 15:1 ratio).

The Sports Wagon (GH-GGB) kept the narrower body (Cd 0.32). In fact, it could just as easily have been taken for an I's Sport with different badging, a bonnet scoop, deeper side skirts and bigger wheels. Amazingly, those larger wheels were unique to the estate. Although they looked very similar, the rim width was slightly narrower at 7J, and close inspection revealed less taper on the five spokes. These alloys came with 215/45 ZR17 rubber.

Inside, the specification was much the same as that for the WRX STi saloon. The front seats (complete with red-stitched logo) were identical, but the rear ones had headrests on the estate (the four-door STi cars didn't have any). The Sports Wagon weighed in at 1430kg (3146lb), the same as the sedan, and 30kg (66lb) more than the Type RA.

The Sports Wagon was available in Pure White, Premium Silver Metallic and WR Blue Mica. The WRX STi, which could cover 0-60 in 5.2 seconds, was available in these three shades, plus Midnight Black Mica; the Type RA came in white only.

Maker options included a navigation system, stereo upgrade,

A couple of shots showing the STi saloon in action.

Advertising for the new WRX and its STi brethren.

tinted glass and HID headlights (not available on the RA). Subaru Tecnica International uprated parts for the 'New Age' Impreza included a pillow bush lateral link set, strut and subframe brace bars, a lowered suspension kit and harder strut mounts, high performance timing belts, sparkplugs, air ducting and radiator hoses, a sports exhaust, a lightened flywheel and competition clutch, a new 'quickshift' and titanium gearknob, rear diff cover, racing specification brake hoses, five-spoke alloys (available with 16-, 17- and 18-inch rim diameters), carbonfibre mirrors, mesh foglight covers, a front lip spoiler, recalibrated instruments (with a 260kph speedo, an 11,000rpm tacho and red pointers), aluminium pedal extensions for automatic cars, and various decals. In fact, a car was shown at the 2001 Tokyo Auto Salon which was fitted with no fewer than 60 modified parts, all available from the STi catalogue.

Wheels magazine tried a Japanese spec STi saloon against the Mitsubishi 'LanEvo' VI Tommi Makinen, and declared: "Driven in isolation, the STi's a master blaster, no doubt, but back-to-back with the mad, bad Evo, it leans more, feels heavier (which it is) and you're not so locked into the point, accelerate and brake a bit.

"It's a less wearing car, especially on the freeway where the sixth gear cuts down engine noise and saves you fuel. The new six-speeder is an absolute joy, by the way, with a light, precise click-click action that first generation WRXers would kill for. Even in clotting Japanese

traffic, the STi is totally unfussed.

"Considering the STi's essentially simple struts, the team has done wonders for handling/ride, while the trademark 4WD once again provides traction and roadholding by the bucketful. The big Brembo brakes feel a bit dead unless you work them hard, though. Fade? You must be joking, but the Evo's brakes do have a more progressive brake feel."

Ultimately, the testers chose the Mitsubishi, as it was the more involving car to drive. In reality, of course, Subaru wanted to make the new Impreza easier to drive for the majority and, in that respect, achieved this goal, albeit at the expense of hardcore enthusiasts. At least tuning parts were available to win back their custom, so all was not lost ...

Stephen Sutcliffe also tried a Japanese STi in the UK, declaring: "To begin with, the only aspects that appear notably different from the regular WRX are the firmer ride (it's hard but not crashy), the slightly heavier and quicker steering, the meatier brakes and the super-short throw gearchange. But the first time you put your foot down and hold it there for more than a second, one very big difference hits you: unlike the regular [European] WRX, the STi goes. Really goes."

While the 20K covered the standing-quarter in 14.7 seconds in independent tests, the STi car could shave over a second off that time. Indeed, comparing the sedan to a Lancer Evolution VII, *Car Graphic* recorded 13.5 seconds for the Subaru, and declared it the better car for average drivers.

On the other hand, racer Takayuki Kinoshita felt the STi could prove a handful for inexperienced pilots when approaching the limit, as strong understeer and oversteer showed through on high speed corners. Another motorsports man, Masanori Sekiya, likened the STi to an ugly girl with a beautiful heart; the Impreza's attraction and undoubted qualities were not immediately obvious.

Just for the record, the STi version got my vote in the annual RJC contest. With my great friend, Nissan legend, Yutaka Katayama, in the passenger seat, I didn't want to push too hard, but even in the short time allowed on these test days I fell in love with the engine note, the great gearbox (all too

A small selection of STi tuning parts available in Japan.

The Japanese market STi cars for 2001. From left to right, we see the Type RA version, the standard WRX STi saloon, and the STi estate.

Cover from the WRX STi Version S brochure.

often nowadays the shift is made too remote - I like to feel something mechanical is happening), and the car's responses to driver input. It was my kind of machine, and, although it didn't win the RJC 'Car of the Year' award, a section of the membership rated the Impreza very highly.

The other Car of the Year group in Japan (COTY), gave the Impreza a Special Award. The reasoning: "It's a sports sedan with the greatest attention to driving pleasure we've seen in recent years, and we were impressed by the safety offered by its highly rigid body."

Another STi option was added in February 2001 - the WRX STi Version S - stripped of lots of luxury equipment like the keyless entry and audio system, aluminium pedals, the trim ring on the gearshift gaiter, and even the special STi key (designed to resemble an ignition kill switch). Of course, items could be put back on via the accessories brochure, but the idea was to make STi motoring more accessible: the basic car (WR Blue only) cost just 3,033,000 yen, and the Version S with HID lights, tinted glass and a front lsd was priced at 3,158,000 yen (the latter was available in blue, white, silver or Blue-Black Mica).

The Third Generation in Europe

The European spec 'New Age' Impreza was launched at the NEC on 17 October - opening day of the 2000 British International Motor Show. Subaru UK exhibited a saloon, an estate and a WRC2001 rally car at the event, the latter reflecting the significance placed on the motorsport programme from a marketing point of view.

The press release noted that the new Impreza took "Subaru's all-wheel drive chassis dynamics to new heights, with the steering, handling and engine even more responsive." It cited "vastly improved refinement, safety and body rigidity," and a "massive advance in interior quality" with enhanced equipment.

All cars came with four-wheel drive, with the 1.6 TS estate providing an entry level machine. Priced at £13,950, the EJ16 engine provided the five-speed station wagon with 95 horses and 105lbft of torque. Even the 1.6 litre model came with a rear spoiler, ABS, PAS, central locking, electric windows, full instrumentation (including outside temperature gauge), a radio/cassette, split rear seat, an alarm, and dual airbags.

The normally-aspirated, two-litre grade was christened the GX. Available as either a saloon or estate, it was listed with 125bhp at 5600rpm, and 136lbft of torque at 3600rpm - just like last year. Moving up to the GX brought alloy wheels (seven-spoke, WRX NA-style items, replacing steel rims with full covers), front foglights, headlamp washers, air conditioning, power mirror adjustment, a radio/CD unit, and sportier front seats. The four-door had a £15,750 sticker price; the five-door body added £500, while automatic transmission was listed for both cars for the princely sum of £1000.

While the P1 was still listed in the UK at the start of the 2001 season, the new WRX certainly generated a lot of interest. The exchange rate was roughly 180 yen to the pound at this time, so the price was substantially higher than in Japan (a crazy situation given the terrific wage difference), but £21,495 for the saloon and £21,995 for the estate (automatic transmission was not available) certainly represented good value.

Below the air scoop on the bonnet, the WRX had a larger intercooler, plus a revised Mitsubishi TD04L turbo and wastegate. With an 8.0:1 compression

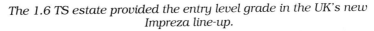

The 1.6 TS estate provided the entry level grade in the UK's new Impreza line-up.

Press shot of the two-litre GX saloon.

official 143mph (229kph) top speed and a 0-60 time of 5.9 seconds, backed up in independent tests, but slightly slower than the old car.

Even so, the WRX was certainly a nice package, featuring a limited-slip differential at the back, ABS with ventilated discs all-round - 294mm (11.6in.) front, 290mm (11.4in.) at the rear - and 7J x 17 alloys (actually the same as those used on the STi estate in Japan, but painted silver) shod with 215/45 Potenza rubber.

The WRX came with air conditioning, a radio/cassette/CD player, an aluminium pedal set, the same leather Momo steering wheel as its Japanese counterparts (with 2.8

The GX Sports Wagon and WRX saloon for the British market.

ratio, the two-litre unit gave 218bhp at 5600rpm, and 215lbft of torque at 3600rpm.

The gearing was different to that of the Japanese model with 3.45 on first, 1.95 on second, 1.37 on third, 0.97 on fourth and 0.74 on top, combined with a 3.90:1 final drive. This gave the five-speed saloon an

The latest WRX estate, pictured at the time of the UK launch.

turns lock-to-lock), and the standard seats (incorporating side airbags) could be swopped for deeper buckets. Interestingly, European cars had a central speedometer with the tachometer taking up a position to the right of it.

The latest Impreza hit the showrooms in late November, and was sold alongside the Justy, Forester, Legacy and Legacy Outback models. Testing the new WRX, *Autocar* observed: "Throttle response is good rather than exceptional for a turbo motor, with boost coming in as low as 2500rpm. But the mid-range isn't as strong as before and, even though the

140

rev limiter is set at 7400rpm, anything beyond 6500rpm and the performance starts to tail away.

"[However, the], Impreza strikes a brilliant balance between refinement and character and makes you wonder why anyone bothers making in-line fours when they're so much rougher than the Impreza's boxer. It may not be as fast as the old car, but with the extra refinement it's almost as satisfying.

"The gearshift and clutch are markedly improved, too. There's less resistance and still a short, snappy throw.

"Brakes have long been an Impreza strong point, and these maintain that tradition. Pedal feel is better than before; they didn't fade once, and they gave every driver real confidence."

The testers were also happy with handling and ride, and especially the steering. The driving position was described as "spot-on," although there were serious concerns about fuel consumption; an average of just 18.7mpg was recorded over a seven day period. All in all, though, the Impreza got a five-star rating: "If you can live with the looks, the WRX remains the definitive affordable performance saloon for the enthusiast."

At *What Car?*, testers praised the "superb handling and performance," but felt the car was "softer and less flexible" than before. In conclusion, the magazine classed the latest WRX as a "great update of a cult classic, but lacking raw edge."

On 23 May 2001, the Prodrive 'UK300' special was announced. Limited to just 300 units, the UK300 was a joint venture between Britain's Subaru concessionaires and Prodrive, with the styling revisions carried out by none other than Peter Stevens.

Key changes for the UK300 included WRC-style headlights, white indicator repeaters and side markers on the front wings, a black front lip spoiler, and a rather unusual rear wing (complete with Prodrive logos). All cars were finished in WR Blue Mica, set off by gold, ten-spoke, 7.5J x 18 OZ alloys shod with 225/40 Pirelli tyres.

Inside, the front bucket seats were trimmed in blue suede-like material with matching door panels. The £24,995 limited edition model also received special carpets and a numbered plaque.

For added exclusivity, the Prodrive WR Sport 'Performance Pack' option could be specified, which gave a useful hike in power and mid-range punch. The £1600 needed to secure it gave the owner a reprogrammed ECU, uprated intercooler piping and a free-flow exhaust system with a single big bore tailpipe, resulting in 245bhp being developed at 5600rpm (at least with 97 Octane fuel), along with 261lbft of torque at 4000rpm. As before, this conversion did not affect the maker's warranty.

The new car in Australia

The latest Impreza range was launched in Australia on 18 October 2000. The line-up consisted of two normally-aspirated grades - the GX and sportier RX, both of which were available with saloon or station wagon body, a manual or automatic gearbox, and four-wheel drive as standard - and the WRX.

For the 2001 season, the entry level GX sedan cost $25,970, whilst prices for the RX started at $30,550 and went up to $32,870 for the two-pedal estate. The turbocharged WRX continued as the flagship model, these five-speed cars costing $43,800 in four-door guise, or $44,250 as a five-door; automatic transmission was not available.

The two-litre 4WD RV estate - an Australian equivalent to the old Outback with its two-tone paintwork (bumpers, wheelarches and door rubbing strips were finished in Grey Opal) - was added in the summer of 2001, but otherwise the range remained the same. First shown as a concept vehicle at the Melbourne Show (badged as an Outback Sport), the RV grade had 16-inch alloys, ABS braking, air conditioning, a radio/CD player, cruise control, foglights, a rear spoiler, and a keyless entry system. Available in shades of white, blue, green or red, and with the option of a manual or automatic gearbox, prices started at $29,990.

The new Impreza in America

After several years of being unkind to Japanese manufacturers, during the early part of 2001 the exchange rate was quoted at a more favourable 126 yen to the dollar, the best return on American currency since 1998. This meant one of two things: either higher profits could be made to make up for

the lean period at the end of the last century, or lower prices could be passed on (or at least held steady), benefiting the customer. Subaru chose the latter route, so that while some equivalent grades were a touch more expensive, others were actually cheaper.

The 2.5 litre TS estate, RS saloon and Outback Sport Wagon grades shared their flat-four engine with the Legacy and Forester. With 165bhp and 166lbft of torque, it was basically a carry-over from the previous generation, and could be hooked up to either a five-speed manual or four-speed automatic transmission.

The TS was the entry level model (available in five-door guise only), with 15-inch steel wheels and disc/drum braking. Moving up to the RS saloon, with prices starting at $18,995, brought a far more interesting specification: while dual airbags, PAS, a radio/CD combination unit, air conditioning, cruise control, central locking, power windows and mirrors, and driver's seat height adjustment were shared with the five-door model, 16-inch alloy wheels with 205/55 rubber, discs all-round (with ABS), front and rear anti-roll bars, a leather-wrapped steering wheel, gearknob and handbrake, and better quality, dark grey cloth trim looked the better bet for enthusiasts.

The Outback was slightly cheaper than the RS at $18,695 with a manual gearbox, or $19,495 in EC-4AT guise, but had its distinctive body mouldings (finished in Greystone metallic), foglights, alloy wheels, and special roof rails, which were different to those of the TS. It also had unique grey trim.

But the big news was the arrival of the 227bhp, two-litre WRX. First displayed at the 2001 Detroit Show, sales of the first turbocharged Impreza for the US market started after the official launch held on 17 March (classed as an early 2002 model year vehicle).

The familiar 1994cc turbocharged four had at last made it to American soil. In US trim, sporting an 8.0:1 c/r, it developed 227bhp at 6000rpm, and 217lbft of torque at 4000rpm, slightly more than that listed for Europe and the Antipodes, but still rather less than available in home market cars. Regardless, the engine cleared America's LEV standard - the key to getting the WRX into the States - thanks to the tumble valve (TGV) system giving

RACE PROVEN, NOT "INSPIRED".

The Impreza section of the US catalogue.

EASY TO GET IN. HARD TO GET OUT.

better burn characteristics at low rpm and the use of three catalytic converters.

Gearing was the same as that listed for Europe on the manual gearbox, although, being America, a $1000 automatic option was listed, and then the gearing was the same as that specified in Japan (2.78, 1.54, 1.00, 0.69, combined with a 4.11:1 final drive); likewise, two-pedal cars were equipped with the VTD-4WD system.

Braking was via discs all-round - ventilated 294mm (11.6in.) items up front with twin-pot calipers, and 266mm (10.5in.) solid ones at the rear - with ABS as standard. The wheels (as fitted to the RS, the Outback had the home market 20K-style alloys) were of a similar design to those of the British WRX, but with a 16-inch rim diameter and shod with 205/55 VR-rated Bridgestone Potenzas.

Covering all the mechanical components was a more aggressive body, with an air scoop in the aluminium bonnet, foglamps in the front airdam, side skirts, a rear spoiler (at least for the Sport Wagon and a $300 option on the sedan), and dual exhausts exiting from the tail. Inside, a Momo leather steering wheel replaced the standard four-spoke item, and a six-speaker sound system (with CD radio and cassette) graced the centre console.

The WRX $23,495 estate was available in Aspen White, Midnight Black Pearl, Platinum Silver Metallic, Sedona Red Pearl and WR Blue Pearl, while the $23,995 saloon version also had the option of Blaze Yellow. Trim was in a black, flat-woven cloth.

Unusual accessories included an auto dimming rearview mirror tha

At last, the turbocharged Impreza found its way to American shores in the form of the new WRX road rocket, which quickly established itself as a car for connoisseurs.

THE NEW WRX DOESN'T JUST HUG CURVES. IT THROWS THEM IN A HEADLOCK AND GIVES THEM A NOOGIE.

doubled as a compass, the uniquely American front 'bra,' and auxiliary gauges (like European models, the US spec WRX had a central speedo, not tacho, by the way).

In its October 2001 issue, *Car & Driver* put the WRX up against the BMW 330xi and Audi S4, as it felt that machinery in the same price bracket wouldn't even come close to the Subaru. Both German cars cost around $15,000 more, so the object of the exercise was to see if the extra money bought a better saloon - interesting.

Ultimately, the WRX came second, pipped at the post by the Audi, mainly on grounds of excessive noise compared to its rivals. It was noted: "We're still arguing the Subaru's second place finish. Two of the three voters put the Subaru in first place, with the Audi second. But one - and he'll remain nameless - put the Audi first and the Subaru last, so when we averaged the scores, the Subaru missed the top spot by just one point."

The article concluded with: "'Subaru got the big stuff right - the motor, tranny, seats, and handling,' wrote one tester in the logbook. That sums up how we feel about this car. One can only marvel at what Subaru could do with another 15 grand."

Able to break through the standing-quarter in 14.2 and clock a 5.6 second 0-60 time (recorded in a *Motor Trend* test), as *Car & Driver* put it, the WRX represented "killer value," and it was certainly popular as a result. First quarter sales alone amounted to over 4000 units, and helped Subaru achieve record annual sales in the States at the end of 2001, the Impreza line accounting for 35,616 of the 185,944 units sold in the year.

Home market additions

A new entry level model called the I's Select was introduced in Japan during April 2001. Based on the front-wheel drive I's, it had a more basic specification, including a steel bonnet, steel wheels with full covers (rather than alloys), different trim, and a

Cover of the I's Select brochure.

143

metallic finish on the centre console. With the five-speed version costing just 1,263,000 yen, the stereo, rear spoiler, foglamps, tinted glass, power mirrors and keyless entry system could be bought separately or as an 85,000 yen package.

Two months later, the I's Sport Special made its debut. In addition to the usual I's Sport goodies, this model (available in two- or four-wheel drive guise with either a manual or automatic gearbox) had a top Kenwood six-speaker audio system with a glass inlayed aerial, chrome inner door handles, and remote control central locking with the answer-back facility. As well as silver, blue and red paintwork options, the Special could also be specified in Midnight Black Mica (new to the I's Sport). Prices ranged from 1,525,000 to 1,798,000 yen.

A New Age rally car
The four-door bodyshell was said to be over twice as rigid as the outgoing car, which naturally helped when it came to fine-tuning the suspension. The bodywork, and interior, as it happens, was once again the responsibility of Peter Stevens.

With the help of an IHI turbocharger (Subaru stayed with IHI - after all, its turbo was well proven, with over eight million in the field), the 1994cc engine developed 300bhp at 5500rpm, and 347lbft of torque at 4000rpm. Prodrive's six-speed gearbox sent drive to electro-hydraulically controlled 'active' differentials at the front, centre and rear.

The 2001 car retained the steering column-mounted gearchange, but the transmission tunnel was now dominated by a huge carbonfibre handbrake which sprouted to the same level as the dashboard.

Suspension was via MacPherson struts all-round, with longitudinal and transverse links at the back; braking came courtesy of Alcon-Prodrive discs with massive four-pot calipers at both ends. Sporting OZ alloys shod with Pirelli rubber, each car cost around US $500,000 to build. Naturally, the WRC2001 weighed in at 1230kg (2706lb), the FIA minimum.

The 2001 rally season
The driver line-up was headed by Richard Burns, with Petter Solberg drafted in as a young prospect. Born in

Norway in 1974, Solberg made his rallying debut in 1996. Within two years, he had become the Norwegian National Champion, and had already made an impact on the WRC scene (his first appearance at this level was on the 1998 Swedish Rally). Getting his first Subaru works drive on the 2000 Tour de Corse, he was immediately on the pace.

One year younger than Solberg, Markko Martin - the Estonian rally driver - was also given a regular drive,

Tommykaira has a long association with the Subaru marque. This advert, dating from summer 2001, shows the 2146cc Impreza M20b, which was endowed with 355bhp.

while Toshihiro Arai deservedly got a more prominent position within the team after several years of plugging away, often with great success, in Group N machinery. Amazingly, Arai, born in Japan in 1966, was the oldest driver in the SWRT. Like other top level forms of competition, rallying was certainly becoming a young man's sport in the new century.

2001 rally record
The new Impreza made its debut on the first round of the 2001 season - the Monte Carlo Rally. Unfortunately, Martin had a problem on the starting ramp, a misfire that finally developed into something more serious; he retired early as a result. Solberg was attacking hard, but perhaps too hard, and he left the road, while Burns was running on three cylinders on the way back into Monaco. SWRT team engineers chose to withdraw the car to investigate what the cause was before the engine was damaged any more.

After a disastrous first round, the drivers could have hoped for better luck, but it wasn't to be. Burns went into a snowbank early on, which doesn't usually present too big a problem, but Sainz had gone off at the same point.

Below & right: The new WRC2001 rally car.

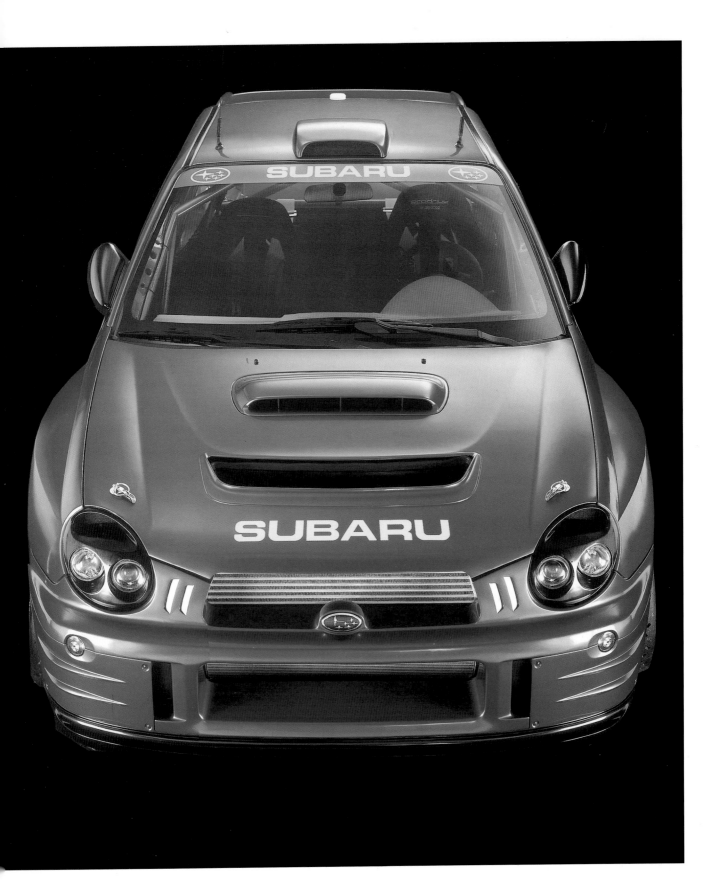

The snow fell on Burns' Impreza, and, with no spectators to help, he lost 13 minutes digging out the car. Martin was again unfortunate as his intercom system broke down, leaving him to drive without Michael Park's help for part of the rally; a buried rock then damaged the suspension. At least Burns was fast on the final day, proving the potential of the new car, and Solberg came home in sixth.

The drivers were met with mud and fog in Portugal, very unusual conditions for the event. Burns had power steering and transmission problems, blunting his hopes of victory. The other Subarus failed to finish; Martin and Arai went off the road, and Solberg succumbed to suspension problems.

There was a closely-fought battle at the top in Spain, but the Imprezas failed to shine on the fast tarmac. Solberg went off the road and into retirement on stage three, while Burns lost some of his gears and then suffered a puncture, putting him further down the field. At least he finished, which is more than can be said for Martin, who pulled out with ignition and transmission maladies.

Burns was running neck-and-neck with Colin McRae in Argentina, but it was the Scot who took the winner's laurels. At least the Subaru driver picked up some valuable points by coming second, and Solberg finished fifth.

Cyprus was pretty much a repeat of Argentina. McRae played a tactical game, taking a penalty to enable him to run second on the road in the final

Motul advertising showing Markko Martin on the 2001 Swedish Rally.

stages - a gamble that paid off in the poor conditions. Solberg's car caught fire, but Arai put in a heroic performance to come home in fourth.

Burns retired with more than a touch of irony in Greece, losing concentration whilst looking at a time board telling him the difference on McRae, and going off the road as a result. Martin had a wheel break, and Arai's car caught fire. At least Solberg put in a decent performance to score a podium finish.

In Africa, Burns landed heavily after a jump, putting a shock absorber

through its top mounting; there wa little choice but to retire. Solberg ha numerous problems, but he wa determined to finish - so determined in fact, that his co-driver risked lif and limb lying on the bonnet to balanc the car after losing a wheel. It was brave gesture but of no use, as to much damage had been done.

All of the Subarus were quick i Finland, although Burns was robbe of victory by a puncture, and Solber experienced problems with his car' centre differential. Martin had bee running third until a heavy landin after one of the event's infamous yump destroyed the exhaust; a spin the delayed him further, so the youn Estonian's fifth place was a good result

George Donaldson became the ne SWRT Team Manager in time for Ne Zealand. Burns duly scored his firs win of the year from ten outings, whils Solberg, having to contend wit overheating and transmissio problems, came seventh after a goo battle with Makinen. Mention shoul be made of 'Possum' Bourne and Tosh Arai, who finished 13th and 14th respectively.

In San Remo, Burns went off on the first stage, bringing his rally to premature end. Solberg hit a rock causing suspension damage and blunting his charge somewhat. Marti was running well until he hit a wall Luckily for Burns, his main rivals in the Championship also failed to shine

Burns misinterpreted his co driver's instructions and damaged his suspension early on in Corsica, but al of the top runners seemed to experienc problems, thus keeping him in with shout. Solberg and Martin let thei teammate through from sixth to fourth while Tommi Makinen and Carlos Sain retired. This turned out to be a critica result in the title chase.

In Australia, McRae was late for meeting in Langley Park which decide starting positions, losing his choic and putting him at a distinc disadvantage before the event got unde way. Makinen, with a bad back and new co-driver following his accident in Corsica, was not on the pace, and Sainz had rear suspension trouble. Al of this and a second place played int Burns' hands, keeping him in touch with the leaders in the Drivers

2001 Rally of Argentina (Burns).

Mitsubishi, although a long way down on Peugeot (the winning marque) and Ford. Richard Burns was declared Drivers' Champion, despite winning only one event all year! Burns later said: "After the Safari rally I did think it was going to be a tough struggle for us to win the championship. Inside, I still had hope, but on the surface I knew that it was going to be difficult." He finished on 44 points, with Colin McRae getting 42 from three wins, and Tommi Makinen scoring 41, also after three victories.

In the Asia-Pacific Championship, Subaru came second, narrowly beaten by Mitsubishi. Peter Bourne's stranglehold on the APC was also

2001 Cyprus Rally (Burns).

Championship; the title would be decided in the forests of Britain.

Burns' run of luck continued on the RAC. Makinen went out early, and Colin McRae rolled into retirement. Burns, therefore, had only to come fourth to secure enough points to claim the WRC crown. Solberg and Martin both failed to finish, but their English teammate came third - good enough to become World Champion.

Subaru finished the 2001 season in fourth position, just behind

broken, but at least Mark Lovell and Subaru took the 2001 SCCA Pro-Rally Championship in America to more than make up for the disappointment.

The 2001 Tokyo Show

The Subaru Traviq - the first visible result of the tie-up with the GM empire - was launched in Japan in summer 2001. Based on the Opel Zafira (the Opel marque was also part of General Motors), this was a compact people mover that usefully expanded the Subaru line-up without the need for massive investment in fresh development costs.

With Kyoji Takenaka in the

2001 Acropolis Rally (Solberg).

2001 Tour de Corse (Solberg).
2001 RAC Rally (Arai).

2001 Rally of New Zealand (Burns).
2001 Rally of Australia (Burns).

President's office (Takeshi Tanaka became Chairman in May 2001), the Subaru stand at the 2001 Tokyo Show was quite spectacular. There were five Imprezas in all, three of which could be held up as being particularly important: a works rally car (registered X15 SRT), an STi Prodrive Style model, and the 250bhp Type Euro Sports Wagon.

The Type Euro, like the Legacy B4 Blitzen (announced in December 1999), was styled by F.A. 'Butzi' Porsche's highly respected Porsche Design concern. It was described as: "a special model in Subaru's line-up. The impression of a massive body coupled with sharp, clean lines give this version

2001 rally record

No.	Driver/Co-driver	Position	Reg. No. (Group)
Monte Carlo (19-21 January)			
5	Richard Burns/Robert Reid	dnf	X2 SRT (Gp.A)
6	Markko Martin/Michael Park	dnf	X3 SRT (Gp.A)
18	Petter Solberg/Philip Mills	dnf	X1 SRT (Gp.A)
Sweden (9-11 February)			
6	Petter Solberg/Philip Mills	6th	X5 SRT (Gp.A)
18	Markko Martin/Michael Park	12th	X3 SRT (Gp.A)
5	Richard Burns/Robert Reid	16th	X2 SRT (Gp.A)
Portugal (8-11 March)			
5	Richard Burns/Robert Reid	4th	X4 SRT (Gp.A)
6	Petter Solberg/Philip Mills	dnf	X6 SRT (Gp.A)
18	Markko Martin/Michael Park	dnf	X3 SRT (Gp.A)
19	Toshihiro Arai/Glenn MacNeall	dnf	X2 SRT (Gp.A)
Spain (23-25 March)			
5	Richard Burns/Robert Reid	7th	X7 SRT (Gp.A)
6	Petter Solberg/Philip Mills	dnf	X1 SRT (Gp.A)
18	Markko Martin/Michael Park	dnf	X8 SRT (Gp.A)
Argentina (3-6 May)			
5	Richard Burns/Robert Reid	2nd	X4 SRT (Gp.A)
6	Petter Solberg/Philip Mills	5th	X6 SRT (Gp.A)
18	Toshihiro Arai/Glenn MacNeall	8th	X3 SRT (Gp.A)
Cyprus (1-3 June)			
5	Richard Burns/Robert Reid	2nd	X9 SRT (Gp.A)
18	Toshihiro Arai/Glenn MacNeall	4th	X1 SRT (Gp.A)
6	Petter Solberg/Philip Mills	dnf	X11 SRT (Gp.A)
Acropolis (15-17 June)			
6	Petter Solberg/Philip Mills	2nd	X10 SRT (Gp.A)
5	Richard Burns/Robert Reid	dnf	X7 SRT (Gp.A)
18	Markko Martin/Michael Park	dnf	X4 SRT (Gp.A)
20	Toshihiro Arai/Glenn MacNeall	dnf	X30 SRT (Gp.A)
Safari (19-22 July)			
5	Richard Burns/Robert Reid	dnf	X9 SRT (Gp.A)
6	Petter Solberg/Philip Mills	dnf	X1 SRT (Gp.A)
19	Toshihiro Arai/Glenn MacNeall	dnf	X5 SRT (Gp.A)
1000 Lakes (24-26 August)			
5	Richard Burns/Robert Reid	2nd	X12 SRT (Gp.A)
18	Markko Martin/Michael Park	5th	X14 SRT (Gp.A)
6	Petter Solberg/Philip Mills	7th	X10 SRT (Gp.A)
New Zealand (21-23 September)			
5	Richard Burns/Robert Reid	1st	X7 SRT (Gp.A)
6	Petter Solberg/Philip Mills	7th	X16 SRT (Gp.A)
18	Toshihiro Arai/Glenn MacNeall	14th	X9 SRT (Gp.A)
San Remo (5-7 October)			
6	Petter Solberg/Philip Mills	9th	X17 SRT (Gp.A)
5	Richard Burns/Robert Reid	dnf	X15 SRT (Gp.A)
18	Markko Martin/Michael Park	dnf	X19 SRT (Gp.A)
19	Toshihiro Arai/Glenn MacNeall	dnf	X1 SRT (Gp.A)

continued ...

The works rally car positioned at the entrance of the impressive Subaru stand at the 2001 Tokyo Show. Concept vehicles displayed at the event included the WX-01 and HM-01.

The Type Euro photographed by the author at the 2001 Tokyo Show.

Advertising for the 2002 model year Impreza I's Sport. It may look like a copy of Renault's 'Size Matters' campaign, but, in fact, the lady is saying that she wants a roomy yet easy to manoeuvre car - the Impreza fits the bill.

No.	Driver/Co-driver	Position	Reg. No. (Group)
Tour de Corse (19-21 October)			
5	Richard Burns/Robert Reid	4th	X20 SRT (Gp.A)
6	Petter Solberg/Philip Mills	5th	X17 SRT (Gp.A)
18	Markko Martin/Michael Park	6th	X16 SRT (Gp.A)
24	Toshihiro Arai/Glenn MacNeall	dnf	X1 SRT (Gp.A)
Australia (2-4 November)			
5	Richard Burns/Robert Reid	2nd	X12 SRT (Gp.A)
6	Petter Solberg/Philip Mills	7th	X21 SRT (Gp.A)
18	Toshihiro Arai/Glenn MacNeall	dnf	X8 SRT (Gp.A)
RAC (22-25 November)			
5	Richard Burns/Robert Reid	3rd	X20 SRT (Gp.A)
21	Toshihiro Arai/Tony Sircombe	10th	X1 SRT (Gp.A)
6	Petter Solberg/Philip Mills	dnf	X17 SRT (Gp.A)
18	Markko Martin/Michael Park	dnf	X10 SRT (Gp.A)

This STi Prodrive Style prototype, photographed at the 2001 Tokyo Auto Salon in January, would find its way into production eight months later.

of the Impreza a sportier appearance, and suggests the car has been sculpted from a huge block of aluminium. The unique, metallic silver body finish emphasizes the luster of the metal."

Meanwhile, the Type B revisions for the Impreza had taken effect in September 2001, bringing with them a modified front mask with a deeper air intake; combined with the existing mesh grille, it gave the car a sportier look. A black, six-star Subaru badge now sat in the centre, with STi models having a discreet STi emblem to the right, one on the tail (by the bootlid lock), and different coloured stickers on the foglight covers.

However, without doubt, one of the biggest improvements was to use dark glass on the HID headlight option, while the standard lights (on all but the basic I's grade) were made to look like the HID units. There was also a matt black cover available to give this most controversial styling element a WRC car look.

In addition, the I's Sport acquired an attractive Astral Yellow paint job (Midnight Black Mica was added to the colour palette a couple of months later), 15-inch wheels and tyres, and a glass inlayed aerial and maplights. All two-litre cars inherited an illuminated ignition barrel, UV-cut side glass, and the option of an electric tilt-and-slide sunroof.

Mechanical changes included modifications for the intake system, combustion chambers, pistons and ignition system on the two-litre NA engine: all non-STi engines received new piston rings to reduce internal friction. The automatic gearbox for the turbocharged models was improved at the same time, giving better fuel economy in heavy traffic, allowing the driver quicker getaways from standstill, and giving smoother shifts once on the move (the final drive ratio on the two-pedal WRX NB was changed to 4.44:1 at the same time). The front crossmember and suspension mounting points were made stronger, while all two-litre cars had EBD to go with the ABS system (with the WRX STi coming with EBD and Super Sports ABS).

While the two-litre range remained the same price as the previous season, the I's was substantially cheaper, the front-wheel drive I's Sport was a lot more expensive, and the four-wheel drive I's Sport just a little more. The WRX could now be painted in either Pure White, Premium Silver Metallic, or WR Blue; the NA also had the option of Gran Blue Mica, and the turbocharged NB offered additional Shiny Red Mica and Midnight Black Mica finishes.

As for the STi cars, the saloon was only 2,895,000 yen now, with the estate commanding 2,720,000 yen; paint and trim options were carried over. The STi

Brochure for the STi Prodrive Style model.

IMPREZA
WRX
& STi WRX/Sports Wagon

WRX STi type RA spec C デビュー SUBARU

IMPREZA
STi
WRX&Sports Wagon

コンペティション・フィールドの頂点へ。
WRX STi type RA spec C 誕生。

戦うように、スポーツしよう。

IMPREZA
STi
WRX

Selected pages from the Japanese 2002 model year catalogue (and pages 150/151).

made its official debut, although sales didn't start until just before the Motor Show. First seen at the Tokyo Auto Salon earlier in the year as a concept vehicle, the show car had full bucket seats and a rather striking paint scheme, not carried over to the

Competition Spec of RA spec C

Type RA, however, was dropped from the line-up for the time being; some say because the Lancer Evolution VII RS was so much quicker around corners that it was embarrassing. But, thanks to the vision of STi President, Masaru Katsurada, plans were already in place for a more potent successor.

On 12 September, two days after the Type B revisions were announced, the WRX STi Prodrive Style Impreza

151

FIGHTING BOXER

筆でしなきポテンシャル。

Competition Spec of **RA**_spec_**-C**

SUBARU MADE 6MT

速さのために、強い6速MT。

Competition Spec of **RA**_spec_**-C**

POWER BODY

マイスターのボディ。

Competition Spec of **R**

ULTIMATE STRUT

ストラットの可能性。

Competition Spec of **RA**_spec_**-C**

brembo+α

ブレンボであること以上の誇り。

COCKPIT & EQUIPMENT

スポーツするためのコックピット。

WRX STi

BODY COLOR

Sports Wagon STi

BODY COLOR

WRX STi type RA spec-C

BODY COLOR

The WRX NB-R: a rather attractive package for enthusiasts.

production models, but it was certainly a nice package for the enthusiast.

The Prodrive Style model featured a number of parts developed jointly between STi and Prodrive in the UK. Compared with the WRX STi it was based on, the main differences were a new front bumper and grille, revised side skirts and a tall rear spoiler (incorporating a high mount rear stoplight), a roof vent, and blue-faced gauges with red pointers. Priced at 3,145,000 yen, it was available in WR Blue Mica or Pure White.

Subaru's answer to the 'LanEvo' - the WRX STi Type RA Spec C - went on sale on 10 December 2001. The main objective with this model was to reduce weight whilst increasing power and fine tuning the chassis. No less than 90kg (nearly 200lb) was shed via deletion of the front subframe, insulation material around the transmission tunnel, both airbags (a Momo three-spoke steering wheel was fitted, combined with a 13:1 rack), the seatbelt pre-tensioners, ISO-FIX anchors, lightening of the driver's seat, and getting rid of the luggage compartment trim and high mount stoplight.

In addition, thinner gauge metal was used on the roof and bootlid, window glass thickness was reduced, and the smaller, 50 litre (11 gallon) fuel tank adopted; the wash/wipe reservoir was also changed, although the

intercooler water spray tank was relocated to the boot (for better weight distribution) and made three times bigger in the process. Other weight reducing measures included a modified front bumper and steering beam, plus revised door beams and mountings for the rear mechanical limited-slip differential.

On the engine front, the ECU, turbocharger (an IHI RHF5HB blower was adopted, the same as that used on the legendary 22B), cylinders and intake manifold all received attention; valve lift was increased, and valve timing revised. The end result was that the Spec C had sharper response and 283lbft of torque at 4400rpm

(maximum power remained the same due to the Japanese voluntary 280bhp limit). Although reducing weight was the key, a transmission oil cooler was added as part of the package.

Finishing touches included revised suspension geometry to make the car react quicker to driver input: the front caster angle was changed to keep more rubber (new Potenza RE070s in the case of the 17-inch wheel and tyre combination) on the road during hard cornering, the front mounts on the rear trailing arms were raised, rear anti-roll bar bushes were hardened, a performance rod was added to locate the lower A-arms, and the front crossmember mounting points strengthened. In addition, different spring rates were adopted and the car was lowered by 10mm (0.39in.). In effect, it was quite a significant re-evaluation of the vehicle's chassis.

Again, a 16- or 17-inch wheel version was listed, the former (priced at 2,713,000 yen) having steel rims and a driver-controlled centre diff, while the 2,953,000 yen 17-inch model had forged 7.5J BBS rims (ten-spoke items) and the uprated Brembo braking system. Both cars were available in white only.

Before the year came to an end, Subaru introduced the WRX NB-R and the I's Select II. Although the latter was basically an I's estate with a CD player, keyless entry and power mirrors, the NB-R was far more significant. Based on the WRX NB, it featured an uprated suspension with inverted dampers, STi-spec brakes, 17-inch STi five-spoke alloys (but painted silver rather than gold), a bigger rear spoiler, foglight

Front, rear and interior of the German spec WRX STi for 2002.

covers (foglights could be fitted as a dealer option), special black trim and an aluminium pedal set. Available in white, silver, black or WR Blue Mica, the five-speed version cost 2,453,000 yen.

The Type Euro station wagon eventually made it into dealerships in late January 2002. There was a 1.5 litre Type Euro 15, a normally-aspirated, two-litre Type Euro 20, and a turbocharged Type Euro Turbo, with prices ranging from 2,028,000 to 2,816,000 yen. The special coachwork could be specified in either Premium Silver Metallic or Midnight Black Mica.

Europe 2002

Naturally, the detail changes applied to home market cars following the Type B revisions filtered through to export markets, but the big news for the

European 2002 season was the arrival of the 265 PS (261bhp) STi models. The WRX STi was announced at the 2001 Frankfurt Show on 11 September, and was scheduled to hit UK showrooms the following January.

The vehicle's arrival was keenly awaited in Britain. As *Auto Express* noted: "The excitement that surrounds the launch of this road-going edition of the car that recently took Richard Burns to his first World Rally Championship title is understandable. Exclusivity is guaranteed, as well, because only two versions of the newcomer will be available: an entry level Type UK priced at £25,995, and the dramatic-looking £27,495 Prodrive edition."

Naturally, the specification of the STi was very close to that of the standard home market version, with gold 7.5J x 17, five-spoke alloys shod with 225/45 Bridgestone RE040 rubber concealing large diameter Brembo brakes, an uprated suspension (including the heavier but stronger inverted damper arrangement), faster steering rack, and Suretrac differentials front and rear. The six-speed gearbox was also a feature, although the ratios on fifth and sixth were different to those specified in Japan: 0.971 and 0.756.

While the run-of-the-mill STi had smoked glass projector beam headlights and a larger air intake as styling features, the Prodrive version also had a deeper front bumper and unique grille, and different spoilers in addition to these features. Both cars came with a single big bore exhaust, better rust-proofing (the English custom of spreading salt on winter roads is not one the Japanese emulate), and an alarm/immobilizer and satellite tracking system in an attempt to deter thieves.

Inside was the familiar black and blue trim, with STi logos on the seats, and red stitching on the steering wheel, gearknob and handbrake lever. There was also the intercooler spray and warning light for when a preset rev limit was reached. The STi cars also adopted the central tachometer, with the Prodrive models getting blue-faced gauges with red needles.

Listed with 261bhp at 6000rpm and 253lbft of torque (at 4000rpm), the STi was available in WR Blue Mica, Blue-Black Mica, Premium Silver Metallic or Pure White, while the Prodrive car was listed in the two darker shades only.

The *Autocar* found that: "far from being a no-compromise tarmac-tearer, the STi is a superb all-rounder with no grave deficiencies and many laudable strengths. It is a better car than the standard WRX Impreza, even taking price into account.

"As for the Evo VII, there's not a road tester among us who'd not rather drive the extraordinary Mitsubishi. But to buy and live with, year after year? As an only car, it would have to be the cheaper, more pragmatic and effective Subaru."

Testing the WRX STi Prodrive Style, *Auto Express* observed: "When you fire up the turbocharged two-litre engine, a deep growl from the exhaust washes through the Alcantara-trimmed cabin. Around 80 per cent of the engine is all-new, and, as a result, the note is more aggressive than the standard model's. In fact, it seems to boast about its 261bhp potential.

"Against the clock, the STi leaps from 0-60 in only 5.2 seconds, hitting a top speed of 148mph [237kph]. That's impressive when you consider the STi has put on more than 100kg [220lb] of weight. This is because of the all-new manual transmission and reinforced crash protection.

"And we can't help feeling that some of those extra kilogrammes are the result of an effort to make the Impreza more refined. Although we noticed greater road noise from the tyres and suspension, few other machines can match the STi's devastating cross-country pace. We suggest no other car can do it with such incredible ease ... the STi is an incredibly exciting driver's car."

Nine months after the STi's launch, Subaru UK stated: "The 'Type-UK' WRX STi and STi Prodrive Style have been a tremendous success, accounting for more than 30 per cent of Impreza sales. All 750 Prodrive Style models are sold and order books are still strong for the standard STi."

Apart from the introduction of the manual only STi models, everything remained much the same in the UK (including prices). In fact, apart from the opening of Subaru Europe (with offices in Belgium and Germany), it wasn't until the summer of 2002 that the next significant event occurred.

Australian update

The Australians gained another new grade for the 2002 model year, the $32,990 2.5 litre RS saloon. With a 99.5 x 79mm bore and stroke, plus a 10:1 compression ratio, the flat-four gave 153bhp at 5600rpm, and 164lbft of torque at 3600rpm. Slightly less than the American spec engine was developing, but still enough to propel the manual saloon from 0-60 in 9.5 seconds. (Automatic transmission was available for an extra $1950.)

The RS had 205/55 VR16s on silver five-spoke alloys, ABS with vented/solid discs and EBD (the latter now fitted to all Aussie Imprezas), aluminium lower A-arms, and a power steering oil cooler. With foglights, bucket seats, a Momo leather steering wheel, a radio/CD unit in the metallic-finished centre console (with screen integrated aerial), cruise control, air conditioning and central locking, it was a nice package.

Wheels compared the new 2457cc sedan with the Holden Astra SRi and declared: "If driving fun tops your agenda, and cost isn't the absolute bottom line, then the Impreza has the Astra beat. The RS reinforces Subaru's sporting focus with excellent dynamics, fine steering and comfort, strong brakes, and a user-friendliness that makes its talents more readily accessible. Judging by current trends, it should have better resale than the Astra, too.

"So instead of some indifferent parts bin special, it turns out the Impreza RS is a bit of a charmer. And a fine drive. All for a fraction of the insurance cost of a Rex. Tell that to your broker."

As for the other models in the normally-aspirated range, prices and specifications were very similar, with manual cars only $20 more than before, and automatics $100 up on the previous season, a small price to pay for the various enhancements and additional safety measures applied to the latest cars.

The WRX (voted 'Best Sports Car' by the NRMA and six other leading motoring organizations in the Antipodes) was actually cheaper, and now available in automatic guise, too: the five-speed sedan was $41,490, while the five-door version was $41,940; choosing the two-pedal option added $1950 to both.

Australia's 2002 model year Impreza RS.

available for the Impreza during spring 2002, and *Motor* Australia voted the WRX STi winner of the 'Bang for you Bucks' contest later in the year; the Impreza had won the title in 1998 and 1999.

Shades of the past

While the S201 marked the end of the last generation, the S202 signalled the premature end of the current cars. Even though it wasn't announced in that way, it suggested something ominous on the horizon. With a number of rumours flying left, right and centre, Kiyoshi Sugimoto taking over as design boss, and ex-Pininfarina and Alfa Romeo

The WRX STi sedan was added to the Australian line-up in December 2001.

The Australians now had a very extensive line-up, and another grade was about to join the range. Having made its debut at the 2001 Sydney Show alongside the automatic WRX, the WRX STi saloon was eventually listed as a catalogue model in December. It certainly caught public imagination, prompting STi Australia to put on a special display at the 2002 Sydney Show.

Meanwhile, the STi was launched at $55,130, and featured all the performance goodies one would expect on a car bearing the hallowed pink insignia: a larger intercooler with water spray, a six-speed gearbox, Suretrac differential at both ends (with a larger R180 unit at the rear in place of the R160 used on the strict WRX model), an uprated suspension with inverted struts, and Brembo brakes (the same massive 326mm, 12.8in., diameter discs with four-pot calipers up front as home market machines, with 10mm, or 0.39in., smaller vented discs and two-pot calipers at the back), as well as a number of luxuries such as a six-speaker stereo and cruise control. Details like the red stitching on the Momo wheel, gearknob and handbrake trim, STi badging on the central tachometer, seats, intercooler, big bore exhaust, and a gold finish for the 17-inch, five-spoke alloys, were also carried over.

The STi, listed with 265bhp at 6000rpm, 253lbft of torque (developed at 4000rpm), and the same gearing as the Japanese six-speed models, was available in WR Blue Mica, Pure White, Blue-Black Mica and Premium Silver Metallic. Trim was predominantly black with the familiar blue and black seats.

February saw the launch of the manual only WRX Club Spec Evo 5, easily distinguished by its orange paintwork, electric sunroof, a top stereo system, and special badging (including a numbered plaque on the console). Just 140 saloons were made available, priced at $43,180 apiece, along with 60 $43,630 estates (the exchange rate was around 70 yen to the Aussie dollar at this time, by the way).

A number of body kits became

man, Andreas Zapatinas, joining the company as Chief Designer a month earlier, a lot of people started putting two and two together. Peter Lyon revealed in *Auto Express* that he'd had confirmation as early as May that a facelifted Impreza was on the cards ...

Meanwhile, the WRX STi Type RA Spec C-based S202 made its debut on 7 May, with sales starting from 3 June 2002. The S202 had a highly tuned engine and a modified ECU, silicone intake ducting, a special exhaust system (with reduced back pressure and using titanium in places to save around 5kg, or 11lb, in weight), and an aluminium oil cooler mounted behind the front number plate.

All told, whilst retaining the 8.0:1 c/r of the standard car, it added up to

Brochure for the S202 launched in Japan midway through 2002.

A couple of shots of the WRX STi Limited from mid-2002.

320bhp at 6400rpm - amazing output for a two-litre road car - and 283lbft of torque at 4400rpm, with better performance at the top end of the rev-band.

To keep the machine in check, the S202 came with pillow ball suspension links at the rear, lightweight grooved brake discs and stainless mesh brake hoses, and forged 17-inch RAYS alloys (gold, with ten spokes and shod with Pirelli P Zero Rosso tyres).

As for the bodywork, there were projector headlights, a carbonfibre rear wing, foglamp covers (the Type RA Spec C had gaping holes where the lights should be) and 'S202' emblems at the front and rear, while the inside featured black seats with the STi logo, special door trim and centre console finish, an aluminium pedal set, blue-faced gauges and the ubiquitous numbered plaque.

Limited to 400 units, the S202 came with air conditioning, power windows and central locking, and was priced at 3,600,000 yen. The promotional paperwork always featured the car in Astral Yellow, but it was also possible to order one in Pure White, WR Blue Mica or Midnight Black Mica.

All 400 S202s sold out in just two weeks, but *Road & Track*'s Sam Mitani was lucky enough to sample one. He said: "As soon as you step on the throttle, all four tyres bite the tarmac, squirting the car forward. When the revs reach 3000, the car finds its true stride, surging forward with alacrity, slamming your torso into the seatback.

"The understeering character of the stock WRX has been all but eliminated. The steering is razor sharp, and the car remains neutral through virtually all types of turns. Stickier tyres also account for the car's excellent cornering ability."

A couple of other special editions were launched at this time to coincide with Subaru's 30 year association with four-wheel drive. The I's Sport Limited featured colour-keyed side skirts, foglamps, exhaust trim, a top six-speaker stereo, dark tinted glass and a few other unique details, but it was the WRX STi Limited saloon that raised a few eyebrows.

The 2,995,000 yen STi Limited had a tuned ECU (keeping power at 280bhp but boosting torque up to 283lbft), a mechanical rear lsd, an STi front lip spoiler and a larger rear spoiler. Available in Pure White, Premium Silver Metallic, WR Blue Mica or Midnight Black Mica, the six-speed Limited saloon was probably a much more practical proposition than the S202 if one of the last third generation vehicles was wanted. Yes, although there was no restriction on numbers for the series, time was running out for the machine in its original form, hence the 'Limited' moniker.

American news
The American Insurance Institute for Highway Safety rewarded Subaru engineers with the top rating for small cars. *Automobile* magazine had voted the WRX its 'Automobile of the Year' for 2001, and it was listed in the *Car & Driver* 'Top Ten' of 2002.

As one would expect, apart from the details introduced via the Type B revisions, little changed for the 2002 model year, as the latest Impreza was still a new machine. However, the WRX was given the option of a fresh set of alloy wheels - 7J x 17 BBS multi-spoke items shod with sticky Bridgestone rubber. Although this wheel and tyre combination cost over $3000, it certainly gave the car a more purposeful look. With the facelifted model on the way, things remained the same throughout the season.

By the same token, with the new Impreza on the horizon, the 2003 models were also very similar, although the WRX had the very latest four-spoke Momo steering wheel with a black centre badge (US cars had a yellow arrow, however, as opposed to a red one for the facelifted machines sold on the home market).

For 2003, the RS was available in Aspen White, Blue Ridge Pearl, Midnight Black Pearl and Platinum Silver Metallic, while the WRX came in the white, black and silver shades plus Sedona Red Pearl, WR Blue Pearl and Sonic Yellow; trim was in black cloth, whatever the coachwork colour.

The 2002 rally season
Although the WRC2001 models were used on a number of occasions, the WRC2002 car had a revised exhaust manifold to give better response in the 4000 to 5000rpm sector of the tachometer (the revs most commonly used in the heat of competition), and minor changes for the throttle body and turbocharger; in addition, the transmission was strengthened and gear ratios revised. The lip splitter on the front bumper was made in rubber instead of carbonfibre (to limit damage) and the anti-roll bar mountings were revised in order to reduce friction.

Official specifications recorded a maximum power output of 300bhp (along with 347lbft of torque at 4000rpm), driven through a Prodrive six-speed gearbox. Braking was via Alcon-Prodrive discs, with four-pot calipers up front (uprated to water-cooled, six-pot items for faster tarmac events); the magnesium alloy wheels were sourced from OZ, shod with Pirelli tyres. Interestingly, 2002 saw the return of 555 sponsorship.

Richard Burns moved to Peugeot for 2002 and was replaced by one of the great all-rounders of the sport - multiple World Champion, Tommi Makinen. Makinen, the 37 year old Flying Finn who started rallying in top class events in 1987, had been with Mitsubishi for a number of years before his move to Subaru. For 2002, Makinen was ably supported by Petter Solberg, who'd proved his worth with the Japanese team the previous season.

The Impreza was voted America's safest small car in 2002.

The WRX certainly took the States by storm. Interestingly, unlike the Europeans and Japanese, the Americans actually gave the Impreza's controversial styling the thumbs up. Many, such as Road & Track's Sam Mitani, were more than happy with the design and, looking forward to the Paris Show, was quick to question the logic of making such dramatic changes in such a short space of time.

The US specification Outback Sport for the 2002 model year.

2002 rally record

As is traditional, the 2002 season kicked off with the Monte Carlo Rally. 55 cars made the start, and, while Solberg claimed fastest time on the third stage, Makinen's consistency resulted in him being the top Subaru driver at the end of the first day (lying second overall). The terrific battle between the Finn and Citroen's

Sebastien Loeb continued on day two, although it was Solberg who was quickest on the final day of competition. However, with Loeb picking up a two minute penalty for changing tyres in an unauthorized area, the victor's spoils went to Makinen on his Subaru debut.

Conditions were difficult in Sweden, with rain falling on frozen snow. Makinen hit a snow bank with the upshot being a blocked radiator that caused overheating and an early retirement. Solberg was sixth at the end of day one, but his engine gave way on SS6 in the following leg, and that was the end of Subaru's challenge.

Both Subaru drivers were fast in Corsica. The changeable weather of day two played into their hands in the early stages, too, but then Makinen aquaplaned off the road and damaged

An Impreza WRX blurring the American countryside.

American advertising from early 2003.

his suspension; he retired straight after. Solberg had been fourth, but punctures ended his charge, and he finished the second day in seventh. However, it's the place at the end of the final leg that really counts, and here, Solberg did not disappoint, claiming fifth and two points.

With Gronholm leading the

Petter Solberg - SWRT's new hero.

Subaru's in-house newspaper featuring Tommi Makinen on the Monte.

Tommi Makinen in the heat of the action, as always.

2002 Cyprus Rally (Makinen).

2002 Tour de Corse (Solberg).

2002 Rally of Argentina (Solberg).

2002 Safari Rally (Makinen).

2002 1000 Lakes Rally (Solberg).

2002 San Remo Rally (Solberg).

Drivers' Championship by eight points, Makinen was joint second on ten, while Solberg, on three, was ninth in the title chase. Of the makers, Peugeot was ahead by a long way, with Ford second and Subaru just four behind the British team in third; Mitsubishi was fourth with its new WRCar.

Having gained a lot of experience in Corsica, the 555 SWRT was confident of a good showing in Spain. However, brake problems slowed Petter, while Tommi overcame gearbox trouble only to go off the road into a ditch. The Finn continued, but naturally lost a lot of time after this excursion and the damaged radiator he picked up cooked the engine. Solberg was the only man to seriously challenge the Peugeots and Citroens, and was rewarded with another two points for his efforts.

A minor mechanical problem cost Solberg three minutes on the opening day in Cyprus, but both Subarus recorded fastest stage times in an event initially dominated by Ford rather than Peugeot. Solberg set a storming pace on day two, although it was Makinen who shone on the last day, claiming a well-deserved podium finish; Subaru's Norwegian driver came fifth - a fine result considering his earlier troubles.

It was Peugeot versus Subaru in Argentina, with Tommi holding second and Petter fourth at the end of the first leg. Covering the same stages on day two, Makinen (who'd won the event in 1996, 1997 and 1998) pulled ahead, only to crash out when the finish and certain victory was in sight; he'd pushed just that bit too hard and suffered the consequences. Meanwhile, Solberg, who had been suffering with stomach pain for most of the trip to South America, inherited second place after Gronholm and Burns (Peugeot) were excluded; Arai came eleventh (second in Group N).

Back to Europe and Athens. Makinen went out early after colliding with a rock; to say that he was fed up with his run of bad luck would be a major understatement! Ironically, with Solberg struggling, it was Toshi Arai in another SWRT car (his first works Group A drive of the season) that led the Subaru challenge at the end of day one. Solberg moved up the field on the second day and continued to fight until the chequered flag, claiming more points for himself and the team along the way.

2002 rally record

No.	Driver/Co-driver	Position	Reg. No. (Group)
Monte Carlo (17-20 January)			
10	Tommi Makinen/Kaj Lindstrom	1st	X28 SRT (Gp.A)
11	Petter Solberg/Phil Mills	6th	X23 SRT (Gp.A)
Sweden (1-3 February)			
11	Petter Solberg/Phil Mills	dnf	X24 SRT (Gp.A)
10	Tommi Makinen/Kaj Lindstrom	dnf	X21 SRT (Gp.A)
Tour de Corse (8-10 March)			
11	Petter Solberg/Phil Mills	5th	X26 SRT (Gp.A)
10	Tommi Makinen/Kaj Lindstrom	dnf	TM02 SRT (Gp.A)
Spain (21-24 March)			
11	Petter Solberg/Phil Mills	5th	X26 SRT (Gp.A)
10	Tommi Makinen/Kaj Lindstrom	dnf	X28 SRT (Gp.A)
Cyprus (19-21 April)			
10	Tommi Makinen/Kaj Lindstrom	3rd	X27 SRT (Gp.A)
11	Petter Solberg/Phil Mills	5th	PT02 SRT (Gp.A)
Argentina (16-19 May)			
11	Petter Solberg/Phil Mills	2nd	X26 SRT (Gp.A)
10	Tommi Makinen/Kaj Lindstrom	dnf	X28 SRT (Gp.A)
Acropolis (13-16 June)			
11	Petter Solberg/Phil Mills	5th	PS02 SRT (Gp.A)
12	Toshihiro Arai/Tony Sircombe	13th	X12 SRT (Gp.A)
10	Tommi Makinen/Kaj Lindstrom	dnf	X21 SRT (Gp.A)
Safari (12-14 July)			
10	Tommi Makinen/Kaj Lindstrom	dnf	X27 SRT (Gp.A)
11	Petter Solberg/Phil Mills	dnf	PS02 SRT (Gp.A)
1000 Lakes (8-11 August)			
11	Petter Solberg/Phil Mills	3rd	X26 SRT (Gp.A)
10	Tommi Makinen/Kaj Lindstrom	6th	TM02 SSS (Gp.A)
Rallye Deutschland (22-25 August)			
10	Tommi Makinen/Kaj Lindstrom	7th	PR02 SRT (Gp.A)
11	Petter Solberg/Phil Mills	dnf	PS02 SSS (Gp.A)
12	Achim Mortl/Klaus Wicha	dnf	X2 SRT (Gp.A)
26	Toshihiro Arai/Tony Sircombe	dnf	X23 SRT (Gp.A)
San Remo (19-22 September)			
11	Petter Solberg/Phil Mills	3rd	PS02 SRT (Gp.A)
12	Achim Mortl/Klaus Wicha	dnf	PS02 SSS (Gp.A)
10	Tommi Makinen/Kaj Lindstrom	dnf	PR02 SRT (Gp.A)
New Zealand (3-6 October)			
10	Tommi Makinen/Kaj Lindstrom	3rd	X27 SRT (Gp.A)
11	Petter Solberg/Phil Mills	dnf	TM02 SRT (Gp.A)
Australia (31 October-3 November)			
11	Petter Solberg/Phil Mills	3rd	PS02 SRT (Gp.A)
10	Tommi Makinen/Kaj Lindstrom	exc	PR02 SRT (Gp.A)
RAC (14-17 November)			
11	Petter Solberg/Phil Mills	1st	X9 SRT (Gp.A)
10	Tommi Makinen/Kaj Lindstrom	4th	TM02 SSS (Gp.A)

2002 RAC Rally (Solberg).

A piece of national advertising released following Solberg's epic victory on the 2002 Rally of Great Britain.

2002 Rally of New Zealand (Makinen).

Makinen, eager to prove a point, led the classic Safari Rally from start to finish on the first day, but suspension problems delayed him before he retired on day two. Solberg had turbo problems early in the event, and was unable to continue after his engine stopped completely on CS4. Subaru stalwarts, Arai and Dor, were also forced out.

Tommi was not on form in his native Finland, lying eighth after the first day, four places down on Solberg and almost two minutes adrift of the leading Peugeot. Solberg dropped back slightly on the second day, but fought back to overhaul Sainz (Ford) and take a podium finish after Colin McRae's retirement; Makinen scored a point despite what - for him - was a disappointing performance.

The next round was the Rallye Deutschland, a new event on the WRC calendar. Petter Solberg was running well on the first day until power steering and driveshaft maladies dropped him down the field. Makinen was slowed by a broken handbrake picked up on SS1. Austrian, Achim Mortl, given a works car, lost a wheel on the same stage, but limped on until an accident on the second day; Arai went out early with a broken gearbox. Solberg retired on day two after hitting a rock, and, to add to the misery, Makinen finished outside the points.

Makinen was forced out of San Remo early with a broken front driveshaft, but Subaru's Norwegian driver continued to race hard, moving up to third by the end of day two - the position he finished in, claiming his first trophy on a tarmac event and consolidating his sixth place in the Drivers' Championship. (Makinen was ninth at this point in the season, with Subaru a comfortable third.)

The WRC circus moved to the Antipodes next, to the fast gravel of New Zealand. The Peugeots were incredibly fast once again, but Makinen finished the first day in fourth; split by a surprise performance from Mitsubishi's Jani Paasonen; Solberg (who nearly went over a cliff!) was sixth at this stage. Tommi remained in fourth at the end of day two, but Petter moved ahead of the Finn, despite hitting a postbox on SS11. Unfortunately, Solberg's charge came to an end on the penultimate stage when his engine expired. At least Makinen continued to claim a podium finish, and 'Possum'

Bourne took Group N honours.

Across the water in Australia there was good and bad news. Solberg had been quick throughout the event, finishing day one in second place, and maintaining that position after the second leg came to an end. However, a lack of grip on day three saw him drop to third at the end. Makinen was

running well, holding fifth going into the final leg despite incurring a jump-start penalty on SS15. He ultimately finished fourth, but was later excluded as his car was deemed underweight: it was a bitter blow.

Going into the RAC, mathematically at least, it was still possible for Petter Solberg to claim

Toshi Arai won the Japanese Alpine Rally in 2001 (with X8 SRT) and again in 2002, as this advert states. Driving X12 SRT on this occasion, Possum Bourne came second to make it a Subaru one-two. There are hopes that the rally can become a round of the APC in the near future, perhaps leading to inclusion in the WRC calendar. Note the new WRC2003 rally car.

Kazuo Ogawa: the man who headed the 2003 model year facelift project.

second place in the Drivers' Championship (although lying in seventh, he was only seven points behind Richard Burns - Marcus Gronholm had already claimed the title). Day one saw Solberg in second place, less than a minute behind Gronholm, but crucially only three seconds ahead of Martin in the Ford; Makinen lost time with a spin early on, but stayed in touch in sixth. While Gronholm rolled out of the event on the second day and Solberg won a few stages, it was Martin who ended the second leg in front, albeit by just 1.6 seconds! Solberg did not disappoint SWRT fans, however, taking the chequered flag and a well-deserved second in the World Championship.

At the end of the 2002 season, the Subaru team finished third, behind Champions Peugeot and second-placed Ford. As for the SWRT drivers, Solberg claimed second, and Makinen eighth; a disappointing result for someone of his calibre, but, given better familiarity with his crew and a new car on its way, next year should be better. Interestingly, Toshi Arai came fourth in the Group N Production Car Championship, just one point off third.

In the Asia-Pacific Championship, 'Possum Bourne' won the Hokkaido Rally (the first APC round ever to be held in Japan), but it was a disappointing year for Subaru in reality. In America, however, Impreza driver, David Higgins, took the SCCA Pro-Rally title after ten rounds, with Mark Lovell claiming third; Subaru came second in the manufacturer's title chase, just a few points down on Hyundai.

The 2002 Paris Show

The Paris Salon saw the world debut of what could be classed the fourth generation Impreza. In a press release issued with a 26 September embargo date, it was stated that "Subaru's strikingly restyled Impreza" would go on sale in the UK during February 2003.

Developed under body specialist, Kazuo Ogawa, (who joined Subaru in 1979, becoming Impreza chief in spring 2001), the "new-look Impreza boasted a totally different front-end that combined an aggressive presence with pedestrian-friendly safety features and aerodynamic efficiency." According to the promotional paperwork handed out at the event, key features for European models included:

- Aggressive, yet more aerodynamic, new front styling.
- Bumper, bonnet, wings and headlamps all new.
- Power boost for WRX - now 225 PS.

- Stronger throttle response for WRX.
- Improved engine cooling for 265 PS STi.
- Revised dampers for most models give even better handling.
- STi gained more rigid front suspension, sharper steering.
- Interior quality upgrade - new cloth trim, revised centre console.
- Safety boost includes active front head restraints, ISO-FIX rear child seat mounts, impact absorbing brake pedal and pedestrian-friendly wipers and bonnet.

Styled for a reason
The facelift is shared with the 2003 World Rally Car, which benefits from a similar reduction in drag coefficient and improved high speed stability.

Unlike some WRC competitors, Subaru has always striven to ensure its road cars inherit the technical and design DNA of its rally machines. Key design changes include a new front bumper, spoiler, bonnet, wings and three-dimensional headlamps. In addition, circular lamps are inlaid in the main headlamp units, which have a striking curved dip to the inner edges.

A strong, flowing character-line sweeps from the lower edge of the circular headlamps and runs over the more steeply sloping bonnet to the windscreen. The top edge of the bumper is rounded, giving a sleeker look with improved airflow.

Early publicity photograph of the 2003 WRX saloon issued at the Paris Salon.

Another view of the WRX, this time in sedan and estate guises (Japan also got a WRX Sports Wagon following the facelift). The drag coefficient was 0.33 for all saloons, 0.34 for the basic estates, and 0.37 for the bespoilered five-door WRX.

The front wings now have a muscle-bound appearance and this menacing presence is complemented by larger air intakes above and below the number plate.

At the rear, all models have new bumpers and light units with a curved dip to the inner edges - similar to the headlamps - to enhance design integration.

The WRX STi gains a larger, high rise rear spoiler, front corner spoilers and new side sill spoilers, all of which contribute to improved high speed stability. Meanwhile, a larger bonnet air intake enhances intercooler cooling.

More power, better handling

Big news for WRX fans is an increase in power from 218 to 225 PS for the turbocharged two-litre 'boxer' engine. Equally important is improved throttle response, thanks to revisions to the exhaust manifold aimed at smoothing the flow of exhaust gases, increased boost pressure and a new engine management system. Both the valvegear and exhaust system were modified for even better durability during extremely hot conditions.

Meanwhile, the cooling performance of the 265 PS STi engine benefits from a change in the shape of the intercooler water spray nozzle and the air baffle plate inside the air scoop.

The STi also has improved front suspension, thanks to strengthened mounts for the transverse linkages and new cross-performance rods. As a result, handling and steering response are even better, thanks to a reduction in geometry change during hard cornering.

Both the WRX and naturally-aspirated 2.0 and 1.6 litre Imprezas have crisper handling characteristics, with increased steering precision; already highly praised by road testers and customers alike. This is due to new, sophisticated shock absorbers. Featuring multiple-layer valves, damping forces were optimized in various speed ranges, with enhanced ride comfort an added bonus.

All new-look Imprezas also have revised steering. Now with a variable capacity steering pump, the system combines even greater straight-line stability at speed with a lighter, more sensitive feel during low-speed manoeuvring.

Interior quality upgrade

New, high quality cloth is used throughout the 2003 model year Impreza range with each model having its own pattern and character.

On all two-litre models the centre console which houses the audio and heating controls is now in a dark metallic shade instead of silver-coloured.

Sporty changes for the WRX include gun-metallic finish wheels and repositioning of the rev-counter to the centre of the instrument display, like the STi. The STi itself gains a new, smaller-diameter (375mm) Momo steering wheel and blue carpets to match the seats and door trim.

All Imprezas continue to benefit from keyless entry central locking and a Category One remote alarm/immobilizer; the WRX STi Type UK also has a satellite tracking system.

Right: The latest STi model displayed very aggressive lines, but, being the basis for the works rally car, function was high on the priority list. Note the larger bonnet scoop compared to earlier models.

The prototype WRC2003 machine (registration TM52 SRT) at the Paris Salon.

Passenger amd pedestrian safety boost
Both occupants and pedestrians are better protected in the 2003 Impreza, thanks to a whole series of safety measures, which include new, anti-raindrop door mirrors, that stay cleaner, improving visibility.

The passenger airbag is now dual stage, providing progressive protection matched to the severity of the impact, and the standard anti-lock brakes (ABS) come with electronic brake force distribution (EBD). This juggles the braking force between front and rear wheels according to load shifts during deceleration.

All WRX models have side airbags in combination with high-backed, rally-type front seats. Previously, side airbags were only available on the WRX saloon when fitted with standard seats.

Like the new Forester, the new-look Impreza has active front head restraints that reduce the risk of whiplash injury. The brake pedal is now energy absorbing, designed to snap away under severe impact, protecting the driver's lower limbs. In the rear seat are two ISO-FIX-compatible child seat mountings.

Outside, pedestrian injury is reduced, thanks to a more rounded

This WRC2003 was displayed at the 2003 Tokyo Auto Salon, held in January. It carried the same plates as the car shown in Paris.

Subaru UK launched the two-litre GX Sport in August 2002 as a sort of final fling for the outgoing model. Available in Premium Silver Metallic, Blue-Black Mica or Dark Blue Mica, the GX Sport had a different headlight treatment and a purposeful-looking rear spoiler, and was priced at £16,000, or £17,000 with automatic transmission.

An Impreza WRX STi Type UK with the Prodrive 300bhp 'Performance Pack,' launched in October 2002. The ultimate Q-car?

While America was readying itself for the all-new Impreza (and getting excited about the forthcoming arrival of the STi, the first time the high performance version of the Impreza had reached US shores, at least through official channels), the outgoing model was still being sold as a 2003 car. This estate was one of several Imprezas featured on the Subaru stand at the 2003 San Jose International Auto Show, held in early January. (Courtesy Ken Hoyle)

 SUBARU

挑み続ける走り—新次元へ。

SWRT（スバルワールドラリーチーム）との
強力なコラボレーションから産まれた、Newインプレッサ。
WRCで勝つために徹底した空力の追求を受けた、その力強いデザインは、
Newインプレッサの意思の表れでもある。
そして今、頂点に挑み続けるその走りは、さらに新次元へと向かう。

photo:（左）WRX STi オプション装着車　（右）WRX

Sports Sensation
New IMPREZA

New IMPREZA WRX STi
- ツインスクロールターボへと進化した2.0 DOHC BOXER ターボエンジンは、2ℓクラス最強の最大トルク394Nm（40.2kg·m）を発生。
- 電子制御により自動的に前後のトルク配分をコントロールするドライバーズコントロールセンターデフを設定。
- 強大なトルクを余裕をもって受け止める、自社製6速マニュアルミッション。

New IMPREZA WRX
- ターボチャージャーのタービンの小径化などで、中低速トルクの大幅な向上を実現した2.0 DOHC BOXER ターボエンジン。
- 倒立式ダンパーや、フロント16インチ対向4ポットブレーキなど、走りの性能をさらに徹底強化。
- 強く、そして速く、全面的に進化した動力性能を余すこと無く最大限に引き出す、スポーツシフトE-4AT。

174

Left & right: Two pieces of advertising from Japan as 2002 drew to a close - the Sports Wagon appearing on one, with the WRX and WRX STi saloons on the other. Similar full-page adverts were run in national newspapers.

Japan's WRX Sports Wagon for the 2003 season.

IMPREZA
Sedan

Pages 176-182: Catalogue for the facelifted Sedan range.

SUBARU

すべては世界で勝つために。

Sports Sensation
New *IMPREZA*

178

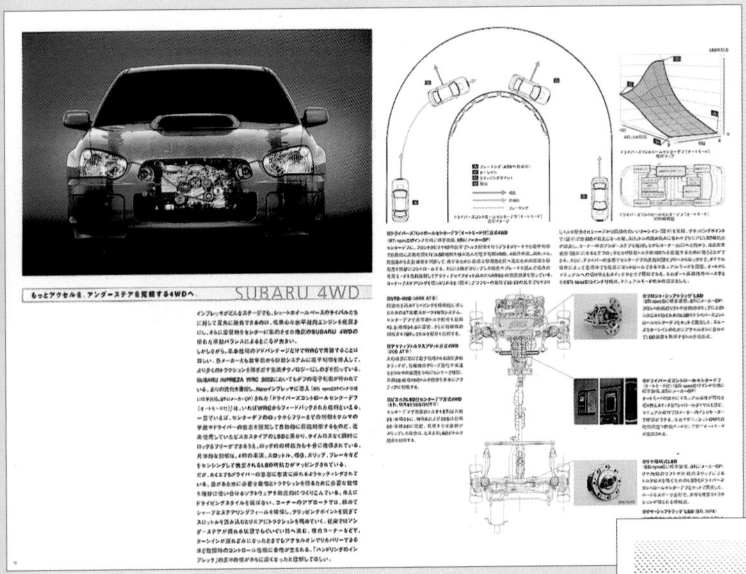
もっとアクセルを。アンダーステアを克服する4WDへ。
SUBARU 4WD

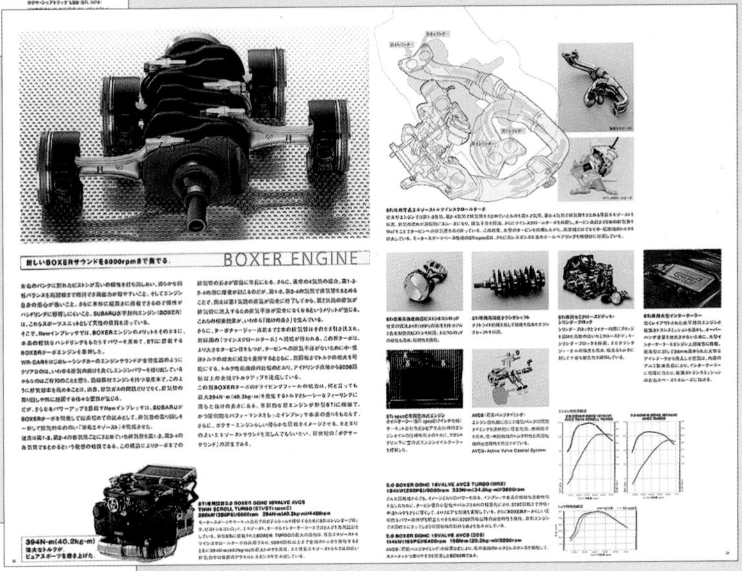
新しいBOXERサウンドを8000rpmまで奏でる。
BOXER ENGINE
394N·m(40.2kg·m)
強大なトルクが、
ピュアスポーツを磨き上げた。

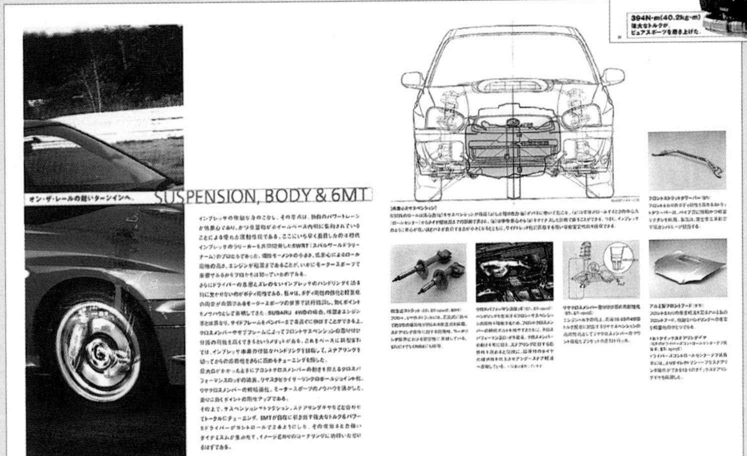
オン・ザ・レールの鋭いターンインへ。
SUSPENSION, BODY & 6MT

BRAKE & TIRE

SAFETY

ACTIVE SAFETY

PASSIVE SAFETY

WRX spec C

REAL COMPETITION

ALL JAPAN CHAMPIONSHIP

MOTOR SPORTS

CONCENTRATION

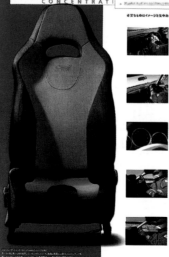

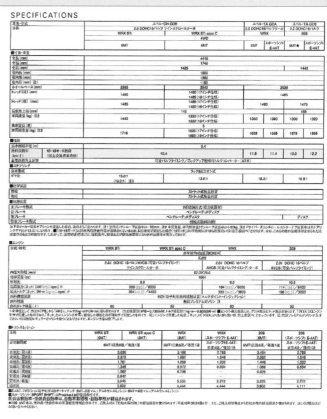

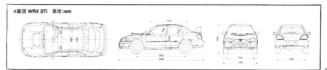

contour to the top of the [urethane] front bumper, a gently curved bonnet and windscreen wipers, which crush, softening any impact.

In its report from the Paris Salon (entitled 'This Time They Mean Business'), the *Autocar* observed: "Headed by the leaner, sharper-looking STi, the new Impreza promises to be even better to drive when it hits UK showrooms in February.

"Big news is the new frontal treatment which finally answers criticisms of the current bug-eyed look of the car launched just two years ago.

"Key to the transformation are new headlamp units which, framed by scallops in the redesigned bonnet, slope aggressively groundwards, giving the car a distinct scowl.

"You could almost call it retro: the

link to past Imprezas is now much greater. However, smoothly integrated bumpers, with larger air intakes, and tweaks to the bonnet keep things looking fresh rather than old-fashioned.

"Rear lights are new, too, and feature prominent fog and reversing lamps within the main unit. The existing car's spoked wheels and bulging wheelarches remain unchanged."

In reality, the styling was not the only reason for change. Yes, fashion was a major factor in the decision to adopt a new design so early in the car's life, but the desire to incorporate new technology and minor updates was just as strong. With the popularity of the station wagon at last wavering in Japan, the time had come to give more attention to the saloons, especially the WRX and STi versions. And, let's face

it, the STi and its arch rival, the Lancer Evolution, had been getting what amounted to a full model change virtually every year, as first one maker then the other upped the ante. With this latest Impreza, Subaru hoped it could stay ahead of the game.

The need for a new, more competitive World Rally Championship contender was also a key factor behind the change. Improved aerodynamics, cooling, and suspension tweaks were incorporated into the latest design, with Prodrive developing the WRC2003 model (also on display in Paris) in conjunction with the road car. In other words, much of the detailing was engineering-led rather than pure styling.

Meanwhile, testing of the WRC2003 car got under way in Spain straight after the Paris Salon debut.

The first test was scheduled to last one week (averaging around 120 miles, or 200km, a day), with drivers Paolo Andreucci and Pasi Hagstrom gradually moving from tarmac to gravel in perfect weather conditions. Early signs show good results from the revised engine and cooling package, the latest chassis, and the vehicle's aerodynamics. With the new car, the vast experience of Tommi Makinen and the blistering pace of Petter Solberg, the 2003 rally season should be an interesting one for SWRT fans.

The UK scene

To clear stocks of the previous generation Impreza before the new car made it into the showrooms in early 2003, Subaru UK ran a special discount offer on 2002 models. As long as the car was registered before the end of the year, an entry level Impreza 1.6 TS Sports Wagon could be secured for as little as £12,495 OTR (a saving of £1455), whilst the WRX saloon and estate were offered at £18,995 OTR, representing savings of £2500 and £3000 respectively.

At the same time (early October 2002), the Impreza STi 'Performance Pack' was announced, the 300bhp version endowing the WRX STi with a 155mph (248kph) top speed, and rendering it capable of dismissing 0-60 in just 4.6 seconds, impressive enough to keep the rivalry between the Subaru and Mitsubishi's Lancer (due to be announced in Evolution VIII guise for 2003) on the boil.

Developed by Prodrive, the 'Performance Pack' gave around 15 per cent more power (300bhp at 6000rpm), plus a significant boost in torque output, up from 253lbft to 299lbft at 4000rpm. The additional horses made for greater flexibility and much swifter progress in all the gears, and all for a fairly small investment of £1995 (including fitting). The kit included a modified ECU, high flow catalyst and sports silencer, and carried Subaru's full three-year/60,000 mile warranty.

Meanwhile, the standard Impreza WRX continued to be available with the popular Prodrive WR Sport 'Performance Pack.' This cost £1600 (fitted), boosting maximum power from 218 to 245bhp, and torque output from 215 to 261lbft.

Looking forward to receiving the new generation WRX, the *Autocar*

noted: "Subaru's updated WRX gets more changes to shout about than its faster STi brother.

"Such as a 7bhp boost in power, taking the maximum to 220bhp. There are claimed improvements, too, in throttle response and the low-down torque characteristics of the familiar flat-four motor.

"Official performance figures won't be released until nearer the February on-sale date, but both acceleration and top speed are said to be better.

"And the WRX's substantial dynamic abilities are promised to be enhanced, too. Steering precision, handling and ride comfort should be even better, thanks in part to new dampers from the Legacy.

"Inside, the WRX gets a neat set of metal-rimmed dials, while the rev counter moves to the centre of the three-clock dash, a treatment previously reserved for the STi model.

"The STi line-up has been simplified to just one model, too. With today's range, buyers can opt for a Prodrive styling kit with a big rear spoiler and body kit; it has proved so popular, it's being made standard.

"Subaru doesn't claim any more power for the restyled STi but engine cooling is said to be better, thanks to the bigger air intakes and detail changes to the turbocharger's intercooler. Expect the 261bhp boxer engine to deliver a marginally improved 0-60mph time of 4.8 seconds.

"Dynamically, the STi has been given a shot in the arm, courtesy of strengthened mounts for the suspension's transverse links and the addition of a strut brace. Subaru says this helps cut down on geometry changes during hard cornering.

"Interior changes are mostly limited to trim tweaks, but the STi finally gets a more manageable replacement for the standard WRX's bus-sized, four-spoke steering wheel."

The STi now had a top speed of 151.5mph (242kph), while the strict WRX - now boasting 225PS at 5600rpm, and 221lbft of torque at 4000rpm - could dismiss the 0-60 dash in 5.6 seconds (or 5.8 for the estate) before running on to at least 143mph (229kph). This increase in performance came with enhanced economy and lower emission levels.

While the WRX engine could now run on either 95 or 98 RON unleaded,

economy was up by around 10 per cent to 39.8mpg on the Extra Urban Cycle. The most significant improvement in fuel consumption figures was accredited to the automatic GX Sport, which gave 43.5mpg on the EUC instead of the previous 37.7mpg.

Ultimately, the success of the run-out campaign (helped by a final push which included a £1000 cashback offer on NA cars, plus free insurance or free servicing) enabled Subaru UK to introduce the new model earlier than expected. The WRX saloon, priced at £19,995 OTR, WRX estate (£20,495) and STi Type UK (£24,995) were in dealerships by the end of January 2003, with the normally-aspirated variants expected in the spring. There was also a luxury WRX 'SL' on the cards, with black leather trim, heated seats and a power sunroof, all for around £1500 more than the standard WRX.

The new car down under

The Australians received the latest Impreza in December 2002, badged as a 2003 model. The GX, RX and WRX grades were available in saloon and estate guises, augmented by the RV Sportwagon, the 2.5 litre RS sedan, and the manual only, old-style WRX STi (all other vehicles were listed with manual or automatic transmission).

Depending on the grade, the new Impreza could be finished in Bright Red, Dark Green Mica, Graphite Black Mica, Premium Silver Metallic, Pure White, Reddish Blue Mica, or WR Blue Mica. Prices started at $25,990 and went up to $45,440; the STi was $55,130 in pre-facelift trim, with the latest version expected in the showrooms during spring.

Incidentally, 2002 turned out to be a good year in Australia, with 6889 Imprezas sold; 297 more units than recorded for the previous season.

Stateside news

As noted earlier, the cars sold during the first part of the 2003 season were basically the same as those offered the previous year. But there was plenty to look forward to, as *Autoweek* observed in its issue of 20 January: "'At least we had the weekend.'

"That's what Mitsubishi folks had to say when, just days after unveiling their 271hp Lancer Evolution [VIII] rally car in Los Angeles, Subaru trumped its competition with the North

American version of the WRX STi at the Detroit Show. The STi comes packing 300hp and 300lbft (versus 273lbft for the Evo). While the STi was no surprise, the power coming from Subaru's 2.5 litre turbocharged flat-four sure was. The machine comes with a six-speed manual tranny, all-wheel drive with adjustable differential, Brembo disc brakes, Momo steering wheel and BBS wheels. The STi goes on sale in May for about $35,000 at a rate of - you guessed it – 300 per month."

Home market viewpoint

The new Impreza went on sale in Japan on 1 November 2002. While the fresh styling was obvious for all to see, and engine and gearing specifications remained virtually unchanged (the STi powerplant, now sporting 290lbft of torque, was the only major difference), there were also many detail improvements under the skin. For instance, 1.5 litre machines got new dampers, while all cars gained a stronger rear suspension top mount, and the positioning of the rear trailing arms now aped that of the limited edition S202.

The I's was now called the 15i, and the I's Sport became the 15i-S. Equipment levels were basically carried over, with two- and four-wheel drive options, and manual and automatic transmissions available on each. Prices ranged from an extremely reasonable 1,198,000 to 1,763,000 yen, bringing the Impreza some rather unexpected rivals at the cheaper end of the market.

The entry level car had new grey trim, but the same steering wheel as before; the 15i-S had revised trim and a slightly different four-spoke Momo wheel. There were minor improvements in the seating, enhancing strength yet reducing weight, and all 1.5 models had dark blue-faced gauges. The 15i-S also received a CD/MD/radio unit as standard.

Normally-aspirated cars were easily distinguished by the chrome bar in the front grille, and there were new coachwork colours, taking the choice to eight shades on some models. As before, various aerodynamic appendages and seat covers were available to upgrade the look of the machines, plus a two-tone steering wheel and gearknob.

The NA became the 20S sedan (featuring a WRX-style front bumper and gauges), while the 20N estate also collected the 20S moniker; the manual sedan was priced at 2,033,000 yen. By the way, all cars in the new range had the same chassis codes as their predecessors.

The turbocharged cars were given a mesh grille for a sportier image. The 20K became the WRX Sports Wagon, inheriting the same 17-inch, five-spoke alloys, inverted struts and uprated brakes (four-pot front, two-pot rear) as the saloon.

The EJ20 Turbo engine was given a bigger intercooler air intake, a 5mm (0.2in.) smaller diameter turbine in the TD04L turbocharger, a lighter valve lifter mechanism with hollow, sodium-filled valves, and a modified exhaust.

Inside, the WRX had gauges with white on black markings and metallic trim rings, and there was a chrome handbrake release button. The steering wheel was the same as that fitted to the 20S on manual cars, but, like the last generation, automatic machines had a similar Momo wheel which featured shift buttons on the top two spokes.

The five-speed WRX saloon had a 2,453,000 yen sticker price, with the estate commanding 2,368,000 yen (automatic transmission adding 153,000 yen on both models). The WRX was available in Premium Silver Metallic, Pure White, WR Blue Mica, Black Topaz Mica or Solid Red, with trim in shades of dark grey.

With the introduction of the WRX estate, a five-door STi model was no longer listed. The standard STi saloon (priced at 2,958,000 yen) had the five-spoke, 17-inch wheels of its predecessor, finished in gold and with the wider taper in each set of spokes. Apart from the obvious styling differences, the STi also featured front corner spoilers, new skirts, and a rather large rear spoiler. Inside, although the black/blue trim looked familiar, the meter panel had illuminated red calibrations on black dials, and there was a small diameter, three-spoke steering wheel.

It was also the STi that received the most attention from a mechanical point of view. The 8.0:1 c/r was retained, and, whilst maximum power was still 280bhp at 6000rpm, peak torque increased to 290lbft at 4400rpm. This came about largely due to changes in the exhaust system to make the most of the twin-scroll IHI RHF55 turbo (the type RHF5HB was employed on the Spec C, incidentally), larger diameter intake ducting and a revised inlet manifold. Cast aluminium alloy pistons were specified, and the block, crankshaft and conrods were strengthened.

The transmission was uprated by way of lighter but harder materials, and the shift linkage was improved slightly. The front crossmember and subframe were made more rigid, thanks to the use of six mounting points rather than the previous four, and the addition of a performance rod. It was much the same story at the back, with a support bracket added for the rear subframe to tighten things, and a ball-joint link was adopted for the rear anti-roll bar.

The WRX STi Spec C, overseen by Michihiro Kawamura, was again available in two guises, with dual airbags as standard (and therefore the same steering wheel as its STi stablemate). The 3,205,000 yen version had the 17-inch, ten-spoke BBS wheels of the earlier car, a driver-controlled centre diff with automatic mode, Suretrac front and mechanical rear differentials, and a quicker steering rack (all optional on the other STi saloon); it also came with an engine oil cooler mounted up front, rather like the S202 again, and a low rear spoiler.

The cheaper 16-inch wheel Spec C car had steel wheels covering the less powerful brakes, a driver-controlled centre diff minus automatic override, and basic seats. In this guise, the Spec C cost 2,740,000 yen and weighed in at 1320kg (2904lb) - 30kg (66lb) less than the other Spec C model, and a massive 120kg (264lb) less than the standard STi car.

As for paintwork colours, the normal STi saloon was offered in the same shades as the WRX, except for Solid Red (which actually had a darker red underneath two top coats to give it a deeper shine), while the Spec C cars came in white only.

Early STi accessories included auxiliary gauge sets (with white on black markings and red needles) or a separate boost gauge, a strut tower bar, and a sports exhaust system.

The press was invited to try the new Impreza on 8 November on the picturesque roads around Mount Fuji. Most testers were impressed with the new car's handling (quite an improvement on earlier models and,

The inside pages of Subaru's brochure produced for the 2003 Tokyo Auto Salon.

according to Tommi Makinen, the difference was evident from the very first high speed corner), and many thought the automatic mode on the Spec C centre differential (ACD) was a real bonus - at least from a marketing point of view.

Peter Lyon wrote the following for *Auto Express*: "Although straight-line performance is impressive, the vehicle's grip is simply astounding. Through long sweeping bends the car refuses to understeer, holding a line with real determination.

"The extra stability comes from a significant redesign of the suspension and axles. Up front, the arrangement is moved 15mm [0.6in.] forward to improve rigidity. Stronger components

are used and there's more crossbracing, allowing engineers to add more negative camber. At the rear, the Impreza has beefed-up anti-roll bars and mounting points to stop it squirming during hard cornering.

"With the new settings, more throttle input results in less understeer. In addition to the centre differential and front Suretrac lsd, Subaru also plans to offer ACD in Japan. This allows the driver to choose how the transmission will deliver the power. The system can also detect wheelspin, and alter its set-up to maximise grip. As a result, corner exit speeds are higher than ever. Sadly, UK cars will not get this modification.

"The only downside, if you can call

it that, is the Brembo brakes. Pedal feedback is not all it should be, feeling soggy and lacking precision. The anchors still bite hard into the discs, but you can't help feeling a little short-changed.

"Overall, however, the changes made to the new Impreza certainly improve the package. Get behind the wheel of one of these and the last thing people will ask about is the headlamps!"

Having sampled the entire Impreza range, a top engineer and good friend of the author's felt the NA two-litre models were superb, but the WRX was perhaps a little too harsh for everyday use and the STi a touch too 'all or nothing' in its power delivery.

However, he was full of praise for

the way in which the marque maintained its individuality, avoiding the temptation to go more mainstream in the quest for high volume sales. And, in a stunning display of its potency, the STi caught up with the record posted by the Lancer Evolution at the Tsukuba race track, knocking almost a full second off the previous best time achieved by a stock Impreza road car. The Subaru versus Mitsubishi fight was back on ...

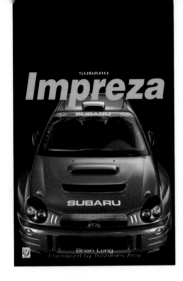

Appendix
Production figures

Production figures

Year	Sedan	Sports Wagon	CKD units	Annual total
1992	11,975	10,786	-	22,761
1993	66,893	48,331	-	115,224
1994	41,815	25,429	-	67,244
1995	36,147	49,695	-	85,842
1996	33,411	51,256	-	84,667
1997	35,023	57,431	1,656	94,110
1998	41,454	52,646	2,232	96,332
1999	42,560	44,184	2,160	88,904
2000	40,154	40,281	3,189	83,624
2001	48,553	53,737	1,428	103,718
2002	47,431	47,960	-	95,301

Export figures

Year	Exports	Cumulative total
1992	1,790	1,790
1993	73,915	75,705
1994	46,419	122,124
1995	35,844	157,968
1996	49,114	207,082
1997	53,480	260,562
1998	55,178	315,740
1999	58,122	373,862
2000	49,371	423,233
2001	76,302	499,535
2002	74,568	574,103

Home sales

Year	Sedan	Sports Wagon	Annual total	Cumulative total
1992	3,989	3,129	7,118	7,118
1993	16,206	15,113	31,319	38,437
1994	14,248	21,668	35,916	74,353
1995	16,101	28,885	44,986	119,339
1996	12,863	27,859	40,722	160,061
1997	11,954	27,032	38,986	199,047
1998	12,119	24,725	36,844	235,891
1999	10,117	19,817	29,934	265,825
2000	9,543	18,674	28,217	294,042
2001	8,268	19,801	28,069	322,111
2002	7,443	17,230	24,673	346,784

Total Impreza production (as of end 2002) - 937,727 units, including 10,665 CKD cars built in Taiwan.

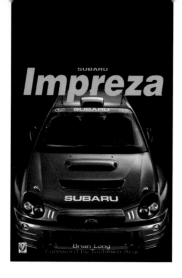

Index

Fuji Heavy Industries (FHI) and Subaru products are mentioned throughout this book, from Chapter One onwards.